AMERICAN SOCIAL ORDER

AMERICAN SOCIAL ORDER

Social Rules in a Pluralistic Society

by Jack D. Douglas

THE FREE PRESS, NEW YORK
Collier-Macmillan Limited, London

THE FREE PRESS
A Division of The Macmillan Company
866 Third Avenue, New York, New York 10022

Collier-Macmillan Canada Ltd., Toronto, Ontario

Library of Congress Catalog Card Number: 70–142360

printing number
1 2 3 4 5 6 7 8 9 10

1577543

Contents

Preface

Sociology has entered a period of creative ferment. Not since the intellectual struggles of the nineteenth century, in which were forged the ideas of classical sociology, has there been such a fundamental challenge to the traditional sociological perspective on society.

As has so often happened in the natural sciences, one element of this challenge to traditional assumptions has come from other streams in Western thought, especially from philosophy and the history of science. For over fifty years sociologists, looking back to Durkheim, Marx, and Weber as the founts of sociological wisdom, have remained isolated from the major branches of twentieth century philosophy—phenomenology and existentialism on the Continent and linguistic philosophy in the English-speaking world. Sociologists have also clung to the image of "hard science" handed down from nineteenth century positivism at the same time most "hard" scientists were increasingly convinced by the works of new philosophers and historians of science, such as Thomas Kuhn's *The Structure of Scientific Revolutions*, as well as by the revolutionary developments in the sciences themselves, that the nineteenth century image of hard science had been a mistake. Sociologists continued to ignore Husserl, Merleau-Ponty, Sartre, Moore, Russell, Wittgenstein, Popper and their co-workers.

Our time of isolation has ended. A rapidly growing proportion of sociologists has begun to use these new perspectives to construct theories and to do research. Moreover, many of those engaged in the growing field of the sociology of sociology have begun to recognize the existence of a "crisis" and have begun to call for new orientations in sociology. The best known of these, Robert Friedrichs' *A Sociology of Sociology* and Alvin Gouldner's *The Coming Crisis in Western Sociology*, have both recognized the great importance of phenomenology and existentialism to this crisis. But they have both also recognized the need for a synthesis of this new perspective with the basic ideas of structural theories, especially those which recognize power as central to the development and maintenance of social structure. While these two works have appeared since this book was completed, there is a remarkable correspondence between the need they recognize in sociological theory and what this book attempts.

Fortunately, thus far there is little tendency to adopt these new perspectives wholesale, and it is to be hoped we shall be spared another era of "schools of thought." Sociology has developed too much careful empirical information to return to an age of philosophical gurus. Phenomenology, existentialism, linguistic philosophy and the new history of science are of value to us mainly because they give us a new perspective for better understanding our society. This *existential perspective* gives us a more systematic and comprehensive understanding of many research findings. Most importantly of all, it has opened new worlds of social research: it has allowed us to see the fundamental importance of the vast realm of everyday situational action (which had previously been subsumed under the rubric of "social structure"). It has further allowed us to see the need to restructure our ideas concerning the nature of "knowledge" and our methods of doing research.

"Deviance," conceived of broadly as the study of social rules as used to construct social order, has been the sociological area in which this new perspective has thus far had its greatest impact. The field of deviance has been of central importance because sociologists have considered the problem of explaining social order and disorder to be the basic problem of the discipline.

Today the field of deviance is one of the most creative and rapidly growing areas in sociology. The theoretical ideas and methods of research which have recently been created in this field, partly as a result of adopting the new perspective, now pose a basic challenge to many of the fundamental ideas that have dominated sociological theory and research since nineteenth century positivism. There are increasing signs that this challenge, coming simultaneously from such increasingly creative fields as the comparative study of social change, is beginning to produce the *sense of crisis* that comes before any revolution in the basic forms of thought of a scientific discipline. While it is possible that the traditional theories may yet meet this challenge, the very uncertainty of the outcome only adds further to the ferment of ideas and the intellectual excitement which one finds among the students of deviance today and among an increasing number of more generally oriented social theorists.

Social theories grow partially out of the everyday experience of their creators. The everyday experience of Americans has undergone a vast transformation in one generation. How would one begin to compare America of the 1930s with that of the 1970s? The transformation in the international situation alone almost surpasses belief. Who in 1939 imagined that within twenty-five years the United States would become the "center" of the world and its unwilling "policeman"? In 1939 few dreams encompassed the moon, or night-mares the nuclear holocaust. There were no electronic com-puters threatening technological tyrannny, and none of their promises both of increased leisure and wealth. Yet the struc-tural-functional perspective that has dominated sociology for the past few decades was created in the 1930s as a variant on the positivistic perspective of the nineteenth century by sociologists who had grown up in an American society even less developed than in 1939. While I believe the relatively simplistic theory they created was based far too much on the limited experience of the ivy-covered colleges and middle-class life, and had little value in explaining even the simpler American society of that day, there probably was a closer relation between the common experiences of rural and small town America and the theory the sociologists created. Rural and small town America was a homogeneous, stable, and closed world with few conflicts and problematic moral mean-ings for its members, at least compared to what we find in American society today—or in the burgeoning cities of the 1920s.

This work is grounded in my own experience of American society, which has been singularly privileged in its great variety and which has predisposed me to see the values of an existential perspective in explaining this society. But this work must be accepted or rejected largely on the basis of its rationality, the objectivity and adequacy of the evidence presented, and of all other evidence the readers can bring to the work. I hope it will stimulate the creative efforts that can produce greater social understanding.

Jack D. Douglas
La Jolla, California

Acknowledgments

This book and related works have been in preparation so long and have been read by so many people in preliminary forms that I cannot possibly acknowledge the help given by most of them. But I am especially appreciative of the fine readings given the work by Peter Manning, Clarice Stoll, Marvin Scott, John Lofland, Carol Warren, John Johnson and John Anderson. In addition, I greatly appreciate the fine editorial help of Clarice Stoll, Irving Naiburg and Carol Warren.

Much of the research that has made this book possible has been greatly facilitated by a post-doctoral fellowship from the American Council of Learned Societies, a small grant from the Center for Studies of Suicide Prevention of NIH, and two small grants from the Academic Senate of the University of California.

AMERICAN SOCIAL ORDER

1. Introduction

Social scientists have begun to reexamine their fundamental assumptions about man and society. Some now believe that social conflicts and moral absurdities are necessary conditions of human existence and have begun to examine the implications of this to explain adequately how social order is constructed. More falteringly, we have also begun to examine the implications of these ideas for realistic social policies.

Symbolic Meaning and Social Order: Freedom and Constraint

Man's intelligence consists preeminently of the ability to think symbolically, that is, to stand back from, to question, to abstract from on-going realities, and to manipulate the resulting abstractions so as to arrive at better solutions to his problems of existence. It is the use of his intelligence that creates the potential of human freedom or of conscious choice; it is the necessity of using this symbolic capacity

1

that makes man *necessarily free*. At the same time, this symbolic capacity must be *developed* if man is to solve his problems of existence. This development consists in acquiring a symbolic universe in which solutions to many problems have been accumulated and transmitted.

Man is the symbol sharer; he is both symbolic and social. Moreover, man's social existence is not governed by instinct. Man's social existence is symbolic and mutually meaningful. Human society is not possible without a shared symbolic universe or shared meanings. Man's symbolic intelligence and his social existence are preconditions of each other and, taken together, are preconditions of man's existence.

The development over the eons of his shared symbolic universe has made it possible for man to solve most of his natural problems of existence. But the solution has itself created another problem for man, which, as the natural problems have receded in importance, has increasingly become the fundamental problem of human existence. This is *the problem of social order.*

Society is only possible to the extent that its members *share* certain symbolic meanings, which they use in common to solve problems. Yet, man's symbolic nature makes him free, for he can study reality and consciously choose from among alternative paths of action. *The necessity of society creates the necessity of constraint, of sharedness, of being like and acting with others; yet the necessity of meaning creates the necessity of freedom, of questioning and making choices, of differentiating and separating oneself from others and from all external realities.* The human condition is thus one of necessary conflict between freedom and constraint, between the demands of individuality and the demands of society. It is this conflict and others which we shall examine that make the problem of social order inevitable.

Social Rules, Social Order and Social Control

The problem of social order is essentially the problem of producing some sharedness of meanings and some coordination of the activities of the members of any society sufficient to allow them to achieve what they consider to be adequate gratification of their needs and desires through their everyday lives. The concrete meanings of "the problem" are themselves problematic for the members of society, since the meanings of each of the major categories—"problems," "ordering," "sufficient," and so on—are subject to dispute. Still, any society must have an ordering of the activities of its members if those members are going to be able simply to live; and coordination becomes more important as the members become more demanding of the outcomes of their social lives. The basic question is how this coordination is achieved.

Once we recognize that human action is *meaningful,* that is, human beings do things because of meanings those activities have for them, then we must expect a coordination of the activities of the members of society will be achieved primarily through sharing of meanings. But a vast number of meanings (ideas, beliefs, values, feelings) are current in any society, and these are shared to different degrees. Is it the sharedness of meanings in general which is of crucial importance in producing whatever degree of coordination is found in a society? Or are there specific shared meanings that produce ordering of social activities?

Nineteenth century sociologists concluded that there is a specific kind of shared meaning that produces social order: social rules, especially moral rules. These sociologists believed that only rules, and probably only moral rules, could produce the degree of social ordering found in societies. As Durkheim concluded, "Society is a moral phenomenon."

was not developed with clarity, it was the
 ustification for the sociologists' concern
 ns," "the violations of moral rules," and
 ntually to become known as "deviance." The
 of social rules was believed to be of significance in
understanding society because these violations have a direct
bearing on social order and the attempts by the members
of society to maintain social order. It was for this reason
that sociological theory always had concern both with social
rules and with social order; and it was for this reason that
the fields of "deviance" and "social control" have always
been of special value to sociologists. The study of both rules
and order was, in fact, so intimately connected that in time
many sociologists were to confuse the two by dealing with
deviance and disorder (or "disorganization," as it became
known in the 1920s) as *identical.* The causal relation between immorality and disorder was implicitly assumed to
exist.

The sociology of deviance and social control was fundamentally concerned with three things:

1) the nature of social rules, especially moral rules;
2) the relations between social rules and social actions;
   and
3) the construction and destruction of social order, with
   special consideration of the parts played by social
   rules in these processes.

This theoretical justification of the connection sociologists
saw between social rules and social order and the great importance later accorded to studies of "immorality" is an ideal-
ization. Early sociologists were unclear about why they believed these things, probably because it seemed obvious,
however vague the exact relations might seem. It seemed
obvious because it was part of common sense in all Western
societies.

There are certain social rules in Western societies that are consciously constructed for the purpose of "maintaining social order." The most obvious examples are laws and the rules of games. The idea of "Law and order," that is, that obeying laws produces "social order" and that violations produce "social disorder," was already a truism among officials and their supporters in the nineteenth century. Basically, "moral rules" are those kinds of rules (*absolutist rules*) whose violation constitutes an injury (socially defined) to the members of society, so that the violation constitutes a form of (socially defined) "social disorder" in that its existence means that the members of society cannot achieve "adequate gratification of their needs and desires." The dominant social meanings of "moral rules" and "social order" so overlap each other that anyone using these ideas to think about society would be apt to see them, at least partially, as identical. Moreover, all of the sociological theories that social deviance produces social disorder (disorganization, disintegration) are little more than intellectualized forms of the ancient belief that "moral decay causes social decay."

Everyone "knows" common-sensically that "Rome decayed because of immoral living." While most members of our society who believe this may be unaware of it, this was the serious (if simplified) argument of Saint Augustine's *The City of God* and, as such, became official dogma: ungodliness destroys society. In the nineteenth century the idea was extended to suicide or self-destruction. Ungodliness (i. e., irreligion, immorality, etc.) causes suicide or self-destruction. At the same time, suicide is a form of immorality and thus causes social destruction. This is what lay behind social science research in the nineteenth century trying to show that lack of religion causes suicide (and all other immorality) and social decay. Durkheim was to argue in sophisticated terms that immorality and social disintegration cause, or are identical with, each other.

These basic ideas of the sociologists about "moral rules" and "social order" were the foundation of the absolutist perspective on society, which was an important part of the traditional common-sense perspective on society, and which, most importantly, was that part of common sense used by the government officials in Western societies to achieve their goals of social control—or "maintaining social order." The early sociologists were implicitly committed to achieving these official goals, used the official information on deviance based on this perspective, and consequently, came to share this perspective. The sociologists eventually developed this perspective into the structural-functional theory of society. This theory assumed social morality (or values) to be unproblematic for the members of society, to be homogeneously shared by all members of society, and to be the basic determinant of a social order that is non-conflictful, unchanging and closed. Such a view of society may have some value in analyzing simple societies that have achieved a rare degree of equilibrium. When applied to American society, or any other major nation-state today, it becomes a distortion.

American society is highly complex and is probably changing more rapidly than any other society (except when under the impact of foreign conquest). It is a society in which moral conflicts have always been intense, in which such conflicts played a major part in producing a terrible Civil War and innumerable lesser conflicts, and in which moral meanings have become even more problematic for its members. These changes are now taking place so rapidly, and with such far-reaching consequences, that they raise serious doubts concerning the possibility of maintaining social order while at the same time preserving personal freedom. We cannot understand such issues or provide the answers unless we can reach a better understanding of the transformations that we and the rest of our society are undergoing. Let us begin by analyzing the traditional perspective on social rules and social order.

2. Social Rules and Social Order: The Common-Sense and Classical Sociological Perspective

The history of ideas has shown that certain ideas can become so pervasive and central to the thought of a culture that over centuries the members of that culture unquestioningly apply these ideas anew in many different ways.[1] These ideas normally form the background for common-sense discourse. The history of ideas has also shown that they frequently constitute much of the substance of serious intellectual work. Though science in the western world was born and developed partly as a revolution against such unexamined and "un-empirical" ideas, recent work in the history of science has led to the conclusion that scientific thought is itself largely the result of just such metaphysical ideas.[2] In the social sciences this close correspondence of many of the

---

1. Arthur Lovejoy's classic study of *The Great Chain of Being,* an idea that dominated much of Western thinking over many centuries, is an excellent demonstration of this ability of certain ancient and fundamental ideas to dominate new forms of thinking.

2. See E. A. Burth, *The Metaphysical Foundations of Modern Science,* New York: Doubleday, 1954. This is one of the early and most important works in what is now a long line of historical and philosophic analyses of science showing the importance of such "metaphysical ideas" in the development of scientific thought.

basic ideas of the scientific disciplines and the metaphysical ideas of common sense is clear and important.

Sociology is profoundly grounded in common sense. There is hardly a modern sociological idea which cannot be found in numerous sources—literary, philosophical, historical, etc. —over the last several centuries. Most of the specific ideas of modern sociology, such as the "social system," the greater tendency of urban men to suicide, the association of downward mobility ("déclassement") with suicide, or the association of the lower class with crime, can be traced to earlier centuries. As I shall show below, many ideas associated with the statistical theories of deviance were worked out two or three centuries ago and had become common-sensical to many men of practical affairs. To some extent these ideas have been transmitted within disciplines by means of formal education; and when they have not been transmitted, they have been "rediscovered" by later generations. The basic reason for this rediscovery is that different disciplines are, to varying degrees, grounded in common sense. Since the ideas are either specifically transmitted from generation to generation common-sensically, or else are constructed out of ideas which are so transmitted, it is easy for members with this common-sense background to come up with them independently of any specialized training. (However, without specialized training, they would not normally use the ideas in the kind of systematic analyses common to the disciplines.)

This grounding of the social sciences in common sense is in no way to be rejected or bemoaned. It is necessary, for *cultural wisdom is the foundation of all social science.* Indeed, all sciences are grounded in common sense. The most mathematical science, physics, relies unquestioningly on common sense to provide the readings of meters and other forms of data. Even mathematics, the ideal in formal thought, has been known since Gödel to rely on certain taken-for-granted ideas of common sense about what is logical. All of science is ultimately bounded by the properties of the human mind; and the human mind is always bounded by a cultural heritage, by common sense, no matter how varied that heritage might be.

The social sciences are also necessarily dependent on common sense in a more important way. Except for the mechanist or pure behaviorist, who would interpret human action entirely in terms of externally perceivable events, social scientists agree that human action must in some way be explained in terms of the *meanings of things to the actors involved.* That is, *human action, especially social interaction, is meaningful action; hence meanings must be considered in any explanation of social behavior.* But there is no way to "perceive" the meanings of things to the actors, to "see" the meanings, in terms of externally perceivable events. (Even a supposedly behavioristic description, such as "he raised his hand," relies on shared, common-sense understandings of the meanings of the linguistic categories "he," "raised," "hand," and the nature of complicated common-sense experience—the nature of possession, the nature of "past" events, etc.—for an adequate communication among scientists.) *Specific meanings can only be gotten at ultimately by sharing with the members of the society some basic meanings, derived from common experience and communication.* Social scientists, then, cannot adequately explain and predict the social phenomena they are studying without making use of their common-sense experience in some way to provide them with the basic meanings of things to the members of society whom they are studying.

There are different ways to *make use of common-sense experience* to provide these social meanings for scientific purposes. There is, especially, a fundamental distinction between taking the *natural (or naturalistic) stance* and taking the *theoretic stance,* as the phenomenological philosophers have long called them.[3] Taking the natural stance consists primarily in *taking the standpoint of common sense,* of *acting within* common sense, whereas taking the theoretic stance consists in *standing back from common sense* and *studying common sense to determine its nature.*

The traditional sociological perspective on deviance, that is, the structural-functional and statistical perspective, was explicitly opposed to common-sense understandings and explanations of such human actions as deviance. It often ridiculed common-sense explanations and opposed them with scientific methods. This was done partly for rhetorical purposes. Just as the natural scientists had for so long rhetorically attacked common sense to demonstrate the need for the independence and the superiority of the natural sciences, so did the social scientists rhetorically attack common-sense explanations to show how "scientific" they were, how much society "needed" the social sciences and, hence, how much they should support and agree with the "superior" understandings of the social scientists.

Remarkably enough, it was in good part because of this opposition to common sense that the social scientists became the captives of common-sense understandings. On the one hand, because they did accept the necessity of getting at the social meanings in order to scientifically explain social actions, they were fated in some way to make use of their common-sense understandings of social meanings in con-

3. There are many analyses of the naturalistic stance and the theoretic stance in the literature on phenomenology and existentialism. See, for example, the discussion of some of these fundamental ideas by Maurice Natanson in his essay on "Phenomenology and the Natural Attitude," in his book, *Literature, Philosophy, and the Social Sciences: Essays in Existentialism and Phenomenology,* The Hague: Martinus Nijhoff, 1962, pp. 34–44. David Matza has supported taking the natural stance by sociologists in his book *Becoming Deviant,* Englewood Cliffs, N.J.: Prentice-Hall, 1969, pp. 3–15. For a discussion of all these issues see my essay on "Understanding Everyday Life" in Jack D. Douglas, ed., *Understanding Everyday Life,* Chicago: Aldine, 1970.

structing their theories. But, on the other hand, *because they were explicitly and emotionally opposed to common-sense ideas, they could not systematically examine the ways in which they used common-sense understandings to provide the social meanings for their theories.* The result was precisely what one finds when there are profound and unconscious conflicts at work in human affairs—an inability to rationally control one's actions because one dares not examine the bases for his actions.

There seems to have been a common pattern involved in the positivistic sociologists' attempts to do "hard science": they excluded common sense while at the same time they *bootlegged the socially meaningful phenomena* back into their works so they would in some way be relevant to everyday life. They normally began their work by constructing a formal definition of the phenomena to be studied and by proposing a formal method as *the* objective method for studying these defined phenomena. Their formal definitions were always in fact largely derived from *some part* of the common-sense meanings of such phenomena, but they always insisted on the difference between this "scientific definition" and the common-sense definition. What the positivists actually did at this stage was to take one small part of the whole range of common-sense meanings, formalize it, and then *substitute* it for the common-sense meanings. *They thus enshrined one part of the very complex common-sense meanings as the "real" meaning and then went on to do their research and theorizing in terms of these ad hoc phenomena which they themselves had constructed.*

While they were studying the world of common-sense meanings, however partially and indirectly, they were also concerned with returning to that common-sense world with "significant" results that could be understood and used for practical purposes. The positivists were, then, forced to shift back and forth in complicated ways among their own common-sense understandings of the phenomena, their constructed *ad hoc realities,* and the more complex common-sense understandings of those phenomena held by other members of the society. Above all, in order to get back to the common-sense world from the ethereal ad hoc realities they had constructed, they were forced to devise *post hoc systems of translating devices* to decipher the "meanings" of their ad hoc findings. These shiftings back and forth between the realms of common sense and the ad hoc realities was almost undetectable to the average reader, who would be quite confused by all the theoretical legerdemain, by the highly complicated procedures involved in any actual statistical study (as opposed to the rhetorical ideal presented in the textbooks on statistics). The complicated bits and pieces of any statistical study and theoretical analysis allow for a great deal of *analytical juggling* to get the pieces to *go together* in some (common-sensically) plausible manner and to get "significant" results. (This is why there have been conflicts among the "findings" of these statistical studies or facile "validations" of opposite positions. The "degrees of freedom" involved in the process allow for wide variations.)

We can see this process at work even in the greatest works sharing the positivistic perspective on deviance, such as Durkheim's *Suicide.* Durkheim began by providing a formal definition of "suicide" in terms of the "knowledge of consequences," which is, in fact, one of the dimensions of meanings we often find in the common-sense uses of the term "suicide." He insisted that this "scientific" definition was necessary to save his "scientific" analysis from the many uncertainties and conflicts among the common-sense definitions of "suicide": He stated clearly his "scientific" contempt for the absurdities of the "average intelligence" and its common sense:

Since the word "suicide" recurs constantly in the course of conversation, it might be thought that its sense is universally known and that definition is superfluous. Actually, the words of everyday language, like the concepts they express, are always susceptible of more than one meaning, and the scholar employing them in their accepted use without further definition would risk serious misunderstanding. Not only is their meaning so indefinite as to vary, from case to case, with the needs of argument, but, as the classification from which they derive is not analytic, but merely translates the confused impressions of the crowd, categories of very different sorts of fact are indistinctly combined under the same heading, or similar realities are differently named. So, if we follow common use, we risk distinguishing what should be combined, or combining what should be distinguished, thus mistaking the real affinities of things, and accordingly misapprehending their nature. Only comparison affords explanation. A scientific investigation can thus be achieved only if it deals with comparable facts, and it is the more likely to succeed the more certainly it has combined all those that can be usefully compared. But these natural affinities of entities cannot be made clear safely by such superficial examination as produces ordinary terminology; and so the scholar cannot take as the subject of his research roughly assembled groups of facts corresponding to words of common usage. He himself must establish the groups he wishes to study in order to give them the homogeneity and the specific meaning necessary for them to be susceptible of scientific treatment. Thus the botanist, speaking of flowers or fruits, the zoologist of fish or insects, employ these various terms in previously determined senses . . . The essential thing is not to express with some precision what the average intelligence terms suicide, but to establish a category of objects permitting this classification, which are objectively established, that is, correspond to a definite aspect of things.[4]

Perhaps because he recognized that the most common everyday meaning of suicide is that of "the intentional killing of oneself," Durkheim was anxious to exclude "intention" as part of the formal ("scientific") definition. "Intention" was

4. E. Durkheim, *Suicide*, New York: The Free Press, 1951, page 41.

seen by all positivists (as by the modern behaviorists) as the most subjective of all common-sense ideas:

Shall suicide be considered to exist only if the act resulting in death was performed by the victim to achieve this result? Shall only he be thought truly to slay himself who has wished to do so, and suicide be intentional self-homicide? In the first place, this would define suicide by a characteristic which, whatever its interest and significance, would at least suffer from not being easily recognizable, since it is not easily observed. How discover the agent's motive and whether he desired death itself when he formed his resolve, or had some other purpose? Intent is too intimate a thing to be more than approximately interpreted by another. It even escapes self-observation. How often we mistake the true reasons for our acts! We constantly explain acts due to petty feelings or blind routine by generous passions or lofty considerations.[5]

It is remarkable that Durkheim never considered how his own *ad hoc definition* of suicide might be related to the definition of suicide being used by the people who provided him with his only source of statistical information.[6] These people, of course, were the official coroners, medical examiners, health officers, police, priests, and so on, of the various nations and localities from which he obtained the official statistics on suicide. As Halbwachs long ago pointed out,[7] and as I have found in a recent study of coroners and medical examiners in the United States (see Chapter 4), these officials were all necessarily making use of their common-sense ideas about persons and social actions to decide

5. *Ibid.*, page 3.
6. I have analyzed this point in my various works on suicide. See especially *The Social Meanings of Suicide,* Princeton: Princeton University Press, 1967. "The Sociological Analysis of Social Meanings of Suicide," *Archives Européennes de Sociologie,* 7 (1966), pp. 249–275; "Sucide: The Social Aspects" in *The International Encyclopedia of the Social Sciences,* Macmillan, and The Free Press, 15 (1968).
7. See Maurice Halbwachs, *Les Causes du Suicide,* Paris: Felix Alcan, 1930.

whether deaths were suicides. This meant, above all, that most officials were classifying deaths as suicides *only if* they first decided that the individual *intended* to kill himself by his action. Durkheim was violating his own severe injunctions. *He was analyzing the most subjective kind of common-sense information, but he was doing his theoretical analyses of this data in terms of an ad hoc definition that had little to do with the data.* Yet his statistical analysis is so complex and so manipulable that his argument proved highly convincing to generations of positivistic sociologists. He had constructed such a powerful argument, by making use of the rhetoric of scientific forms (numbers), that few succeeding sociologists saw this fallacy in his arguments.

In this way the traditional perspective on deviance took from common sense a number of fundamental ideas about deviance that became the unexamined background, the metaphysics, of the sociological analyses of deviance. The *ad hoc* nature of the approach and the complex *post hoc translation devices* then hid the common-sense nature of these assumptions from the sociologists, making it almost impossible for them to analyze the most fundamental aspects of their theories. In this way they became the captives of common sense, rather than scientists trying to use and study common sense to construct better understandings of social phenomena. It is now important to analyze these metaphysical assumptions and to show how these assumptions, which are either wrong or very distorting when taken out of the whole context of common-sense discourse and action in which they were created and used, must be replaced by a more existential perspective on deviance.

The Assumption of Moral Absolutism

One of the basic assumptions of common sense in the earlier centuries of Western societies, and very probably in all reasonably simple societies, was *the assumption that the moral rules and other meanings of the society are absolute.* There are at least six basic properties to this assumption of absoluteness concerning any social meanings (i.e., ideas, beliefs, feelings, values, etc.). First, the meanings are assumed to be completely *homogeneous* (or the same) for everyone (or, at least, for all normal, adequate persons). There can be no variability or relativity of morality, beliefs, etc. Second, the meanings are assumed to be *unproblematic,* so that everyone can be assumed to know without question or uncertainty what is right or wrong at all times and for all situations. Third, the meanings are assumed to be *external* to the individual, independent of his own will, so that they in no way depend on him for their existence or meaning. Fourth, the meanings are assumed to be *necessary*: There can be no escaping them or choosing not to invoke them. Fifth, the meanings are assumed to be a *necessary part of reality,* derived from the very substance of Being or God. Sixth, the meanings are assumed to be *timeless* or eternal. They are always the same; they do not change or go into abeyance.

These assumptions have been made not only by men acting from common sense, but, more importantly, by officials seeking to control the members of Western societies in accord with their own morality. This *official moral absolutism* and its consequences will be discussed later (especially in Chapters 3, 4, and 7), but it is important to note here that official control agencies in Western societies take a more absolute view of morality than do most men of common sense in these same societies. For reasons to be discussed later, the officials themselves do in fact violate the supposedly absolute morality for the ostensible purpose of enforcing it, and they necessarily reinterpret it as their situations change; however, this does not prevent them from acting *as if* the morality they are enforcing is absolute. Official moral absolutism is important for our purposes here because the sociologists from the eighteenth century up to the twentieth century were sometimes official agents of control and, more often, were engaged in helping officials to find better ways to "solve social problems," which largely meant enforcing the supposedly absolute morality. The traditional sociological perspective on deviance, then, was largely developed within an official context, so that the sociologists tended more strongly than most men of common sense to assume the absolutism of morals, beliefs, and other social meanings.

These early sociologists unquestioningly accepted the official assumption that there was something necessarily "immoral" about such actions as suicide, divorce, or theft; they implicitly assumed that the meanings of such terms as "moral," "immoral," "crime," and "suicide" could be taken for granted. These assumptions led them and succeeding generations of sociologists to adopt a theoretical perspective on these forms of behavior that assumed such behavior must be studied *as violations of moral rules* and that the meanings of these social categories, including "moral rule" itself, are unproblematic. These theoretical assumptions have had far-reaching consequences for sociological studies of social rules and social order; and repudiation of these assumptions has been one of the most important reasons for the creative developments in recent years in the field of deviance and in the theory of social order.

The Social Relativity of Moral Rules. In relatively simple, homogeneous, and stable societies the members of the society generally *take it for granted* that their many social meanings are right and adequate. To them it is "obvious" that reality has one and only one meaning; it is also obvious that any man of "good will" with "adequate senses" will "see" the meaning of things in just the way any such member of that society sees them.

The members of simple societies have little reason to see

things differently. Most of their communications are with other members of the little society in which experiences have been largely homogeneous. Such an *absolutist view* of one's way of life probably makes the group more successful in its attempts to compete with other groups and to preserve itself. Most contacts with other groups involve actual or potential conflict, which tends to encourage an absolutist view of one's "way of life" and a view of one's way as obviously superior to that of the enemy "barbarians," the inferior outsiders. Also, most records of events are simply transmitted personal memories, which is the form of recording that is most subject to reconstruction to fit the demands of any current social situation.

We must, of course, be careful not to fall victim to the same tendency to accept a polarized view of the "barbarians." There have probably always been primitive philosophers, marginal men, diplomats with dual allegiances, and cynical politicians who questioned the rules of their societies; but there is a real difference in the frequencies and degrees to which members of different societies take their social meanings for granted and as absolute. Generally, *the more simple, homogeneous, closed, stable and internally unconflictful a social group, the more the tendency of its members to take their social meanings for granted and as absolute.* The converse seems equally true: *the more complex, variegated, open, changing and internally conflictful a social group, the more the tendency of its members to see their social meanings as problematic and relative.*

Even when members of a society come to see tastes, motives, and beliefs as relative and subjective, even as legitimately varying for different groups, individuals and situations, they resist seeing social rules as similarly relative. There are no doubt many reasons for the tenacity of this belief in the absoluteness and universality of social rules. Rules are seen as basic or ultimate: they form much of the basis on which the accepted differences in motives, tastes, and beliefs are regulated or coordinated. Because of this, any questioning of the rules is generally seen as posing a threat to the ordering of one's social life and, thus, arouses deep anxieties. In the Western World the *moral rules* have been seen as the most absolute rules of all. Because the moral rules were believed to be given by God (the *one* God), and were believed to be unalterably known to each individual through his God-given conscience, they were seen as absolute, universalistic and unproblematic. Given the great dominance of Christian thought in moral matters for more than a thousand years, this absolutist view of moral rules (and of the crucial importance of moral rules to social order) pervaded most social thought, so much so that it was taken for granted by most social thinkers.

From the sixteenth century on, the rapid increase in involvement with non-Western cultures, combined with increasing religious differences between and within nations in the Western World, led to an increasing rejection of the absolutist view of other societies. Though the theories of evolution tried to show that the other cultures were moving in the direction of Western culture, social thinkers increasingly accepted the diversity of moral and other rules *between* cultures. By the early twentieth century anthropologists had been reasonably successful in showing that there is tremendous diversity in the rules found in different cultures, so much so that one can almost always find exceptions to any rule which was once thought to be universally shared. Sociologists readily accepted the "relativity" of rules *between* cultures; but until quite recently they have continued to take an absolutist view of moral rules *within* Western societies.

The Problematic Nature of Moral Rules Within American Society.   Throughout most of the early history of sociology the assumption of the absolutism of rules was so strongly taken for granted that deviations from the rules were called "pathology," and there developed a specialized field of study concerned with such deviations, called "Social Pathology." [8] The supposed deviations from the rules were implicitly assumed to be relatively unusual or rare, and harmful to the individuals involved and to society.

The assumption that *only* one set of rules is important in explaining behavior in any given society was felt to be so essential to sociological analyses that Durkheim himself had considered any disagreements over these rules among the members of society to be "pathological." [9] Yet it was apparent to any French intellectual, especially to one as well acquainted with Romantic literature as Durkheim, that there was a great deal of disagreement in France over the moral meanings of suicide. The arguments over the morality of suicide were intense and bitter. On one side, the conservative social thinkers, aligned with the Church, considered suicide to be absolutely immoral, with no consideration of the "extenuating circumstances" of situations. On the other side were the Romantics, aligned with most members of the intelligentsia and the urban, upper classes, who not only accepted certain situational circumstances to be extenuations of moral blame, but in many instances glorified suicide as the mark of the free man who refuses to submit to the constraints of an evil world. This view led the conservatives to attack them for causing "suicide epidemics" among their young readers. Between these extremes ranged every type and degree of opinion. In spite of these obvious moral disagreements, Durkheim felt it essential to assume that there was some absolute moral rule against suicide which did not

8. See the classic article on this by C. Wright Mills, "The Professional Ideology of Social Pathologists," *American Journal of Sociology,* 49 (Sept., 1943).

9. See E. Durkheim, *op. cit.,* pp. 297–392. Durkheim's argument about "pathology" was very rightly and thoroughly criticized by Roger Lacombe in his classic work on *La Methode sociologique de Durkheim: Étude Critique,* Paris: Felix Alcan, 1926.

vary significantly from one group to another within French society. In order to justify this assumption in the face of the moral disagreements, he argued that such individual disagreements were "pathological" and temporary and, therefore, need not be taken into consideration in a sociological theory of suicide.

Durkheim had attacked the Church and its supporters, who believed that moral rules were absolute *because* God had decreed them as part of the structure of being. But, agreeing with the conservative position that only moral absolutism makes social order (or "social integration") possible, Durkheim replaced the moral absolutism of the Church with the moral absolutism of society. As he put it so pointedly, "It is necessary to choose between God and society." For him each served the same purpose: each provided the absolute moral rules which he believed essential for maintaining and explaining social order within any society.

Durkheim's theory of moral absolutism was soon challenged by one of the greatest works of analytical and historical sociology, Albert Bayet's *Le Suicide et la Morale*.[10] In the introduction to this detailed analysis of the moral meanings of suicide in French society, Bayet argued that Durkheim had not actually attempted any analysis of the mass of evidence concerning the moral meanings of suicide in French society, but had, instead, simply *assumed* that these moral meanings were whatever they had to be to fit the preconceptions of his general theory. Bayet concluded from his own historical analysis of expressions of moral feelings in books, laws, magazines, newspapers, and other such sources that there was a great deal of argument, much of it bitter, over the morality and immorality of suicide in French society, espe-

10. See A. Bayet, *La Suicide et la Morale*, Paris: Felix Alcan, 1922. For some reason, this great work of analytical and historical sociology disappeared from the works of sociologists, not only in the English-speaking world, but in France as well.

cially in the nineteenth century. In general, he concluded that on one side there was the *simple* (or absolute) *morality* of the more rural, lower class, uneducated, religious groups which viewed suicide as categorically evil, without consideration of any situational circumstances; and on the other side there was the "nuanced" or *situational morality* of the more urban, upper class, educated and unreligious groups which viewed suicide as either moral or immoral, depending on the types of situations in which it occurred. This finding was later accepted by Maurice Halbwachs' in his important work on *Les Causes du Suicide* and extended into a general criticism of Durkheim's method of analysis in *Suicide*.[11] Essentially, Halbwachs argued that systematic differences in the moral meanings of suicide cross-cut all of the important relations Durkheim found between suicide and other social phenomena, such as rates of divorce; that these differences in moral meanings constitute a fundamental part of the differences in "ways of life" that are the actual causes of the relations found by Durkheim; and that, consequently, Durkheim's attempts to validate his theory of suicide empirically cannot be accepted.

Unfortunately, these important conclusions from the works of Bayet and Halbwachs were almost completely unknown to sociologists concerned with deviance until quite recently, especially in the United States, where deviance was becoming an important and specialized field of study. Sociologists continued to assume that the members of society experience no significant problems in knowing what rules to apply to any given situation and what exactly they *should* do in view of these relevant rules—in general, sociologists continued to assume the rules and their meanings were absolute.

The *social disorganization theory* of deviance, which was

11. See Maurice Halbwachs, *op. cit.* Also see the chapter on "Halbwachs' Sub-Culture Theory of Suicide" in *The Social Meanings of Suicide, op. cit.*, pp. 124–131.

developed by the Chicago school of sociologists, and which for many years was the dominant theory of deviance in American sociology, implicitly assumed that the moral rules of American society are universally shared, unproblematic in their meanings, and must constitute the basic factors in any explanation of deviance. In addition, the important works proposing the social disorganization theory of deviance, such as Thrasher's famous work on *The Gang*,[12] assumed that laws are logically derived from these homogeneously shared moral rules, so that the relations between moral rules and laws would have to be unproblematic as well.

This assumption of an unproblematic congruence between the moral rules and laws of society was successfully challenged in the 1930s by Lind, Sellin, and others. Lind argued that in urban areas, where there are many different ethnic groups, some of the groups have moral rules that are in conflict with the laws, which have been enacted by legislative bodies dominated by other groups.[13] This led Sellin and others to argue that sociologists must clearly distinguish between the social moral rules (or "conduct norms") and the laws.[14] This line of thought had gone a long way toward recognizing the problematic nature of moral rules in our society, but it remained largely submerged for at least two more decades.

The social disorganization theory of the Chicago School was largely displaced by the *functionalist* theory of deviance,

12. See F. Thrasher, *The Gang*, Chicago: The University of Chicago Press, 1927.

13. See A. W. Lind, "Some Ecological Patterns of Community Disorganization in Honolulu," *American Journal of Sociology*, 36 (1930), pp. 206–220. For a general critique of many of these urban studies of deviance, see Terrance Morris, "A Critique of Area Studies," in *The Criminal Area*, London: Routledge and Kegan Paul, 1958, pp. 92–105, and David J. Bordua, "A Critique of Sociological Interpretations of Gang Delinquency," *The Annals of the American Academy of Political and Social Science*, 338 Nov., 1961), pp. 120–136.

14. See Thorstein Sellin, *Culture Conflict in Crime*, New York: Social Science Research Council, 1938.

especially as proposed by Robert K. Merton in his famous essay on "Social Structure and Anomie." [15] Drawing heavily on Durkheim's theory of society and deviance, notably as presented in *Suicide*, this approach was in complete agreement with the earlier theories concerning the nature of moral rules. The functionalists implicitly assumed that moral rules are homogeneously accepted and are unproblematic in American society.

Merton's theory of anomie, social structure, and deviance makes several assumptions concerning the unproblematic nature of social meanings in American society. He argues that all individuals in American society are after the same goal, that is, "success," but that individuals have different degrees of legitimate opportunity for success available to them because of social stratification. Merton assumes, first of all, that all members of the society, and certainly all sociologists reading his work, will understand without problem the meaning of "success." In one way he is probably right. It is reasonably clear from the context of his work that by "success" he means "financial success" or, at least, "socio-economic success." He is arguing, then, that all Americans are socialized to desire "financial success" or "socio-economic success" and it seems likely that most Americans, certainly most people reading his essay, would understand this and would have some idea about the nature of financial success. Beyond this, however, there is little reason to expect that Americans would agree.

There is no prima facie reason to believe that Americans would agree very widely on who is or who is not a "financial success" in our society. We would probably find that people are able to agree on those at the pinnacle of "success" and on those at the bottom. But even here there are some obvious problems. For example, would all Americans agree that the

15. Robert K. Merton, "Social Structure and Anomie," *American Sociological Review*, 3 (Oct., 1938), pp. 672–682.

present generation of Rockefellers are "financial successes"? Certainly everyone would agree that there are few people in the world who are wealthier. Yet most Americans would probably consider an individual to be "successful" only to the extent that he has "achieved" something, only to the extent that he is a "self-made man." Seen in this perspective, it would be difficult for people to decide whether the present generation of Rockefellers is "financially successful." It should be apparent, then, that there are a number of different dimensions of meaning involved in an idea as seemingly simple as "financial success," so that individuals would have serious disagreements in trying to classify the members of our society on these terms.

The meanings of "success" are far more problematic than the meanings of "financial success." There are almost as many *kinds* of "success" as there are important lines of activity in our society: "political success," "success in living," "athletic success," "family success," and so on. While the functionalists might like to believe that all of these bear some simple and logically structured relation to each other, so that it would be possible to construct some "index" of "success," this simply does not seem to be the case. Success in any line of activity is commonly seen by members of our society as in fundamental conflict with "success" in other lines of activity. For example, such popular works as *The Man in the Grey Flannel Suit* have described the common-sense conflicts between being a "business success" and being a "successful family man." This particular work has also made it clear that just how these different kinds of "success" are related to each other is highly problematic for the members: it is something they must worry about, feel anguish about, and make decisions about, all largely in darkness.

Even the meanings of such simpler social conceptions as "poverty" and "wealth" are problematic in our society. This is apparent from the great conflicts that are raging among "experts" and "politicians" over the formal definitions of "poverty." Each "expert" has his own criteria for specifying "what poverty really is," so there are many different definitions. As a consequence, estimates of the frequency of "poverty" differ by as much as forty million individuals.[16]

On first consideration, both the Durkheimian and the Mertonian theories of anomie and deviance might seem to imply that there are certain necessary problems of meaning in our society. Each would seem to imply that some individuals for various reasons come into conflict with the values and ideas of the rest of the society. However, closer examination of these two theories reveals this denial of absolutism to be only an apparent one. In one of his several interpretations of the meaning of anomie, Durkheim argues that anomie is a failure of social meanings, especially of moral meanings, which leads to deviance, especially to suicide. However, the ideas about meaning involved here did not lead to any conclusion that there might be conflicts or disagreements among the members of society over the meanings of things; nor did it lead to any idea that members might ever be free to create new meanings for situations. Instead, Durkheim argued that this "failure" in meaning caused the individual to commit suicide quite independently of his will. Anomie, therefore, was a *proof* both of the lack of problems of meaning and of the lack of independence of the individual from the absolutism of society.

Merton's theory of anomie rests upon his assumption that in a society in which individuals have the same goal, that is, "success," but in which there are differences in the legitimate opportunities for success available to individuals, there will exist a strain within individuals, an anomic strain, which will

16. For one of the better discussions of the problems encountered in trying to define "poverty" officially see Ben B. Seligman, *Permanent Poverty: An American Syndrome*, Chicago: Quadrangle, 1968, pp. 21–40.

produce an increasing tendency to deviance as the strain increases. His theory too might seem to rest upon certain differences in the *meaningful* opportunities, perhaps in the perceived opportunities, available to individuals; but he circumvents this possibility by treating stratification as an "objective variable," that is, as a variable which could be perceived by the omniscient sociologist, but which need not be perceived by the individual. Moreover, when we look at the functional theory of social stratification, we find that stratification differences themselves are supposed to be the result of unproblematically shared values in the society: the values on achievement, the means to achievement, and so on.

Rather than constituting or implying meaningful problems for the members of society, these theories of anomie involve a denial of such meaningful problems, even of the possibility of such problems. (Besides, the only alternative admitted to *the* absolute social meanings is ·'meaninglessness," so that at most violations and disagreements could only be "meaningless.")

To those sociologists who share the traditional structural-functional perspective on deviance, one of the great beauties of anomie theory is that it appears to explain the violation of the rules of society in terms of the absolute rules themselves; thus, it gives the appearance of explaining seeming rejections of the values of society in terms of an absolute acceptance of the values. The apparent disagreements and conflicts in social meanings disappear in a grander synthesis of social meanings; social divisions vanish in a greater homogeneity of society; and social disorder is explained by an insuperable social order. What might appear to be unsocial or anti-social, and what might appear to be instances of freedom, "really prove" the absolutism of society. There is no way out of the closed system.

The first major break with the functionalist assumption

that moral meanings are unproblematic to the members of our society came from the *sub-culture* theories of delinquency. The students of delinquency implicitly assumed along with the functionalists that there is a dominant set of moral rules in American society, a middle class morality, that must be used as the point of departure for any sociological theory of deviance. It also seemed apparent to them that there were some important differences between the moral rules of juvenile gangs and the so-called conventional morals of middle-class groups. Cohen,[17] Kobrin [18] and others attempted to resolve this conflict by assuming that lower-class delinquent gang boys are ambivalent about middle-class rules: they accept them but cannot achieve in terms of them, so they attack these rules by developing some kind of "inverse" moral rules. The problem with this interpretation is that there is almost no good evidence to indicate that gang boys are "ambivalent" about middle-class rules. It seems much clearer that they simply *reject these conventional rules for some purposes and accept them for others.*

Matza argued that delinquent boys seem to be committed to conventional moral rules, but that our society provides these boys with plausible justifications ("techniques of neutralization") for certain kinds of violations of these rules.[19]

17. Albert K. Cohen, *Delinquent Boys*, Glencoe: The Free Press, 1955.
18. See Solomon Kobrin, "The Conflict of Values in Delinquency Areas," *American Sociological Review*, 16 (Oct., 1951), pp. 653–661. Among the other important theorists in this tradition of thought are, for example, Walter B. Miller, "Lower Class Culture as a Generating Milieu of Gang Delinquency," *Journal of Social Issues*, 14 (1958), pp. 5–19. For a thorough critique of the theory that the sub-culture of poverty as a cause of crime see Charles A. Valentine *Culture and Poverty: Critique and Counter–Proposals*, Chicago: University of Chicago Press, 1968.
19. The first publication presenting this point of view was that by Gresham Sykes and David Matza, "Techniques of Neutralization: A Theory of Delinquency," *American Sociological Review*, 22 (Dec., 1957), pp. 664–670. The most developed form of the theory appears in David Matza, *Delinquency and Drift*, New York: John Wiley, 1964.

More recently, the Schwendingers,[20] Werthman [21] and others have tried to show that there need not be any important interactions between conventional rules and rules associated with violations of these conventional rules. The same individuals can and do accept "conflicting" moral rules, yet need not experience any conflicts between these different rules because they *apply them to different situations in their lives.* The rules are *situationally meaningful.*

This line of thought and the work of the labelling theorists (see Chapters 5 and 6) have led increasingly to the realization that there are many different and partially unrelated *situational moralities* in American society. Very importantly, the students of deviance have increasingly rejected the assumption that moral rules are homogeneously shared by the members of our society. They have come to see that American society is a *morally pluralistic society* because it is made up of a large number of groups, especially ethnic groups, that have different moral rules, and because even within groups the individuals have come increasingly to have different situational moralities.

The Assumption of Moral Determinism

Another implicit assumption of the officials and sociologists concerned with studying and solving "social problems" in the nineteenth century was that social problems must be studied and solved from the standpoint of morality. They were assuming, then, that "immoral actions" were the result

20. Herman and Julia Schwendinger, "Delinquent Stereotypes of Probable Victims," in Malcolm W. Klein, ed., *Juvenile Gangs in Context,* Englewood Cliffs: Prentice-Hall, 1967, pp. 91–105.

21. Carl Werthman, "The Function of Social Definitions and the Development of Delinquent Careers," in *Task Force Report: Delinquency and Youth Crime,* the President's Commission on Law Enforcement and Administration of Justice, Washington, D.C.: U.S. Government Printing Office, 1967, pp. 155–170.

of moral decision-making on the part of the individuals who committed them. If one assumed that each individual performing any action knows absolutely the moral meanings of that action and bases his decisions on how to act in terms of those moral meanings, then it makes good common sense to assume as well that *an immoral action can be adequately explained in terms of its immorality*. This was the *assumption of moral determinism* that is so basic to both the traditional common-sense and sociological perspective on deviance.

Modern sociologists became firmly committed to this assumption of moral determinism by their acceptance of functional theory. Functional theory was partly a revolt against the assumptions of the utilitarian theories of human actions. These utilitarian theories argued that the attempt of the individual to achieve his greatest self-interest would lead to the greatest interests of all individuals, which would include the maintenance of social order. Durkheim, in his first important work, *The Division of Labor in Society*, rejected these utilitarian assumptions, as found in Herbert Spencer's sociology. Durkheim argued that such unbridled pursuit of self-interest would lead to social chaos, rather than to social order. He argued that the utilitarians had overlooked the importance of social values in upholding and making effective any form of utilitarian contractual relations, such as those found in the economic bargaining of the marketplace. Further, he stated, these values were simply taken for granted by the utilitarians and were actually crucial in producing social order. (This will be discussed in greater detail in Chapter 7.) As we have already seen, Durkheim then went on to make these social values the basis of society and the fundamental determinant of social order. For Durkheim, society was a *moral* order. It was this line of thought, developed further by the later functional sociologists, best represented by the works of Merton and Parsons, that made the assumption of moral determinism an integral part of the traditional sociological perspective on deviance.

As the sociology of deviance developed, this implicit assumption of moral determinism was incorporated by almost all sociological explanations of deviance. The sociologists did not consider whether morality might be an irrelevant aspect, or, perhaps, simply one factor which an individual took into consideration in deciding what to do. They wound up focusing their attention almost entirely on the question of *why* an individual would *choose* to do "immoral things."

Once we recognize that ours is a pluralistic society, that there are basic disagreements over morality (especially between the officials who are defining deviance and those officials who are defined as deviants), then we can see that this assumption of moral determinism is necessarily wrong. While it still *might* be the case that individuals are committing actions primarily because of the nature of the moral considerations that they give to the action, it would not make any sense to try to look at the moral decision-making of an individual categorized as "deviant" from the standpoint of the moral beliefs of the officials who are defining his actions as immoral. Yet, even the relatively recent work by Sykes and Matza on "neutralization processes" [22] and delinquent acts assumes that the delinquents share an absolute morality with the officials who are defining them as delinquents, so that they must go through some kind of process by which they neutralize their "feelings of guilt" before they can commit the "immoral action."

When we also see that members of our society experience real problems in determining the specific implications of abstract morals for their actions in any concrete situation, as, indeed, we shall argue is the case (see, especially, Chap-

22. See Sykes and Matza, "Techniques of Neutralization," *op. cit.*

ter 5), then we can see that, even if individuals in our society shared all of the same morals, there would still be an indeterminacy in the relations between these abstract morals and the actions of individuals. Each individual would be forced to take into consideration factors other than the morals themselves in deciding what he should do in a given situation.

We shall find, then, that in our highly complex and morally pluralistic society there can never be any simple determinant relations between a given set of morals and the real actions of individuals. We shall find it necessary to bring in many other forms of social meanings and meaningful phenomena to explain why individuals do perform those kinds of actions considered to be deviant by some important group in the society and, indeed, why such groups consider those things to be immoral. For one thing, in complete opposition to functional theory, we shall find it necessary (in Chapter 7) to consider the factor of *power*, both social power and physical power, as fundamental in explaining the making of rules, the applications of rules, and the relations between rules and social order in our society.

The Assumption of the Omniscient Sociologist

At the same time that sociologists assumed the moral meanings of society to be absolute, or unproblematic, for the members of society, they assumed that the social meanings of the members of society could be determined unproblematically by the sociologist. This assumption by the positivistic sociologist was especially striking in its contrast with the extensive consideration given to the *problems of determining social meanings* by the historical sociologists, especially those in the tradition of Dilthey and Weber. These historical sociologists were, in fact, concerned with the fundamental problems of early phenomenology, which took the meaningful phenomena experienced by individuals in everyday life as the basic reality of their study and argued that the "objective" determination of these phenomena is problematic for anyone. It was no coincidence that Weber defined "social action" itself as "subjectively meaningful action" and the basic method he used to analyze the subjective meanings was "understanding." [23] Unfortunately, Weber's formalized method of "understanding" involved the construction of "ideal types," which were not meant to represent directly what the members of society take to be reality, but, rather, what the sociologists considered to be the *essential* features of social reality. He did, of course, seek to determine the meanings of things to the members of society and, to some extent, to construct his ideal types in the light of this determination. But, in the end, he, too, failed to see how fundamentally problematic the determination of the social meanings is for the sociologist, probably because he did not see how problematic the meanings were to the members of society themselves.

There is a great difference between Weber's weak assumption of sociological omniscience and the assumption of sociological omniscience made by the positivistic structuralist. To the structuralists, such as Durkheim, Merton and Parsons, any problems that sociologists might have in determining the meanings of things to the members of society were seen as so small that they warranted little consideration. In a very real sense, they assumed the sociologists to be omniscient,

23. I have previously discussed Weber's treatment of social meanings in *The Social Meanings of Suicide, op. cit.,* pp. 235–246. There are innumerable examples of the "arrogance of sociologists" in imposing their own meanings on the members of society to be found in the structural-functional literature, the many discussions of the "dysfunctions of bureaucracy" serve as an excellent example. See, for example, the essay by Robert K. Merton, "Bureaucratic Structure and Personality," in *Social Theory and Social Structure,* Glencoe: The Free Press, 1957, pp. 197–200.

to be able to see, for example, what purposes were "really" served by the actions of the members,[24] whereas the members were often assumed to be either ignorant of such things or irrational in their understandings. The sociologists would impose their understandings of the social world upon society and what the members might say about these understandings was irrelevant. It was in this way that the sociologists were able to divine the "real functions" of social forms.

We have already seen this assumption in one of its more extreme forms in Durkheim's *ad hoc* construction of a formal definition of suicide that not only violated the common-sense meanings of suicide, but, by doing so, made his own analysis of the official statistics on suicide irrelevant. The other examples of this assumption at work are extremely numerous, but two brief analyses will serve our purposes sufficiently.

We have already seen how Merton assumed the meanings of success to be unproblematic for the members of society. Implicitly, of course, he was assuming that the sociologist would know what "success really means" and that any sociologist who wanted to study success, perhaps to "test" his theory of deviance, would be able to do so without facing any serious difficulties in defining the meaning of "success." But his assumptions about the meanings of deviance itself are even more pertinent. Merton argued that there are five distinct "types of deviance." [25] He then constructed these types in a logical fashion in terms of whether the members accept or reject the normatively-defined goals of society and whether they accept or reject normatively-defined means for obtaining those goals. He argues that anomie will lead to a tendency toward any combination of these five different types of deviance. The theory does not actually contain any means for specifying what kind of anomie might

24. See Albert Cohen, *Delinquent Boys, op. cit.*
25. See Robert K. Merton, "Social Structure and Anomie," *op. cit.*

be related to what types of deviance. As the theory is stated, then, any sociologist who wanted to determine whether anomie was actually producing deviance would have to determine not only whether there was such anomie, but also whether it was associated with any changes in the amount of the five different types of deviance. This would mean that the sociologist would have to know when the five different types of deviance were occurring. For example, he would have to be able to specify exactly when the form of deviance he called "ritualism" was taking place. Ritualism was defined as accepting the "means" of society, while rejecting, or not being concerned with, the goals of society. The primary example of concern to him is that of bureaucratic behavior in which the means are supposed to displace the ends, so that individuals ritualize the behavioral forms, while forgetting about the goals these behavioral forms were originally intended to achieve. But how is the sociologist to know when a bureaucrat is maintaining the means, such as the behavioral forms of bureaucratic practice, while not relating this behavior to the ultimate goals toward which the bureaucracy was originally oriented? Is he to ask the bureaucrat whether he is no longer concerned with the purpose of the organization? Surely not, for anyone would expect common-sensically that the bureaucrat might simply lie about it. Instead, Merton assumes that the answer is obvious. The sociologist will look at the operations of the bureaucrat and of the bureaucracy as a whole and he, the sociologist, will specify whether "ritualism" (deviance) is taking place. The sociologist, not the members, will say whether the members are living up to the goals of the organization. Most importantly, the sociologists' imputed meanings will be treated as objective (scientific) facts, not as problematic ideas derived from his own common-sense understandings.

Merton's theory of deviance also assumes the omniscience of the sociologist in another important way. We noted that

Merton's theory does not include any way of specifying which of the five types of deviance will be associated with any particular anomic strain. Yet, Merton himself never attempted to show that a given kind of anomic strain, such as that supposedly experienced by the urban poor, leads to an increase in all types of deviance, or, say, to an increase in some types and a decrease in other types. He never looked at the five different types of deviance when he was considering the supposed anomic strains of the poor. Instead, he assumed, in line with the middle-class common-sense assumptions about the poor, that the poor would tend toward the form of deviance represented by crime, which in turn could be, he assumed, represented by official information on crime, such as delinquency statistics. So his own suggestions for testing his theory were limited almost entirely to assuming that there exists some specific relationship between a given anomic strain, which he assumed to exist, and a given type of deviance, which he assumed could be unproblematically specified, even though this was a violation of his own far more complex theoretical argument. (It did not even seem to occur to him that old people, who are one of the poorest groups in our society with the fewest "opportunities of success," are also those who commit the fewest crimes.)

The only way in which this can be seen to be a reasonable deduction from the theory is to assume that in some way the sociologist is omniscient enough to be able to disentangle the potentially complex relations between any given anomic strain and the five different types of potential deviance. This is also a necessary assumption for any sociologist wishing to take Merton's theory seriously, since the theory is quite untestable as stated and could only be made to appear testable, in terms of the ordinary criteria of statistical tests accepted by Merton and the other structuralists, by assuming that the sociologist knows, without even having to carefully analyze the situation, how to cut away almost all the complexities and to get at the few essential "facts" that constitute *the* relations between anomie and deviance.

Albert Cohen's sub-cultural theory of delinquency [26] has been one of the most influencial structural-functional works in recent years. It is probably the best known attempt to explain deviance in terms of Parsons' theory of social action. It is also one of the rare attempts by a Parsonian theorist to come to grips with the problem of determining the meanings of social actions to the actors themselves.

Cohen's fundamental method of determining the social meanings to delinquent boys of their own actions is to work backward from the actions they are observed (or supposed) to have committed. One of the most important examples of this *backward analysis of social meanings* is his analysis of the "non-utilitarian" nature of delinquent acts. He first argued that many of the actions of delinquent boys are of the nature of vandalism (desecration of principals' offices and so on). He then argued that even in the case of theft delinquent boys often give away the stolen property, destroy it, or in other ways do not "make use" of it. He immediately concludes from these that the delinquent acts of the boys— even the acts of theft—are "non-utilitarian."

Cohen's method assumes that the sociologist can determine the meanings of the actions to the actors themselves simply by observing the actions, comparing a few of them, and "inferring" the meanings. Apparently he saw no need to determine what the boys themselves had to say about their actions. If we look carefully at the actions of the boys and consider whether they themselves might see some utility in their actions, I think we can see, common-sensically, that there may be forms of "utility" which have not occurred to Cohen. For example, we know common-sensically, as well as from Whyte's analysis of *Street Corner Society,* that many

---

26. See Albert Cohen, *Delinquent Boys, op. cit.*

groups of young men in our society have strong norms in favor of sharing one's wealth with the other members of the group. We also know in the same way that the sharing of wealth is subject to a norm of reciprocity; that is, an individual who gives something away to another individual can reasonably expect or demand things from that individual in the future. Giving away stolen goods, therefore, could be seen as quite "utilitarian," even from the standpoint of middle-class understandings of usefulness. It would be comparable to giving business gifts. Again, it is possible that the boys saw the destruction of stolen goods as very "useful" because they thought it was a way of getting revenge on other people or of avoiding detection by the police for having stolen property in their possession.

The point is that Cohen, like most of the positivistic, structural sociologists, has assumed that he, as a sociologist, can unproblematically determine the meanings of social actions to the actors themselves. He has assumed that the sociologist is omniscient about the social meanings of action. The truth seems to be, rather, that we as sociologists must view the meanings of actions as far more problematic than the ordinary members of society would do in their everyday actions. In fact, *we must take the problems of objectively determining the social meanings of actions to the actors as the fundamental problems of sociology.* This is the foundation of the theoretic stance toward common-sense meanings which sociologists must take. If they fail to take this stance, then they can hardly be said to be studying society objectively. Instead, they are taking the naturalistic stance of common sense. They are *acting within common sense* and are imposing their own *ad hoc meanings* upon the actions of other members of society in roughly the same way in which ordinary members of the society do in their everyday interactions. The only difference is that these sociologists are assuming sociological omniscience by wrapping the mantle of science about themselves and asking for special deference to their ideas because they have seized this mantle.

The Assumption of the Statistical-Hypothetical Perspective

The primary source of information used by sociologists to construct and test their statistical theories of deviance has been the official information on deviance, constructed and published by the official agents of control. We shall see (in Chapter 3) that there were many important reasons why sociologists became so committed to using these official statistics on deviance; we shall also see (in Chapter 4) the ways in which the use of these statistics bias the sociological theories of deviance. But the use of the statistical-hypothetical method in social research on deviance is partially independent of the use of official statistics and must be briefly examined.

The hypothetical approach assumes that one should make all basic decisions about how data will be classified, analyzed, and validated *before* one begins the research. The purpose of this is to eliminate bias in the collection and analysis of the data used in testing any theory. Another assumption of the hypothetical method is that one should "deduce" a hypothesis about some given phenomenon from an abstract theory intended to explain that phenomenon and then analyze statistical data to determine whether the hypothesis is true or "verified." If the hypothesis is upheld, then the theory is considered to be acceptable (though never absolutely "proved"). By its very nature the hypothetical approach assumes that *one must know (or assume for research purposes that he knows) the general truths about social phenomena before he begins his research,* or, at least, the statistical part of his research. *One must know the whole truth before he can know the particular truths.*

How he is supposed to know that whole truth before he

begins his research is left unanswered. Suppose one looks at the process as one of approximations, in which hypotheses that are rejected by analyses of the data then lead to the rejection of the theories or to some change in the theories. It is still apparent that ultimately one must have arrived at his ideas about society on some basis other than a statistical-hypothetical approach. This approach, therefore, cannot be a self-contained method and must be based upon some other, more fundamental approach. What that approach is to be is never made clear by sociologists, but what it is in fact seems much clearer: it has been the common-sense understandings of the particular sociologist deriving the hypotheses and doing the testing. Since sociologists, like members of any other group in our pluralistic society, have somewhat different common-sense understandings of our social world, they begin by assuming different general theories to be true, so they arrive at different hypotheses to be tested. The consequence is that we have statistical-hypothetical theories that are in considerable disagreement with each other.

Once again, we can refer to Merton's essay on "Social Structure and Anomie" for illustration. Merton took it for granted in this essay that human actions are fundamentally goal-oriented and that frustrations in achieving those goals would lead to some kind of action to eliminate the frustration. Rather than look first at the deviant behavior to determine whether this assumption would be valuable in explaining the deviant behavior, he *assumed* goal-orientation and the rest and then tried to deduce some hypotheses from it which could be tested by the official information on deviance. The phenomena are subjugated to the general theory.

Furthermore, the hypothetical approach in practice (as opposed to the *ideal* of the method developed by the statisticians and methodologists) often allows the investigator freedom to make his decisions on classification, methods of analysis, and so on after he has begun the research and even after much of his analysis is done. As noted above, it is primarily the complexity of the approach which allows for this kind of theoretical freedom, and it is this freedom of analysis which furthers theoretical juggling in statistical works. This theoretical juggling, combined with the arrogance of the statistical methodologists, has led many people in our society to believe that "you can prove anything with statistics." Although certainly this is an exaggeration of the truth about the method, it is nevertheless a close approximation.

3. Official Information and Official Control

In most intellectual disciplines certain ideas seem to most practitioners to be so necessary and so obvious that they become taken-for-granted. These ideas, which Thomas Kuhn has called *paradigmatic ideas*,[1] become the background ideas of the discipline. Normally, they are not themselves examined critically; rather, they are used as the basis for critical examinations of other ideas. In fact, the entire discipline seems to depend so completely on these background ideas that any critical examination of them seems to threaten the discipline itself, thereby arousing the anxieties one feels when faced with chaos or with the loss of a secure social status. They provide the basic order that constitutes the discipline's perspective on the relevant realm of reality; to deny or destroy them seems to many to destroy any possibility of order.

1. See Thomas S. Kuhn, *The Structure of the Scientific Revolution*, Chicago: The University of Chicago Press, 1962.

Introduction to the Nature and Use of Official Statistics on Moral Phenomena

In the sociology of deviance the idea that one must use statistical rates has been one paradigmatic idea. For well over one hundred years sociological thinkers in this field have used statistical rates of categories of actions as their basic information, both as their causal variables and as their variables to be explained. By the middle of the twentieth century this statistical-rate approach had become taken-for-granted. Sociologists used the approach—and the official statistics on deviance which alone filled their need for statistical data—with almost no analysis. Yet, in almost every case in which sociologists did investigate the official statistics, they concluded that these official statistics were so unreliable as to be useless. Such conclusions were widely met by a professional conspiracy of silence: The commitment to the statistical-rate approach was so great that the fact of overwhelming evidence against the use of the only available source of information for this approach, the official statistics, simply could not be faced.

In the classical works of Graunt, Süssmilch, and others in the seventeenth and eighteenth centuries, there were two main reasons for using a statistical approach to the study of social actions. Most importantly, these men lived in an age when the mathematical feats of classical mechanics seemed quite miraculous, an age in which men sought blindly to apply "the magick of number" to all natural and, indeed, all supernatural phenomena.[2] When Johann Peter Süssmilch, the first recognized "moral statistician", applied the early statistical thinking of the "political arithmeticians"

2. See my essay on "The Rhetoric of Science and the Origins of Statistical Social Thought," in Edward Tiryakian, ed., *The Sociological Phenomenon*, New York: Appleton-Century-Crofts, 1970.

to moral phenomena, such as divorce, crime, and suicide, he did so with the conviction that numbers were the appropriate way to study the "divine order" in human events; [3] that is, one uses a divine method to study a divine order. A second reason for using a statistical approach must be taken more seriously. It was apparent that one must have order if one is to do any kind of scientific study; and the order which Graunt, Süssmilch, and their successors discovered in human action was constituted by this statistical data or, as they assumed, was *revealed* by this statistical data. Like almost all men of common-sense, they had taken it for granted that moral actions are the result of choice or free will. (This, of course, is a necessary condition of common sense for any action to be legitimately subject to moral evaluation, as I shall later argue. They apparently expected from this that moral actions, and probably human actions in general, would either show a lack of order or, at least, would not show clear numerical patterns. When they discovered numerical patterns and reasonably stable relations between these patterns in the official statistics, they were astounded at the degree of order "revealed" to them. This astonishment and joyful awe was to be experienced many times in the early nineteenth century as Guerry, Quetelet, Wagner, and many other famous social analysts made the same discovery and worked to clarify the numerical relations and to explain them in terms of scientific "laws." They had "discovered" a lawful order in human actions which ordinary mortals could not divine or accept because of their "blind" belief in free will and uniqueness. Never was the Olympian feeling of a higher knowledge better expressed than in Quetelet's *Physique Sociale:*

"It is curious to see man, who with pride calls himself The King of Nature and who believes he rules all by his free will, submit

3. Johann Peter Süssmilch, *Die Gottliche Ordnung in den Veränderungen des Menschlichen Geschlechts,* Berlin, 1761.

without knowing it to the laws to which he is subject more rigorously than any other creatures. These laws are so wisely coordinated that they even escape his attention."

These early social scientists were quite right in arguing that there is an order to official statistics on "moral" phenomena. In fact, as was shown by the series of works by the moral statisticians, especially those by Wagner, Morselli, Oettingen, Bertillon, and Durkheim, the patterns that can be "discovered" are exceedingly intricate. With the advent of more sophisticated statistical techniques in the twentieth century, beginning with the analyses of the official statistics on suicide by Miner [4] and Halbwachs [5] and coming up to the very complex analyses by Henry and Short [6] and Gibbs,[7] it has proven possible to "discover" an ever increasing number of statistically "significant" patterns in these relations. As ever more sets of official statistics are considered, and as ever more variations in the patterns are found, the number of "significant" patterns that can be "discovered" seems to be infinite, limited only by the number of man hours, and computer hours, available. As these methods and the explanation of results have been extended to other forms of "deviance," each new special area has been defined by some new *official category of "deviance"*—"juvenile delinquency", "marihuana use", and so on. Consequently, this centuries-old statistical approach to deviance has blossomed into a massive "science" which could certainly go on making new "discoveries" over many centuries. Since this statistical approach to *officially defined "deviance"* has itself increasingly become an integral part of official procedure, officially sanctioned and

4. See J. R. Miner, "Suicide and its Relation to Other Factors," *American Journal of Hygiene*, Monographic Series, #2, 1922, pp. 72–112.

5. See Maurice Halbwachs, *Les Causes du Suicide, op. cit.*

6. See Andrew F. Henry and James F. Short, *Suicide and Homicide*, Glencoe: The Free Press, 1954.

7. See Jack P. Gibbs and Walter T. Martin, *Status Integration and Suicide*, Eugene, Oregon: University of Oregon Press, 1964.

financially supported,[8] criticism of the approach has itself become an act of "deviance", though the sanctions for this "deviance" thus far involve little more than scorn and difficulty in funding research. (There are not yet any official statistics, but this might someday become an important index of "cognitive deviance.")

When we consider the growing rhetorical power of mathematical symbols in our technological society [9] and its combination with such powerful official sanctioning, it becomes apparent that we could be witnessing the development of a new Ptolemaic astronomy destined to spin out over the centuries ever more complicated mathematical calculations of heavenly "epi-cycles". But there is a basic weakness in this analogy. The observations that formed the foundations of such early sciences were admittedly crude by modern standards, and certainly early scientists were not aware of the ways in which "subjective factors" and "uncertainty effects" become important determinants of scientific observations; yet these ancient forms of astronomical data were veritable models of scientific data compared to the official statistics on deviance. Unlike even ancient data in astronomy, official statistics on deviance have been created and controlled by officials, not by social scientists, so that our prima facie expectation must be that this information has been created in accord with the demands of official work, not in accord with the scientists' principles of observational controls. Second, and most importantly, those social scientists who have used the official statistics on deviance to construct and test their theories have almost never critically examined the nature of these official statistics, and have not determined how they are created.

In general, these social scientists have been guilty of the

8. The massive studies of "juvenile delinquency," most of which have been supported by official funds, are excellent examples of the way in which officials fund research on their own officially defined categories.

cardinal sin of science: they have not critically, systematically investigated the nature of the information they were using to determine the state of nature and to try to control the methods by which their information was generated so that it would be more valid and reliable. The consequence is that they have had no basis for expecting that their theories of deviance would be valid. In fact, when we do systematically investigate the nature of these official statistics, we find that they are not simply unreliable, but rather, *give a completely false idea of the nature of deviance in our society, so that only false (official) theories will be "statistically verified" by them.*

The Origins of Official Information on Moral Phenomena

At least two developments led to the emergence of official statistics on deviance in the eighteenth and early nineteenth centuries. The first was the spreading application of quantitative ideas to human phenomena; the second was the rise of systems of *moral accounting* by Western bureaucracies.

The rudimentary ideas of quantifying phenomena which have social meanings in terms of these meanings, especially the "values" given to them in society, were first developed for the practical purpose of managing economic matters by *economic accounting*, or keeping a record of economic transactions.[10] There are at least two different types of *accounts*. Perhaps the simplest form is the *memory device*. For example, while the exact uses of early double-entry bookkeeping records are unknown, it is entirely possible that their

10. Economic accounting was common practice in Greece and Rome, but it had to be re-invented in the European societies, probably sometime in the 10th or 11th century. Economic accounting is one of the few areas of social accounting for which a history which has been developed. There is a large literature here on such topics as the English pipe rolls, double-entry bookkeeping, and so on.

primary use was as memory devices for the businessmen to keep track of who owed whom what and what the balance was present. But the use of accounts as memory devices soon led to (if this is in fact the order of development) the *moral definition and sanctioning of accounts.* That is, certain records came to be socially defined as the means of "proving" what had happened and, therefore, when put into the context of the general social understandings, what "should" be done by whom toward whom, such as who "in fact" owed whom what. This form of accounting was especially found in the central governments of Europe to manage taxation problems. In England, for example, long before reading and writing were widely enough known to be used as the means of keeping records, the king's tax collectors used the lengths of sticks to account "legally" for how much a given individual had paid; these *analogue records* constituted "legal proof" of one's payments and debts to the king.

The use of these two types of quantitative accounts, but especially the non-morally defined (or *actuarial record,* as Bittner and Garfinkel have called it [11]) was greatly expanded from the fourteenth century onward as *quantitative comparisons between societies* developed. As Jacob Burckhardt pointed out, much of this kind of quantitative comparison was done at first for the purpose of "proving" which Italian city was the best through showing which had more works of art. This kind of comparison was soon extended to nations as a whole, and by the time of Machiavelli the power of different nations, such as France and England, was compared in terms of the number of troops, agricultural wealth, and other indices of power. This was the beginning of what was to be highly developed as *political arithmetic* in the seventeenth century. It was because men of practical affairs, especially rulers, came to believe that quantitative compari-

11. See Harold Garfinkel, *Studies in Ethnomethodology,* Englewood Cliffs, N.J.: Prentice-Hall, 1967.

sons of social populations was important as a way of knowing how politically powerful nations were and thence, what policies should be followed to make them more powerful than others, that officials began to create quantitative accounting systems for population, wealth, etc. For example, it was in order to get better information on the properties of the population, its causes, and its potential usefulness in political struggles that the Prussian officials paid Süssmilch to do his massive work on population in the eighteenth century. *From their very beginnings official statistics were policy-oriented and determined primarily by the political goals of the officials.*

An early example of *moral accounting systems* was found in the Church bureaucracy. Accounts of heresy and many other phenomena had been collected for many centuries, and presumably served as the model for the recording of legal accounts when the governments began to rapidly expand their legal work. (Church officials, as the educated men of the society, were much involved in keeping all state records.) However, Church accounts were not systematically reported, centralized, and tabulated until some time in the early seventeenth to the early eighteenth century, depending on the nation, when the *amount of "immorality"* came to be seen as relevant in determining the wealth and power of the nation. More specifically, the number of "confined" individuals and their activities became a basis for determining not only the wealth and power of the nation but also for *showing* the adequacy of the performance of the officials in charge of the rapidly spreading houses of confinement.

Beginning in England in the early seventeenth century, houses of confinement for all who for any reason could not, or, worse, would not work spread throughout Europe. As Foucault has argued, this massive confinement, which has persisted to the present day for various forms of "social pathology," was primarily a response to the prolonged depression throughout Europe during this period. Later it became a standard policy for dealing with non-workers, for the officials inevitably found a new reason for maintaining and expanding their bureaucracies:

Throughout Europe, confinement had the same meaning, at least if we consider its origin. It constituted one of the answers the seventeenth century gave to an economic crisis that affected the entire Western world: reduction of wages, unemployment, scarcity of coin—the coincidence of these phenomena probably being due to a crisis in the Spanish economy. Even England, of all the countries of Western Europe the least dependent on the system, had to solve the same problems. Despite all the measures taken to avoid unemployment and the reduction of wages, poverty continued to spread in the nation. . . . It was feared that they [the poor] would overrun the country, and since they could not, as on the Continent, cross the border into another nation, it was proposed that they be banished and conveyed to the New-found Land, the East and West Indies. In 1630, the King established a commission to assure the rigorous observance of the Poor laws . . .

But outside of the periods of crisis, confinement acquired another meaning. Its repressive function was combined with a new use. It was no longer merely a question of confining those out of work, but of giving work to those who had been confined and thus making them contribute to the prosperity of all. The alternation is clear: cheap manpower in the periods of unemployment, reabsorption of the idle and social protection against agitation and uprisings. Let us not forget that the first houses of confinement appear in England in the most industrialized parts of the country: Worcester, Norwich, Bristol; that the first *hôpital général* was opened in Lyons, forty years before that of Paris; that Hamburg was the first German city to have its *Zuchthaus*, in 1620. Its regulations, published in 1622, were quite precise. The internees must all work. Exact records were kept of the value of the work, and they were paid a fourth of it.[12]

12. Michael Foucault, *Madness and Civilization*, New York: Pantheon Books, 1965, pp. 49–51.

While this great confinement was spreading throughout Europe, we find the beginnings of the whole idea of *"police work"*, *a totality of morally sanctioned ideas and practices aimed at "rationally" controlling the lower classes so that they would work and not endanger the lives and interests of the upper classes:*

Confinement, that massive phenomenon, the signs of which are found all across eighteenth-century Europe, is a 'police' matter. Police, in the precise sense that the classical epoch gave to it— that is, the totality of measures which make work possible and necessary for all those who could not live without it; the question Voltaire would soon formulate, Colbert's contemporaries had already asked: 'Since you have established yourselves as a people, have you not yet discovered the secret of forcing all the rich to make all the poor work? Are you still ignorant of the first principles of the police?' [13]

Over the centuries police work was to be expanded by hundreds of other official bureaucracies dedicated to "rational" control of the lives of citizens, notably those of the lower classes who might not work willingly, pay taxes, serve in the military, be "decent" in public, and be "orderly" at all times. These bureaucracies grew steadily, but they made quantum leaps in size and power primarily in those periods when the "dangerous classes", as they were to be called in the nineteenth century, were believed by the upper classes (the "respectable classes") to threaten "public order". (This, for example, was most especially the case in the early nineteenth century when our "modern police forces" were established in the large cities, especially those with masses of poor immigrants.)

We have here, then, the beginnings of the *bureaucracies of official morality*. From their very beginnings in the early seventeenth century they were dedicated to the ideas of

13. *Ibid.*, p. 46.

"rational control" of their charges by means of "rational" procedures. From the very beginning they, like all official organizations, were *responsible* to the political rulers. Unlike officials of an earlier day, the growing size and complexity of Western societies made it very difficult for rulers to check directly on their operations. For this reason the rulers believed that some form of *accounting information* was necessary. That is, they needed some form of information which could be *legally and morally sanctioned* as the basis for *judgments* of the work of officials, and which could, therefore, be used to decide whether officials were doing their jobs morally and legally, how funds should be allocated to produce the desired results, and so on.[14]

At first, moral and legal accounts could be effectively rendered by way of *paragraph presentation* of information: The relevant information was simply written out in linear form, one item of information following another as in a paragraph, without attempting any special order. We find this in all of the early forms of information, even in those forms of economic information for which numerical estimates were already used, as in the English tax rolls. Subsequently, the growing size and complexity of information led to the development over the centuries of *tabular presentations*, or presentations of information in terms of tables or columns. This makes information more easily observed, but it does not appreciably eliminate the amount of information to be considered. Only *categorical presentations* in tabular form will do the latter, and they were quickly utilized. *Presentation of information in terms of categories brings together information on the basis of characteristics that presumably*

14. It should be clear at this point that we are in need of far more detailed information on the specific decisions and ideas of rulers or officials concerning the construction of this kind of information. We do not at present have much of this kind of information simply because historians and others have not seen it as important.

*are relevant to the purposes of the people constructing and
using the information.*

In our everyday experience we use *categories,* especially
the symbolic categories that constitute our primary means of
communication with other persons, in much the same way.
These categorizing practices alone make it possible for us to
live in a world that is infinitely complex: we have to reduce
our world of experience in terms of a small set of categories
that tell us what is relevant to our interests and problems
in living. Without thus selecting and ordering a tiny slice of
life's potential experiences as relevant to us, we would respond with random, even frenetic, responses to the innumerable stimuli. Hence, linguistic categories make human life
possible.

In everyday life we use what any official would see to be
an impossibly large number of categories. For example, we
have thousands of words referring to different types of
people and social situations, and we use them in combinations and with shades of meanings communicated by tones
of voice, emphases, facial expressions, or hand gestures to
construct complex *concrete meanings* in concrete situations.
We do this in most of everyday life because we are deeply
concerned with the concrete situation, person, and experience; we are held responsible by others for these concrete
phenomena. For example, while it is both true and necessary
that other individuals hold us responsible for killing someone
in terms of the abstract category "murder", it is also true
that they use these catagories to construct concrete meanings
for the person killed, the killer, the reasons, the weapons, the
intentions, and so on.

In the beginning bureaucracies of official morality made
use of roughly the same common-sense categories to construct more specific, concrete descriptions for their own
use. But over the centuries these bureaucracies have moved

steadily toward fewer and more isolated categories, rather than combining categories to construct more concrete descriptions. In addition, the categories used by the officials have become increasingly rigid and abstract, less affected by changing situations. Many would be tempted to see this reduction by officials of the amount of information, and the growing rigidity of the information, as the result of a steady increase in specialized knowledge concerning such actions and the persons involved. But this is ridiculous. Few social scientists would make claim to having developed specialized knowledge to the point where they *know* which categories actually constitute the scientists' *fundamentum divisionis* (or fundamental classification of phenomena in terms of their scientifically important characteristics), and certainly the non-scientific officials lack any such knowledge. Instead, officials seem to have developed at all times an *official fundamentum divisionis of types of actions and persons that allows them to manage the practical problems they face in attempting to enforce their official morality, most especially those practical problems involved in accounting for their responsibilities to the political rulers who determine their fates as officials, and, secondarily, those practical problems involved in managing increasingly complex bureaucracies of official moralities.*

It should be apparent that the more massive the information conveyed to the political rulers (and to the general public in a democratic age), the harder it is for them to see what is "really" going on and, thereby, to judge the "adequacy" of it in terms of their intentions. As governments became more complex, this problem grew at a great rate. Probably for this reason, the basic purpose of official information, that of accountability to the political rulers to whom the officials are responsible, led to the decrease in information and to its increasingly rigid nature. Second, as the bureaucracies of official morality grew, proliferated, and became more complex, the problems of handling information within the bureaucracies and the closely associated problem of managing the activities of the members of the bureaucracies. grew. These internal problems could also be solved both by reducing the amount of information that must be managed and by making that information more rigid. (Rigidity of information reduces the information that must be managed *in a given time*.) A third reason for the acceleration in the reduction of information and for its increasing rigidity in the last century seems to be the emergence of mass democracies and their attendant need for officials to "educate" the public in those matters for which they are responsible to the public. Ellul, Galbraith and others have very likely been right in arguing that the rise of mass democracy and technological society has produced a need for officials to develop highly effective propaganda—"public relations" and "political persuasion"—to manage and stabilize public responses to their official policies.[15] One of the basic rules of all effective propaganda in a mass society is that the message be simple (i.e., contain little information and, even more, that it be repeated over and over or sloganized, i.e., be rigidified). *The bureaucracies of official morality, then, must make use of the same categories and the same ideas about the categories if they are to use public relations effectively in persuading the public about the "dangers to the foundations of society," the need for more money to fight crime and delinquency, "the menace of dangerous drugs," "the rising crime wave," "the way the Mafia is destroying the moral fibre of the nation," and so on.* This need has become even greater as they have sought with increasing success to control the legal definitions both of forms of deviance and of the means they are to use in

15. Many of these arguments have been presented and analyzed in my essay on "Freedom and Tyranny in a Technological Society," in Jack D. Douglas, *Social Problems in a Technological Society: Freedom and Tyranny,* New York: Random House, 1970.

controlling it.[16] We are, then, presented with the apparent paradox that *the more massive and complex the world which the bureaucracies of official morality are trying to control, the simpler their pictures of that world and their practices for dealing with it have become. And, the more democratic the societies have become, the more rigid and autocratic the information forming much of the foundation of the administration of justice has become.* This paradox is explained by the administrative needs of officials and the requirements of accountability to which they are subject. (In American democracy public officials are held more accountable for their actions than businessmen or others. This greater accountability then becomes merely a greater pressure to become more autocratic in dealing with the public and rendering one's accounts.)

The Origins and Effects of the Quantification of Moral Phenomena

From the standpoint of common sense, few things would appear to be less subject to *quantification* than morality and immorality. Indeed, as the moral statisticians themselves realized, all social action has been traditionally viewed by men using common sense as non-quantifiable because they thought that all social actions are seen as the partial result of "free will." In addition, as I have argued in the preceding section, men of common sense are concerned primarily with the concrete. Acting from common sense, men of the Western societies have for many centuries seen moral phenomena as the most "free" and as requiring the most concrete description and evaluation (because the consequences for immorality have been so severe).

16. The police, like other special interest groups in our society, have sought to construct a social image of themselves as experts with specialized knowledge in their area of activities. The police have probably been more successful than other such groups in doing this.

Although there is still some of this common-sense belief today, there is a world of difference between the way people react today toward official statistics on human actions and the way they acted before the nineteenth century, that is, before both formal education in technological society and the officials had trained them to think differently. The contrast between the modern and the traditional attitudes of Western men is shown well in Ariès' description of the great resentment and resistance produced over several centuries by the practice of trying to record "age":

A man of the sixteenth or the seventeenth century would be astonished at the exigencies with regard to civil status to which we submit quite naturally. As soon as our children start to talk, we teach them their name, their age and their parents' name. We are extremely proud when little Paul, asked how old he is, replies correctly that he is two and a half. We feel in fact that it is a matter of importance that little Paul should get this right: what would become of him if he forgot his age? In the African bush, age is still quite an obscure notion, something which is not so important that one cannot forget it. But in our technical civilization, how could anyone forget the exact date of his birth, when he has to remember it for almost every application he makes, every document he signs, every form he fills in—and heaven knows there are enough of those and there will be more in the future. . . In the Middle Ages the Christian name had been considered too imprecise a description, and it had been found necessary to complete it with a surname, a place name in many cases. And now it has become advisable to add a further detail, the numerical character, the age. The Christian name belongs to the world of fancy, the surname to that of tradition. The age, a quantity legally measurable to within a few hours, comes from another world, that of precise figures. In our day our registration practices partake at the same time of all worlds. . . .

(The recording of births in parish registers was imposed on the priests of France by François I, but to be respected this order had to be accepted by people who for a long time remained hostile to the rigour of abstract accounting. It is generally agreed that it was only in the eighteenth century that the parish priests began keeping their registers with the exactness, or the attempted exactness, which a modern state requires of its registrars. The personal importance of the idea of age must have grown in proportion as religious and civic reformers imposed it in documentary form, beginning with the more educated social strata, that is to say, in the sixteenth century, those who had a college education.)[17]

How was this resistance to the *official quantification of everyday life* overcome? After the triumphs of the natural sciences in the seventeenth century many educated people urged quantifying and analyzing everything, as we can see in the extreme cases of Derham's physicalistic theology and Spinoza's geometrical analyses of morality. Yet deep faith in the power of mathematical analysis, which actually went all the way back to Plato, was by no means sufficient to explain the growing commitment of officials to the numeration of moral phenomena. No doubt, few of them were such believers, and men such as Süssmilch had to rely on more mundane officials to provide them with numbers. In addition, the rhetorical power of mathematical analyses was probably not at that early time sufficient throughout most of society to make this a good reason to quantify official information.

Clearly, one factor closely associated with this faith in number and its later rhetorical power was the analytical and calculating form of thought of the growing bourgeoisie. This form of thought which was so basic to their world view that Weber made it part of his famous definition of "the spirit of capitalism" in his study of the "rationalization" he believed had occurred over centuries. This rational and analytical approach contributed at least two elements to the eventual official quantification of moral phenomena. First, it con-

17. Philippe Ariès, *Centuries of Childhood*, New York: Alfred A. Knopf, 1962, pp. 15–16.

tributed the view of men and their actions as *absolute categories* (or absolute typifications). That is, rather than see men and their actions as the continuous, situation-bound, concrete persons we normally assume for our purposes of everyday interaction, it saw them as *discrete,* discontinuous phenomena that are independent of time and situations. It is this set of properties which is necessary before one can validly apply real numbers and mathematical analyses to human beings and their actions; it is this assumption that generates the *pigeon-hole perspective on man* known to all students of introductory methods in the social sciences. It is the contrast between this "bourgeois" (or technician) perspective and the natural attitude of everyday life (a more "existential perspective") which Desan has put so well in paraphrasing Sartre:

For the bourgeois, men are like peas in a can, all alike, juxtaposed, each of them equally available for an examination by the *analytical* mind, that is, able to be defined, classified, and categorized. Thus is man analyzed and placed. The bourgeois philosopher never thinks of the living dialectic, of the movement of reciprocity which links man to man. He does not see man as free creativity, man made by a fundamental 'project,' which affects his every gesture, every word, and every deed.[18]

Second, this calculative attitude was fundamental to the development of the *rational policy orientation* of officials and rulers that made official information the means of "testing" and "proving" the effectiveness of official policies. Just as the calculation of the return in relation to the investment (i.e., the profit) was so fundamental to the "spirit of capitalism," so was the calculation of the *effects* of official action relative to the policy-determined *practices* (i.e., effectiveness) so fundamental to the development of all official information. Just as the *Werkmeister* in the German asylum in

18. Desan, *Marxism and Existentialism.*

1622 established a work plan for the inmates, kept records on the work, and determined by checking those records at the end of each week whether that plan had been carried out, so did the officials check on each other (and the rulers checked on them all) by examining the official records, normally through an annual report, a practice which continues to this day.

These two factors, then, appear to have been pre-conditions leading to the quantification of moral phenomena and of human beings. Once again, the pervasive problem of limiting the amount of information seems to have been crucial. The numeration of categories of moral phenomena and of persons shows at a glance *how* effective the officials have been, *how* threatening crime is, and so on. At the same time, quantification itself strongly supports the further reduction of the numbers of categories, so that the relationship is reciprocal. More importantly, even the simplest forms of comparative analyses are made easier by the use of quantities of categories, so that the pressure toward quantification has increased along with analyses of the official information.

The Early Commitment of Sociologists to Official Statistics on Moral Phenomena. By the early nineteenth century official statistics on moral phenomena were already well-established, but the greatest strides in their development and use were made at this time. It was also at this time that the early sociologists studying and theorizing about moral phenomena became committed to their use.

This period was, as we have already noted, the great age of classical science and the age of positivism in social thought For a little more than a century, from the first quarter of the nineteenth century until sometime during the age of crises of the world wars, most educated men in the Western societies believed—and convinced the general public—that the classical forms of the natural sciences, especially the mathematical forms of analysis and verification, would provide man with an "objective" knowledge of *all* "real" phenomena. Eventually there would be an absolute knowledge independent of human biases (and even of the properties of the knowing mind itself), knowledge that would someday solve all of man's problems, perhaps even banish the spectre of death. The Western World, though thought of as a common universe by educated men and spanned by several universal institutions, was rent by so many basic differences and conflicts, both within and between nations, that there was a fundamental need of such an object-like knowledge to resolve its otherwise interminable conflicts. It was the fundamental methods of science, those of experiment and verification above all, which promised knowledge independent of the particular social perspective of the knower and, hence, rightfully enforceable upon all as *the* truth; it was the mathematical forms which embodied and communicated the methods of producing absolute knowledge. (In fact, though Gödel's proof and other developments in the twentieth century have undermined the "absolute rationality" of the classical mathematical analyses of real numbers, this form of analysis remains the ideal of "absolute rationality" and lies behind the insistence of classical science that the world of experience can be subjected to rational ordering.)

In no realm is some agreement more necessary in our pluralistic societies than that of political activity, especially when concerned with the issue of *what to do about social problems*. All of our differences are focused in the political arena, and they must somehow be worked out there if we are to avoid open conflict, an ever present possibility which has often been realized with extreme results. And those matters dealt with as "social problems that must be solved by organized political action" focus these differences and conflicts most intensely, for they call not only for the usual costs in taxes, but also for action on the part of some members of the society against other members of the same society (those who are believed to either constitute the problem or to be the causes of it). Consequently, even when there is some general consensus on what constitutes a "social problem," as there appears to have been in the nineteenth and early twentieth century, there is still disagreement over the political issue of how it is to be "solved," what the best solution is, what is "causing" the problem. In the nineteenth century there was intense conflict throughout Western societies concerning the "causes" of social problems (crime, suicide, prostition, poverty, etc.) and, hence, over the best solutions to these problems.

It was precisely such conflicts that the "absolute certainty" of scientific method promised to resolve. If one could show with the *certainty of numbers and mathematical method* that any given problem was caused by certain factors and could, thus, be solved in particular ways, then who could disagree with his analysis of the problem and his proposed solutions? Any individual who sought understanding of and solutions to social problems might have a sincere interest in the possibility that science could provide him with certain knowledge. Nevertheless, it is also apparent that science, especially the mathematical forms of scientific method, presented one with an immensely powerful *rhetoric,* a means of *convincing* others of the absolute truth of one's ideas regardless of the sincerity of one's motives.

When we look at the early works in moral statistics and the related forms of statistical analyses of social phenomena, we find that, with hardly an exception, they are concerned with the *use* of official statistical information and of statistical methods of analysis *to get at the causes of social problems and, hence, to show that certain solutions are better than others.* Guerry, for example, began and ended his classical work on moral statistics with strong statements about how crucial such certain ("scientific") knowledge is in resolving policy questions and in serving as the "means of control." In the second paragraph of the book he begins the work with what one might have expected to be its hopeful "conclusion":

The use of the method of observation in the study of moral and political questions not only leads to the progress of science, but has an effect as well on mattters of possibly the greatest and most immediate importance. In our day theories of any sort do not long remain vain abstractions; from writings they pass into the public and soon penetrate institutions, exercising either a benign or harmful influence on society. It is, therefore, to introduce as much as possible into the study of moral sciences the rigid method of the natural and physical sciences; to direct attention to the facts, to collect them, to take note of them, to increase knowledge of them, and, thereby, to destroy false theories at the same time as instilling useful truths.

Statistics already, by clarifying great questions of criminal legislation, has shown the fertility of its application and the success which one could hope from investigations of the same kind. Until now one was limited almost exclusively to assembling the facts concerning the movement of population of a nation, and to the knowledge of its commercial or agricultural wealth. No one had yet dreamed of collecting in a special volume those which reveal the moral state of its inhabitants. Persuaded of the importance and the usefulness of such a work, we believed it worthwhile to undertake it.[19]

Examples of this call for research could be extended almost endlessly, since almost all the thousands of statistical studies included some such exhortation. The expected value in deciding policy matters for governments was stressed from the time of Graunt and Petty in the seventeenth century, and Süssmilch in the eighteenth, up through Durkheim,[20] and then through to modern American sociology. Only in the last several decades, after sociology became predominantly an academic discipline in the United States (with over 80%

19. Guerry, *Statistiques Morales de la France*, Paris, 1831, pp. 1–2.
20. E. Durkheim, *The Rules of Sociological Method, op. cit.*

of American sociologists being supported primarily by teaching jobs in the universities) did any significant number of sociologists begin to consider sociology as a goal in itself, and even then only the most esoteric sociologists expressed such a view. Additionally, those who did express such a view tended to be non-statistical (i.e., humanistic or theoretical) sociologists who were unsupported by government agencies. Indeed, the notion of "value-free sociology" itself was developed earlier by the academically based and *humanistic* German sociologists, who were strongly opposed by many of their peers, probably including almost all the statistically oriented sociologists.

Even if the practical orientation of the social sciences turned them strongly in the direction of the statistical approach, there was no reason why they could not have *tried* to get their own statistical information on "social problems," sources not subject to the biases of official information. We find, in fact, that certain nineteenth century social scientists tried to collect statistical information on "social problems" independently of the official agencies, though this was not concerned with the kind of morally defined information we would consider to be information on deviance. Booth's massive statistical studies of the poor in London is undoubtedly the best known example. Booth undertook a detailed study of representative households, collecting immense amounts of information which was analyzed statistically in various ways. He directed it toward what he saw as the "social problems" of poverty, to provide information that could be used politically in implementing solutions to these problems. There was a long tradition of analyzing the poor in terms of official information, one in which the poor generally came out looking like the "dangerous classes" which the upper classes already believed they were, but *Booth was trying to show something that could not be shown by official information so as to support political action which could not be plausibly supported by official information.* Official information was constructed for the purposes of the established governments and it supported the kinds of policies they supported, but Booth was trying to change these official policies. (While there had been various parliamentary investigations of poverty, such as those leading to the famous "blue books" which were used to support radical political programs, the official agencies did not normally produce this kind of information.)

In contrast, the early social scientists, such as the moral statisticians, used official information and derived policy conclusions from it that supported the general goals of official agencies (such as doing away with "crime," rather than changing the laws to make some behavior legal) because *they were committed in various ways to the official agencies and their policies.* Undoubtedly, feelings of social class lay behind much of this: Social scientists were almost always from the more well-to-do classes, especially in a society in which education was very much the privilege (and control device) of the richer members of society. It was no doubt also true then, as it often is today, that the easiest way to get some change was to direct one's work toward the officials to try to change them, rather than try to produce a social movement and turn them into enemies. Perhaps more importantly, *the early social scientists doing statistical studies of deviance and other social problems were themselves very often officials or were directly and indirectly involved in official work.* This was true of many moral statisticians and other early social scientists, such as the "public hygienists." For example, Parent-Duchatelet was a "public hygienist" (official) who worked with other officials throughout Europe in publishing a massive two-volume statistical study of prostitution in the 1840s, which went beyond any other statistical study that has ever been done on the subject. It included the maps, tables, ecological studies, and so on that were to be rediscovered almost seventy-five years later by the Chicago sociologists.

To the degree that this is true, then, *statistical sociology, especially statistical studies of "social problems" such as deviance, was created by officials (and by those working with officials) for the purposes of better understanding and solving the officially-defined social problems.* In this light it should not be surprising that they used the officially-constructed information. It was precisely this official information that best suited their purposes in developing more abstract or theoretical analyses of the social problems, that fit the needs of a bureaucratically rationalized form of work directed at the social problems, that would yield the kinds of "solutions" sought by officials, that would be the most rhetorically powerful in general, and, at the same time, powerfully support the official agents themselves. These mathematical analyses would show that the officials were doing the right things because they provided *scientific* (hence, absolute) justification.

The historians of sociology and the other social sciences have overlooked the role of the *official origin* of sociological research, especially of statistical research. Instead, they have looked to the philosophers as the prime source of sociological ideas; yet without the research base with its mathematical forms social scientists would still have been looked at as philosophers. That which was most distinctive of the social sciences and which most justified their being considered sciences, rather than philosophy, was the statistical research, most of which consisted of analyses of official statistics on deviance. (Recall that Durkheim chose to do a statistical study of suicide to prove that sociology was in fact a science and an independent discipline. In fact, many sociologists still use *Suicide* precisely for this purpose in introductory sociology courses, where they are apt to meet unbelievers.)

Durkheim relied almost exclusively on the earlier official statistical works for most of his own theory of suicide, merely carrying the argument about society as an independent level of existence further than anyone else had done. As I have previously argued at great length,[21] on the most general level the task Durkheim set himself in *Suicide* was that of *systematically relating the already established statistical relations between certain official statistics on official categorizations of individuals (such as married, divorced, etc.) and certain official statistics on suicide rates to the egoist-anomie theory of immoral actions developed by certain Romantic authors.* This previously had been attempted only partially by Boismont and Morselli.

For the past several decades Durkheim's *Suicide* has served as the paradigm for sociological studies of deviance in the United States and the rest of the world. Yet, even before American sociologists had institutionalized this paradigm, they had moved in its direction. In the 1920s the Chicago sociologists had utilized the early participant-observer method of studying deviance and had produced some classical studies using this method. At times they even gathered some statistical data as seen in such works as Thrasher's study of 1313 gangs. Then, as American sociologists became more directly involved with government agencies and with officially defined policy problems (e.g. controlling delinquency) they rapidly became more oriented toward using the official statistics. At first, the Chicago sociologists who used the official statistics were aware of their problems and warned of the biases, the ecological fallacies, and so forth. For example, both Cavan and Schmid dealt with such problems concerning the official statistics in their works on suicide, and both believed that one had to use individual cases to counterbalance the official statistics. However, as Ameri-

21. See *The Social Meanings of Suicide, op. cit.,* pp. 3–78.

can sociology "progressed," such considerations disappeared from the works on suicide and individual cases were never used, in spite of the fact that the later works were using highly developed statistical tests that could be far more easily affected by biases in the statistical data.

Official Determinants of All Statistics on Deviance. Another basic reason sociologists who are committed to a statistical approach to deviance have relied almost exclusively on official statistics is that they are almost the only statistics available. This has been due, in part, to the great difficulty and cost that would be involved in creating statistical information on deviance independently of the official agencies and their information resources. On the other hand, when we consider both the recognized problems of official information and that one would generally only need a sample of a few thousand to do most such studies, it becomes apparent that there must be something more to this reliance on official information.

This something more, which has rarely been explicitly stated in the works on deviance, has been the social moral meanings and practical implications of information on deviance. *According to the legal definitions in our society, most forms of deviance today cannot be said to exist until they are legally (officially) defined in concrete cases.* That is, crime, suicide, and so on, exist only when the legal procedures have "certified" them. Until the officials (district attorneys, coroners, etc.) have "proven" these acts of deviance to have been committed, they cannot be legally said to exist; individuals can actually be sued for "accusing" someone of having committed a crime when this is contrary to "fact" as legally defined. Basically, then, most forms of deviance today are constructed by official action and by law. Thus, the social scientist who seeks to study deviance independently of official information, for example, by using anonymous self-reports on acts of deviance,[22] is necessarily studying something different; although he may be relying on a more ancient definition of the acts, he will not be studying what are legally defined as deviance and deviants.

But the point is broader than this. *All information, all "facts" purporting to be information about deviance have moral meanings (and sometimes legal meanings), and consequently, are subject to social sanctioning.* To know of, purport to know of, believe, or suspect that an act of deviance has occurred or might occur: all these possibilities have many moral meanings which depend upon the situation, especially one's relations to the act and person. One may have an obligation to trust one's relative or friend, therefore not to suspect him of evil doing; one may have information concerning evil doing which one is legally obligated to report, personally obligated to distort, or wise to forget; and one may have a right or not to information on deviance.

Since knowledge is power, and control of social information gives one social control. Perhaps the most crucial step in the development of the power of officials has been their legal status as the controllers of information on deviance and other forms of social behavior. This official control over information on social behavior has grown over the centuries as the state has sought to extend its power over its citizens. *By becoming the legally-sanctioned creator and controller of social information, and by making that social information the legally-sanctioned basis for individual accountability (guilt, family responsibility, etc.) and social decision making, the state has steadily increased its powers throughout society.* Not only does the state, through legislative bodies in Ameri-

22. There is now a large literature involving the study of self-reported deviance. The most important early study was that by James F. Short and F. Ivan Nye, "Reported Behavior as a Criterion of Deviant Behavior," *Social Problems*, 5 (Winter, 1957), pp. 207–213.

can society, construct the definitions of legal deviance (insanity, delinquency, etc.), as Becker has argued,[23] and through the organizational practices of the officials determine the concrete "instances" of deviance and deviants, as Cicourel has argued,[24] but, most importantly of all, the state in every way has expanded its controls over the background conditions in which social information can be constructed and over the ways in which it can be used.

This control over information and the power it gives officials over society has been accelerating so rapidly in recent years, under the guise of the "foreign threat", that certain of its extreme forms, especially that of "official secrecy" and "classified data", have come to be seen as "pathologies" of "intelligence"[25] which require new laws to enforce "public disclosure" of more official information. Yet over the centuries the growth has been so slow that it has been assimilated as part of our taken-for-granted understandings of everyday life. It is largely for this reason that sociologists have generally failed to see the profound ways in which the use of official information on deviance determines the nature of their theories of deviance and of society more generally. Indeed, in some instances in which they have been aware of this possibility, as Cloward and Ohlin were,[26] they have sought to justify the use of official information by arguing that the study of "official deviance" must itself be of great importance to sociology. They have, presumably, failed to see that, by committing themselves to this study of "official deviance," they are actually putting themselves in the service

23. See Howard Becker, *Outsiders*, New York: The Free Press, 1963.

24. See Aaron Cicourel, *The Social Organization of Juvenile Justice*, New York: John Wiley, 1967.

25. Probably the most important work on the "pathologies of intelligence" is that by Harold Wilensky, *Organizational Intelligence*, New York: Basic Books, 1967.

26. See Richard A. Cloward and Lloyd E. Ohlin, *Delinquency and Opportunity*, New York: The Free Press, 1961.

of the officials and lending the prestige of "science" to the officials' attempts to control those they define as deviants.

Yet, as I have been arguing, the attempt to study deviance statistically yet independently of official information appears doomed to fail. This is due most generally to the moral meanings of the information. Not only does revelation imply possible degrading of the self for the deviants, but there are also some forms of information whose meanings are changed by the very fact of being known to others, regardless of whether the other thinks badly of you or remains the "cold scientist". For example, in our society all sexual behavior is socially defined as "intimate" behavior and is supposed to be known only to the participants. To tell others about it violates intimacy, makes it "public knowledge" rather than "private knowledge" and, thereby, destroys the relationship of intimacy. To reveal such information, then, is seen as immoral, as a severe violation of the self, *regardless of the motive for the revelation.* (Members do distinguish degrees of violation and immorality in this matter—so that telling friends is not so heinous as telling strangers.) As a result, anyone seeking information on the most intimate of matters, sex, is asking people ("subjects") to take part in an immoral transaction. This is a reason why so many people respond with a sense of horror to "scientific" studies of sex.

But, in addition to the effects of these general moral meanings of information, there are official factors which will inevitably determine the nature of sociologists' attempts to study deviance statistically. First, there is the obvious factor of possible legal involvement of the sociologists in the deviance, at least as accessories. Second, there is the related factor of fear on the part of the informants that their identities will somehow be disclosed. The costs to them of exposure are very great, so that even slight distrust can lead to hiding or lying. Only drastic change in the legal

definition of research, giving sanction to all research informants, would eliminate all of this; and the legal definitions
would still be indirectly structuring the observations. Third,
and most important of all, *the information on officially defined deviance is legally defined as controllable by the
officials.* This means that, for most forms of legal deviance,
citizens are responsible for reporting suspected violations
and information that *might* pertain to violations (e.g., med-
ically unattended bodies) to the "appropriate authorities",
which generally means the police. *The officials, then, are the
legally defined gate-keepers of information on legal deviance*
and they have the authority to decide which reported cases
of "possible deviance" will and will not be investigated, how
they will be investigated, who will and will not do the investigating, and what the disposition of such investigations will
be. This means that any sociologist wishing to study that
kind of behavior will have to negotiate with the officials to
get access to it. The outcomes of such negotiations will determine the nature of the sample because the officials will
already have structured the situation before the sociologist
has observed it, (or they will determine how the observing
is to be done). Finally, officials determine at least partially
what can be done with the information.

All of these forms of official and unofficial determination
of sociological observations can, for example, be seen in the
attempts by sociologists to study suicide independently of
officials. Let us consider, for example, the steps that sociologists might take, and sometimes have taken, to study
suicide independently of the officials, but in such a way as to
collect a representative sample and more reliable statistics
on suicide.

A first possibility is to go directly to the deaths to investigate them. This would mean going to the scenes of both
serious injuries, since these might result in death, and of

deaths themselves. Otherwise the study would have to rely on some combination of reconstructions of events by the non-officials and officials present. It should be noted that even if one in fact did get to the scenes of injury and death, one would still have to rely on some reconstructions by the members present to determine what happened and whether there was any "intention" to kill oneself. In this case, then, even natural observations could rarely involve direct observation of the events by the scientist: the scientist almost inevitably relies upon the members to give him the basic information about "what happened". Since almost all scenes of interest come first to the attention of the police or medical officials, it would be up to the officials to determine whether the sociologist would be allowed on the scene in the first place. There have in fact been some attempts made by sociologists to go to the scenes of death. In one case, one of America's largest cities, the officials decided that a court order would be necessary and this could not be obtained. In a similar case, that of a small Midwestern town, the sheriff was very willing to have a sociologist go along with the deputies to investigate unattended deaths.[27] My own study of county coroners in one major state showed that officials differ greatly in their choices of how to interpret the laws about public disclosure of information (and there is a very real choice involved here). As a result, while in some instances sociologists have been able to negotiate excellent cooperation, they could not themselves choose which cases to study. They could not come up with a representative sample even remotely meeting statistical criteria.

Another possibility would be to make-do by using a repre-

27. This is a study being done by Alfred Bradshaw. While he found the sheriff willing enough to let him observe investigations of unattended deaths, he found them relatively unwilling to call him in on such cases. This, however, may have been due entirely to the practical problems of finding time to call him.

sentative sample of the cases actually investigated by the officials themselves. After all, is there not a realistic hope that individuals will obey the law and report all "unattended deaths" to the officials so that these reports could be used to get at all "real suicides"? In the first place, this would leave out of consideration all instances of deaths that are suicides "concealed" or "unrecognized" by the doctors. To go directly to the doctors, rather than using only reports of unattended deaths, would get a sociologist involved again in the problem of having to negotiate, only in this case he would have to negotiate with every individual doctor or some representative sample of them. Second, he would quickly discover that the laws defining "unattended deaths" vary greatly, and that the interpretations of these laws and the actual practices vary even more. Further, the decision over whether the death is "unattended" or "attended" is generally made at the first step by questioning police on the scene over the phone and deciding for that specific situation whether a doctor should be called, whether the hospital should handle the case, or whether some representative of the coroner should subject it to an official investigation. (In some cases, as in one major city I studied, this initial, gate-keeping decision is made by a "morgue attendant".)

It should be apparent, then, that any attempt by the sociologist to study officially defined deviance by statistical means, but independently of the officials, will in fact be structured by official action. The case of suicide is, if anything, less subject to these problems than other forms of official deviance; the other forms are usually subject to penalties of imprisonment, commitment, or fine and are mainly subject to police action, which is normally far less open to outsider observation except on their stringent terms.

In recent years sociologists have used one other statistical approach in an attempt to get at official deviance independently of official structuring. This is the *self-reporting method.*

Most of these studies have been of crime or delinquency,[28] but the President's Crime Commission also made use of a method of self-reporting on having been "victimized" by crime.[29] This approach too is subject to the biases resulting from the moral and legal definitions discussed earlier (distrust of the interviewers, fear of disclosure, desire to "brag") and there is no evidence thus far that the supposed anonymity of the interview situation actually eliminates them. It is also subject to all of the biases to which all questionnaires are subject.[30] In addition, it fails to consider the variations in meaning given to most terms used to designate legal violations; that is, "assault", "embezzlement", "grand larceny", "rape", and so on, have very different meanings, even in legal codes and among police, and certainly among the general public. (One would even find that a significant percentage of initial reports of "crimes" reported to officials are not considered by them to be "crimes" subject to prosecution.)

If sociologists are going to do statistical studies of deviance, especially of those forms subject to official action, they will necessarily be using either official information or information structured by official definitions and official actions. We must, then, thoroughly investigate the nature of official statistics and consider the alternatives.

Conclusion

When sociologists knowingly or unknowingly commit themselves to the kind of practical activity implicit in the nature of official information on deviance (or any other

28. See for example, James F. Short and F. Ivan Nye, "Reported Behavior as a Criterion of Deviant Behavior," *op. cit.*

29. See *Crime in a Free Society*, the President's Crime Commission Report, Washington, D.C.: U.S. Government Printing Office, 1967.

30. For a general analysis of the fundamental biases of questionnaire defined categories of social events, juvenile delinquency is one of those categories that was created by officials earlier in this century without any significant prior basis in common-sense discourse.

phenomena), then they are commiting themselves to *doing official action.* Allowing one's theories to be predetermined in this way by the nature of the official information used defeats the whole purpose of science. I do not mean by this to argue that we must seek some kind of "absolute" knowledge that is free of all predetermination by the nature of methods and the nature of values. We now have every reason to believe that this kind of absolute knowledge is impossible. As I have argued before, we must recognize that all knowledge is to some degree situation-bound, that all knowledge can at best be *useful-knowledge* because it does implicitly assume certain properties of the information used and certain general goals.[31] *But it is of crucial importance that one seek to control and to minimize such effects and to make his knowledge of society as generally or universally useful as possible.* Only when one does this is he doing science, as opposed to more immediately practical, situation-bound kinds of activities.

The kind of theory based on official information, especially on official statistics on deviance, is of little value or is actually dangerous to most of us. This is true partly because it makes the theory so situation-bound, so completely dependent on assuming the perspectives and goals of official organizations in our society, the generality of the knowledge involved is exceedingly limited. In a complex society such as ours it is very difficult for policy makers to honestly know what is going on in all of the important parts of the society, nonetheless to understand the complex relations among these parts. For this reason, anyone who would be an effective policy maker (i.e., who will in fact run the society so that people become more rather than less satisfied) must have some highly reliable and valid information. In addition, in a society changing so rapidly as ours, any effective policy

31. See my essay on "The Relevance of Sociology" in Jack D. Douglas, ed., *The Relevance of Sociology,* New York: Appleton-Century-Crofts, 1970.

maker must have generalizable rather than situation-bound information, because only the former will allow him to anticipate the nature of *future* possible states of society. Situation-bound information on the so-called "status-quo" will necessarily distort any such futuristic, policy-oriented thought and decisions based on it will produce more or less unhappy results. The need for generalizable information constitutes the real social justification of social science. Committing ourselves to the official perspectives and goals implicit in official information necessarily prevents our reaching such social science.

But it is also true that *official-knowledge* produced by social scientists can be *dangerous-knowledge* because it provides a powerful rhetoric to the officials that they use in achieving their goals, which generally consist of a further standardization of life. This in turn has the effect of making their mathematical information more reliable and valid as a description of the society, so that the more effective they are in achieving their social goals, the more they are able to provide an *ex post facto validation* of their kind of *official-knowledge*. The officials have understood well the power of this mathematical rhetoric, and, as I have already argued, this is a basic reason for creating and using the official statistics in the first place. The imprimatur of the scientific disciplines on one's side is even more important as a rhetorical device. Then it is not merely the officials, who are suspect in any society that values individual freedoms, but it is also the "scientists" who support the official policies and general perspectives. The rhetorical power of this "expert" status is great and growing in our increasingly technological society, so it is valuable to officials to have the experts on their side, quite independently of any truly scientific information they might have.

In our world today the officially-controlled mass society and the official-statistical knowledge of "social problems" are necessarily interdependent. Each can exist only to the extent that the other does; to create one makes the other possible. For social scientists to create such official statistical "knowledge" is, then, to make official control more possible. In addition, since the sociologists disavow control of such knowledge by selling it through the consulting relationship, they make it almost completely amenable to the specific goals of the officials in control.[32]

If sociologists are to fulfill their purpose of creating scientific knowledge of social phenomena, such as moral phenomena, then they must remain free of all of the basic assumptions of official information, the implicit goals of such information, and of the organizations which create it. They must, instead, construct their own information about the phenomena, controlling the methods used to get the observations on which such information is ultimately based. Above all, they must control these observations in such a way as to have the least possible effect on the observations. *We must be as true as possible to the phenomena we are studying.* Only in this way can we possibly build a valid science of human beings and human society. If we cannot or do not remain as true to the phenomena as possible, then we can only do pseudo-science which can be used to control human beings, but not to make them freer.

32. See *Ibid.*

4. The Biasing of Official Statistics on Deviance

We have seen the basic properties of official organizations, their social situation, and the underlying properties of the official statistics themselves which would lead one to expect that the official statistics would be very untrue to the phenomena. It is equally important to see the specific ways in which these official statistics are biased and, more importantly, distortions of the phenomena. This will help to show why certain kinds of theories of social rules and social order have been so common in sociology and have been so wrong. It will also help us to see better what kind of information and theory must be used.

The Officially Biased Meanings of the Categories of Deviance

One assumption underlying the sociological use of official statistics to study deviance has always been that the official categories are representative of fundamentally meaningful social categories, so that the official statistics can be taken as a representative sample of the specific *socially meaningful actions* being studied. For example, sociologists assumed that the legal definitions of crime could be taken as directly representative of homogeneously shared social meanings of crime. This was important because they were interested, like we are, in studying the actions of the members of society from the standpoint of the actor: that is, they assumed that the actor committed a crime with full knowledge that it was a crime, that this criminal meaning of the action was relevant for understanding why he did or did not commit the act, and that the official categories of crime involved the same meanings as the meanings the actor would give to the act. Again, sociologists studying suicide were concerned with studying the relative willingness of types of individuals in different social situations to choose death rather than go on living. This, for example, was the reason why Halbwachs argued that we should be equally concerned with the attempted suicides, since these too had a bearing on the degree of willingness to choose death over life.

Related to this assumption were two others: (1) the social meanings themselves were assumed to be the same for all members of society, including the officials who constructed and imputed the categories, so that one could expect a direct relation between the official meanings and the general social meanings; and (2) the social meanings were assumed to be non-problematic for all members, including officials. While both of these assumptions were discussed in Chapter 2, it is useful to consider certain evidence against them here.

Many bits of information over the years lead one to deny the validity of the assumption that the meanings of official categories are the same for all members of society. It is common knowledge among lawyers that the legal definitions of official categories vary greatly from one governmental area to another within our society. For example, states commonly have different legal definitions of specific forms of crimes, even though the same words are used. Cressey found an excellent example of this in *Other People's Money*, a study of embezzlement. He found that states legally define "embezzlement" so differently that he could not find any behavioral element common to even most of the cases of convicted "embezzlers".

Some of the findings from my research on coroners' and medical examiners' imputations of suicide as the cause of death in one of the most populous and urbanized states in the United States illustrate the highly problematic meanings of suicide for officials. One of the most important conclusions from this study was that an adequate understanding of the official organizations and procedures involved in the classification of suicide as a cause of death can be gained only when one understands the ways in which the laws are interpreted and made use of by the officials in their everyday work activities. Being a "home-rule" state, the state has general laws covering coroners' and medical examiners' offices and also county laws, especially county interpretations of state laws, regarding these offices. As a consequence, the laws and the interpretations are very complicated. When one also begins to consider the number of judicial decisions that become important precedents in a common law system, the complexity can be seen to be very great indeed. I found that coroners and medical examiners differ greatly in the degree of knowledge they have concerning the laws and the interpretations of these laws. In one instance a doctor who had been a coroner in a rural county for 25 years stated flatly that there were no laws concerning the operation of the coroner's office. He said that he had tried to get the district attorney in that area to determine what the laws were but the district attorney reported there were no laws. At the other extreme, I found a county coroner, a funeral director, who knew a great deal about the laws of the state, about the changes that had been made a few years earlier, and so on. Most of the coroners and medical examiners, however, know relatively little and do not seem particularly concerned about what the laws are.

My findings led me to several conclusions:

1) First, it seems clear that the laws are too complicated, too abstract, and too removed from the everyday lives of the coroners and medical examiners to have much effect on their activities. I was especially concerned from the beginning of my research to determine whether the coroners and medical examiners were making use of any shared definition of suicide to classify suicide as a cause of death. In each case I specifically asked, and returned in most cases to ask several times, whether there was any legal definition of suicide or, if not, whether there was any formal definition of suicide that they were making use of in arriving at their decisions on how to classify the cause of death. *In no case did they know of any law defining suicide in this state or any other state.* In a few cases they said they believed there were formal definitions of suicide in textbooks on pathology, and named a famous one. However, in one of America's largest cities the pathologist, who was also a university teacher, did not know what that definition might be. In most instances respondents simply seemed surprised at my asking what the formal definition of suicide might be. It appeared clear that *they expected me and any other knowledgeable member of our culture to know what suicide is. They were relying on their own common-sense meanings of suicide, expecting me to do likewise in deciding whether any given death was caused by "suicide".*

My next concern was to determine what they considered suicide to be. In most instances it was apparent that this was not something the respondents had really thought about. *The meanings of suicide were taken-for-granted; they were background meanings in their everyday activities.* When they did think about it, in almost all instances they provided some definition of suicide in terms of the *intentional taking of one's own life.*

2) Second, the attempts of the State Department of Health to communicate the nature of the law, in particular, some changes in the laws made two years earlier, had had little effect because the laws were either unknown or not seen as important in carrying out the task. *The task of classifying suicide as the cause of death was seen primarily as a practical activity to be gotten done within the practical restraints, notably those of time, space, effort, and, I suspect, human anguish.* The laws were seen to be important only insofar as they became practical constraints which had to be dealt with. Since there were relatively few, if any, possible consequences for not complying with the law, in most instances it was no constraint on the coroners and medical examiners. The law, therefore, could in no way provide the kind of patterns to activities that would be necessary to produce comparable information.

3) Third, no matter what the law is in the abstract, it must still be interpreted in specific situations before it can have any effect. Interpretations are made in such a way as to solve the far more important (as they see it) practical problems which they face, such as getting a sizeable amount of work done in a very short period of time. *The result is that there are as many specific interpretations of the laws as there are specific combinations of practical attempts to solve problems faced by the specific organizations.*

4) Fourth, no matter what the specific situational interpretation of the law, what is seen as the law would
be explicitly violated if it interferes with the conception the officials have of how to do their job,
assuming the present lack of consequences. At least,
this is clearly true in some instances. For example, a
funeral director-coroner, who was the most knowledgeable of all respondents about the law, was himself specifically violating what he saw as the laws, yet
this did not in any way disturb him. Sometimes he
violated the recent law which made it mandatory to
have a doctor certify cause of death. In this instance
the coroner himself was not a doctor, yet did not in all
cases use a doctor's decision regarding the cause of
death.

In general, it was clear that the coroners and medical
examiners, along with most of the rest of us, expect that there
are laws which apply to the operation of their official offices
and which should have some definite effects in determining
the nature of their activities. For this reason, they treat the
issue of whether there are laws governing their activities as
being a serious question that has to be answered. This,
presumably, was why they would offer to look up the laws for
me, ask their secretaries to do it for me, or tell me where
I could send to get the laws. *The general presumption would
seem to be that the laws are somehow absolute and govern
one's action even when one doesn't know what they are.*
Perhaps the laws are taken as a frame that determines the
limits or possibilities of their actions, so that the *respondents
assume, and expect the questioner to assume, that, although
the laws may not specify just what they do, they at least
specify what they are not doing. They assume that the laws
will fit their common-sense conceptions of morality and
of law in such a way that, whatever the content, the*

laws will legitimate what they in fact do. This interpretation could be based upon the assumption that one is an adequate and legitimate official doing what officials are supposed to do, and, therefore, one's activities will be in accord with the law. (This seems a better explanation than the alternative that the meanings of the laws are "indexically" provided by their practical use, since the laws are not "used.")

What is true for the official category of suicide appears to be true for almost all categories of deviance: there appear to be essential differences in the official definitions from one political unit to another, *and* even when there are comparable *paper definitions,* as is often the case within one state, the officials are not aware of just what those paper definitions are. There is a large difference between *paper laws* (or legal codes) and *folk laws,* the laws as actually understood by practicing members of society. David Riesman long ago pointed this out when he argued that the law as learned by law students has little to do with the way law is actually practiced by lawyers and judges, if for no other reason than that the practicing attorneys and judges no longer know the precedents and written minutiae. Further, there is good reason for them not to know: To make use of them would not only be irrelevant, but would also lead to violations of what the local publics consider moral. One also finds that, regardless of the paper definitions of crimes, individual policemen, who must ultimately determine what kind of action is taken, do not agree about the legal definitions; and we would probably find similar disagreements at the level of district attorneys who bring the charges against individuals. Indeed, we know that courts themselves frequently disagree with each other over the meanings of paper laws, and, in fact, *our entire system of legal appeals is based on the assumption that this will be the case.*

There are a few official categories of deviance with definitions that can be applied with precision, such as blindness and deafness. These categories have precise legal definitions in our society at the national level, perhaps because officials make use of medical texts to categorize individuals precisely in these terms. But this high reliability in categorizing such stigma can be purchased only at the expense of making the categories invalid representations of the common-sense meanings of the categories, and, therefore, in no way representative of the social phenomena that sociologists are most interested in. These categories have been defined so that the officials can use them to achieve the controls they seek. As Robert Scott has argued so persuasively, these controls are often directed at achieving their own ends:

> In constructing these definitions there was an important factor that had to be taken into account. Conditions such as total blindness, total deafness or severe retardation are rare ones in the population. It would not be possible to justify national or state programs for people with these impairments if the programs were to be limited only to those who are most severely impaired. It would only be possible to maintain or expand these programs if the populations in need were large ones. Moreover, it seemed desirable to offer such services not only to those who were totally impaired, but to the severely impaired as well. The definitions of stigma that were developed had to take this problem into account. The question is, how far toward "normal" should one go? In order to answer this question it was necessary to construct highly technical definitions of impairment. The "legal" definition of deafness that was adopted specified the precise level of decibel discrimination that an individual had to be able to make in order to become eligible for services. . . . Legal blindness was defined as "Central visual acuity of 20/200 or less in the better eye with correcting lenses; or central visual acuity of more than 20/200 if there is a field defect in which the peripheral field has contracted to such an extent that the widest diameter of visual field subtends an angle distance no greater than 20 degrees."

A striking feature of these definitions is that there is not a direct correspondence between them and the ones that a layman would use to determine if he or another person were physically or mentally impaired. Indeed, in order to determine if an individual who has a severe problem seeing is "legally blind" it is necessary to give him a careful, clinically controlled test of vision acuity. This test requires not only an exact determination of maximum levels of vision discrimination, it also requires that his discrimination levels be ascertained after he has been fitted with glasses that correct his vision to its best possible level. Disagreements about "best corrected vision" are common among people who are experts at measuring visual acuity. It is not surprising then that there is no direct correspondence between an expert's definition of blindness and the visually impaired person's subjective experience of his seeing trouble. This suggests that the closer one is to the point where the experts' demarcation lines are drawn between normalcy and impairment as it is legally defined, the less correspondence there will be between expert definitions of these conditions as stigma and the lay person's subjective experiences of them as stigma.[1]

It should be apparent, then, that the official categories are not and probably cannot be defined by some formal method in any way that would lead one to reasonably expect that the officials are using the same abstract definition of the categories in their categorizations of deviance. That is, the categorizations cannot be very reliable because the categories (or the official knowledge of them) are not very comparable. We shall soon see that the problematic nature of the social meanings means that no single category can be applied across the society as a whole and that, in fact, *no single categorization will normally be accepted even for one event by all members of the society.*

1. See Robert Scott, *The Making of Blind Men,* New York: Russell Sage Foundation, 1969.

Operational Biases in the Imputations of Official Categories

Most of the criticism of official statistics and official information on deviance has concentrated on the biases at the operational level, the level of actually imputing the categories to individuals and groups of individuals. Since there has been so much on this, we will consider this topic briefly.

Probably the most important operational biases, because they have the most pervasive influence, are those in the official categories that result from the necessarily political nature of the legislative processes producing the legal definitions of categories, the policies of enforcement, the laws concerning enforcement, and the distributions of funds used to enforce laws. Undoubtedly the most important group here is that concerning the legal categories of crime.

Few common-sense categories are seen as more homogeneous and absolute than those concerning "crime." This is reflected in the social strategy for dealing with crime: if the nature of "crime" is seen as a necessary part of reality, as being unarguable and beyond the control of man, then committing a crime is indeed a horrible thing, even an affront to God to be punished by eternal damnation. In addition, this absoluteness is important in eliminating any conception of the laws as arbitrary or unequal at their foundations. Because law-makers generally have a practical understanding of the importance of the absolutist conception of laws in maintaining the authority of the law and its enforcement, they commonly use many presentational devices to create the appearance of absoluteness where they themselves know how subjectively and arbitrarily the laws have been enacted and enforced. Just as ancient legislators generally "discovered" the laws engraved in stone in holy circumstances, modern legislators generally try to rig public testimony so that only "reasonable experts" will be heard and, if this fails, they then may try to suppress (i.e., to keep private) information concerning the disagreements. For example, in her study of legislation on prostitution Pamela Roby found that the disagreements and arguments among the "experts" were not reported. Presumably, the reader of the legislative reports would conclude that the evidence and reasons for the laws were absolutely clear.

This conception of the laws as absolute is so widespread that even the convicted criminal generally finds it difficult to challenge the laws in his own mind. Rarely does he argue that the laws are immoral or wrong in any way. Even those deemed so dangerous that they are isolated from other prisoners seem not to challenge the basis of the laws, but rather concentrate their anger on what they believe to be corrupt middle-level officials who have misused the laws.[2]

Further, professional criminals, such as con-men, shoplifters, and prostitutes, have clearly developed ideas about the social processes lying behind the specific laws: They seem to be aware of the ways in which the interests of specific groups with power lead to the enactment of some laws rather than others. Consequently, they are alienated from the laws, feel no moral compunctions or embarrassment about violating them and feel no need to justify their behavior to themselves or others. For example, Daniel Bell saw this in the confrontations between moralistic senators and cynical professional gamblers in the senate racket hearings.[3]

Rarely, however, can the cynical deviant stand back to see the social processes that go into the construction of the legal definitions of crime. It has been hard enough for social scientists to do, and their structural theories of crime have almost universally assumed the absolutist attitude toward

2. See Richard H. McCleery, "Authoritarianism and the Belief System of Incorrigibles," in Donald Cressey, *The Prison*, New York: Holt, Rinehart and Winston, 1961, pp. 260–306.
3. See Daniel Bell, "Crime As An American Way of Life," in *The End of Ideology*, The Free Press: New York, 1961.

crime. But sociologists have come increasingly in recent years to see that the definitions of "crimes" are themselves the outcome of a political struggle. As Turk,[4] Quinney,[5] and many others, especially the labelling theorists, have argued, the legal definitions of crimes are constructed primarily by those few groups who control the political power of the state legislatures and who purposefully use the criminal laws to try to control those forms of activities which they find detrimental to their own interests, including everything from *their* moral feelings to their material interests. This is very evident in the legislation against "crimes without victims." A classic example is the enactment of the Prohibition Amendment to the Constitution, which made most forms of drinking a criminal offense. As Gusfield, Timberlake and others have shown, this was largely a middle-class, rural, Protestant movement aimed at controlling the lives of the lower class, urban, Catholic immigrants through official action. This whole orientation led to a concentration on *legislating control of the morals* of the lower-class groups. (Troy Duster has also found this to be a basic goal of anti-drug legislation.[6])

For the most part, middle and upper-class groups, who control the power of state legislatures, use the legal definitions of crimes in an attempt to control the kinds of things lower-class individuals commit against them, in particular, property crimes and certain acts of violence. The result is that *these acts defined as "crimes" in our society will almost always be precisely the kinds of activities committed by lower-class individuals.*

4. See Austin T. Turk, "Conflict and Criminality," *American Sociological Review*, 31 (June, 1966), pp. 338–352.

5. See Richard Quinney, "The Conflict Theory of Crime," in Jack D. Douglas, ed., *Crime and Justice in America*, Indianapolis: Bobbs-Merrill, 1970.

6. Troy Duster, *The Legislation of Morality*, New York: The Free Press, 1970.

What we find is that *when legislators want to control activities they pass criminal laws against those activities committed predominantly by lower-class individuals but pass civil laws against those acts committed predominantly by middle and upper-class individuals.* So that even if official statistics on "crimes" were reliable and valid, they would, nevertheless, show a very biased state of affairs: namely, that "criminal violations" are committed almost entirely by lower-class individuals, which is what they show. The fact is that these categories simply do not cover the kinds of "violations" committed by higher class persons.

In some instances the legal statutes defining "crime" do *potentially* cover the kinds of activities committed in the higher classes, yet ways are found by legal devices to avoid categorizing these activities as crimes, at least on a standardized basis. For example, the federal anti-trust laws make violations subject to either criminal or civil procedures. As Sutherland found, almost every major American corporation has been found guilty at some time of such violations, which cost the American public billions of dollars in higher prices, amounting to more than all the petty theft of the lower classes. In almost every instance the Justice Department officials have decided to try the cases as civil rather than criminal cases. One exception was the infamous "great electrical conspiracy," which involved many of the top executives of most of the big firms producing electrical equipment. In this case several executives were tried and found guilty of criminal charges of violating the anti-trust laws.[7]

More importantly, even when middle and upper-class types of violations are defined as "criminal", the laws are made unenforceable or are simply not enforced. For example, probably the single greatest form of "theft" in our vast consumer society is that of "consumer fraud" committed by

7. See Richard Austin Smith, "The Incredible Electrical Conspiracy," *Fortune* (April, 1961), pp. 132–180, and (May, 1961) pp. 161–264.

companies and salesmen. Although legally defined as criminal, it almost never leads to prosecution. It is not that the prosecuting attorneys choose not to prosecute, but rather that state legislatures have passed and maintained laws that make it almost impossible to prove fraud. It is necessary to prove "intent" to commit fraud, and to prove "intent" is almost impossible, even though various means of easily "establishing" intent to commit burglary and other such lower-class crimes have long been established and routinely used. Consequently, there are almost no official statistics showing the vastness of this form of "theft".

When the laws against the kinds of violations committed by middle and upper class individuals are potentially enforceable, then it is generally found that the state and local budgets and the policies of police departments lead to non-enforcement of the laws. Obvious examples of this are the discrepancies between money and man-power devoted to such lower class activities as narcotics or vice and those devoted to business fraud or professional crimes. Every significant urban police force has a vice squad and a narcotics squad, but no police force has a "professional squad," a "medical squad," or a "lawyer squad". Doctors, lawyers, and other professionals and businessmen are allowed to police themselves, so that their criminal activities do not often become officially categorized as crimes, whereas the lower classes have their policing done for them by the police.

This non-reporting extends all the way down the scale of business. As Melville Dalton found in his study of three large chemical firms, at the executive level there are various forms of misappropriation of funds, which are potentially treatable as embezzlement, but which almost never lead to any action at all. At this level the reason for such non-reporting seems to be that the *potentially-categorized thefts* are treated as side payments, perhaps secretly accepted forms of the "tax-dodge", so that what is honest and what is dishonest becomes shadowy or problematic for both the individuals involved and any outsiders, such as the police.[8]

This form of employee *potential-theft* extends all the way from executives down to the more petty forms that are probably universal in American industry. As Cameron found in her study of shop-lifting, probably over 90 percent of the shop-lifting that goes on in our society is unreported to police, though it is more often reported to the insurance companies; a high percentage of this shop-lifting is almost certainly done by employees.[9] Liebow has shown how it works even at the lowest level of jobs as a standard part of the job, so much so that employers appear to take into consideration the theft potentials in deciding on the wages. But, as usual, this kind of lower-class theft appears also to be more often publicly disclosed, either by firing for theft or by reporting to the police.[10]

In addition to these factors, we must also consider the effects of formal and informal police policies on the discovery and reporting of crimes. Not only are the police provided with the legal mandate and the financing to seek out primarily lower-class crimes, but they also appear to develop their patroling and enforcement policies for this purpose. More clearly, the police as individuals know that they must be careful not to "roust" or "arrest" individuals who might bring complaints or suits for false arrest against them, since, even though the possibility of winning such a case would be small, it would not look good on their "records". The lower-class person, lacking the knowledge or the means to bring suit has traditionally been the ideal target (though the

8. Melville Dalton, *Men Who Manage*, New York: John Wiley, 1964, pp. 194–195.

9. Mary Owen Cameron, *The Booster and the Snitch*, New York: The Free Press of Glencoe, 1964, pp. 38–39.

10. Eliot Liebow, *Tally's Corner*, Boston: Little Brown and Co., 1967.

development of civil rights protections for the poor may be changing this now). Since the police have operated very largely as secret organizations in our society, there is very little evidence on this matter; but Cameron did find that the private police in department stores were explicit about the danger of rousting "well dressed" patrons, so much so that professionals, who are aware of the meanings of the "respectable front" to the police, take advantage of this by dressing respectably.

Another form of biasing, which makes the official statistics highly incomparable from one area to another, is differences in the local organizational policies and in discretionary policies of individual officials. For example Goldman found that in the towns surrounding Pittsburgh the police departments had very different policies concerning the disposition of cases of reported or discovered delinquency. These policies, which resulted in very different official rates of delinquency, were related almost entirely to individual factors, primarily the relation between the police officials and the local communities, rather than to the nature of the crimes.[11] Other researchers, such as Cicourel,[12] have found similar variations in the official disposition of juvenile cases. He also found that the official statistics are incomparable even *within* agencies, since policies and personnel change within the same agency.

I found such incomparability of official categorization policies to be even greater in the case of suicides. In *The Social Meanings of Suicide* I argued that the official statistics on suicide are summings up of numbers of classifications of suicide which are not comparable and, therefore, which are neither reliable nor valid. The most general and striking finding of my research on coroners was that the official organiza-

11. See Nathan Goldman, *The Disposition of Juvenile Arrests by Urban Police,* New York: Social Science Research Council, 1964, pp. 588–590.
12. See Aaron Cicourel, *The Social Organization of Juvenile Justice, op. cit.*

tions are more different from each other than I had expected. For example, I had expected that there would be greater similarity in the organizations and procedures to be found in large urban areas than proved to be the case. I had been misled by the use of the general name, "Medical Examiner's Office," to cover the official organizations classifying suicide as a cause of death in large urban areas. I had assumed that "medical examiner" would designate only a professionally-trained pathologist with a professionally-trained staff. I had expected the medical examiner's office would function under roughly the same legal status so that they would, for example, be able to carry out autopsies whenever they had any suspicion of suicide. I did not find this to be the case. In this state the differences in medical examiners' offices is very striking. I found one of the largest cities in the United States at one end of the spectrum, at least in terms of professional training and resources dedicated to the carrying out of the medical examiner's duties. This city has its own medical examiner's office as a result of special state legislation. Although it is true that even in this city some important decisions, especially that regarding whether the medical examiner should be called into the case, are left to non-medical personnel, such as the police and even morgue attendants, it is quite obvious that this city is more carefully surveyed by professionally-trained pathologists for any instances of "non-natural" causes of death than is any other major American city. This medical examiner's office is not only headed by a famous pathologist, but is itself a famous organization. This medical examiner's office has the power to order an autopsy in any case where the examiners believe the cause of death may be non-natural, and they have the resources to carry out these autopsies. As a result, there appears to be a far higher percentage of autopsies and toxicological examinations in this city than one would find in the other large cities of this state. At the other extreme, one finds coroners in large rural counties who work on a part-time basis for a small salary of several hundred or a few thousand dollars who have no direct contact with pathology or training in pathology, and who must cover a huge area, sometimes eighty or a hundred miles long. In a coroner or medical examiner's office of this sort one would normally find great financial constraints on performing autopsies, or even toxicological examinations.

While we would not expect to find much similarity in the organizations or procedures of such a large city and a relatively unpopulated rural county, we would have expected much greater similarity between this largest city and the other major cities of this state. There was similarity in one large city, but not in others. To illustrate, in one of these cities the medical examiner, who was an appointed official and had been medical examiner for many years, was a trained pathologist who took an active part in administering the operations of the office and in training the doctors who went out to do the on-scene investigations. In another large city the doctor who ran the medical examiner's office had no training in pathology and took no active part in running the operation involved in the medical examinations or training of personnel. In this latter office the medical examiner also served as a county health officer and performed many other local medical duties. He had to rely almost entirely upon young doctors just entering upon their own practices who wanted to make a few thousand extra dollars a year. These men normally have had no training in pathology and remain employees of the medical examiner's office for relatively short periods, many of them, according to the medical examiner, being fired or relieved of duty for not performing the duty adequately.

In addition to the lack of comparability between cities in the nature of their organizations, I found that the legal situation of the county medical examiner's offices differed greatly. As a "home-rule" state, the county attorney's office is important in interpreting the nature of the laws for various local health officers. As a result, in one large city with a majority Catholic population, the county attorneys' office has told the medical examiner that autopsies can be legally performed only when there is very clear evidence of violence. This stringent interpretation of the law has led the medical examiner's office to place great restraints on ordering any autopsies, and consequently there are very few autopsies. In other cities a very different interpretation of the state law has been provided, so the percentage of autopsies performed is not too different from that found in the largest city.

It is further clear that differences over time lead to greater incomparability than differences between one place and another today. In the English common law countries, such as the United States, the coroner's office was originally a political and legal office second in importance only to that of the sheriffs. As the coroner's duties of investigation have been taken over by police, sheriffs, or district attorneys' offices, the coroner's office has come to concern itself with the classification of the cause of death and with the attendant investigations. In line with this development the coroner role has been filled by medical doctors, who often are trained pathologists.

Hence, throughout the state I studied there has been increasing reliance upon doctors to classify suicide as a cause of death. But these changes have been very erratic. Some areas, such as the largest city, changed in this way years ago. Yet some small rural counties have not changed because they say they do not have the money or the amount of work needed to make these changes. As a result, in this state today there are counties that use mechanics and funeral directors as their coroners and there are cities or counties with world famous medical examiners' offices. When one looks at the present situation and at the changes that have been taking place, it seems necessary to conclude that the amount of variability is so great that the official statistics on suicide within this state would inevitably be very incomparable over time and place.

There is, then, a great deal of evidence to show that official agencies are legally and bureaucratically structured very differently, that they have different (non-comparable) policies for their normal operations, and that these differences normally generate stable differences in the rates of deviance recorded in their official statistics. All of this is quite sufficient for rejecting official information and statistics as information on deviance. Yet, as if these were not sufficient, we also find that *all available evidence indicates that officials normally manipulate or corrupt the statistics for their practical purposes.* Above all, they manipulate the statistics to justify their policies and their personal actions to the public and to political leaders. For example, Niederhoffer, himself a policeman turned sociologist, has analyzed the corruption of police statistics:

With monotonous regularity the statistics reported are collated, and often manipulated, so that they prove how successfully the department is performing its duties. If newspapers complain that delinquency is rising, the next police report will inevitably reveal a great increase in arrests of juvenile delinquents. When a safety council alleges that motorists are speeding dangerously, "by coincidence" the police publish statistics of a tremendous number of summonses issued for speeding violations . . .

Members of the force themselves realize that statistics are artificially regulated to make monthly and annual reports appear more impressive. When a commanding officer tells them that a new policy of enforcement is to be followed, the patrol force is skeptical, interpreting the purpose behind the change as the desire to build up a record on paper, rather than to meet the actual need for police services.[13]

It has long been known by both the police and criminologists that the police at the lowest administrative level, the precinct, systematically manipulate the statistics to make their precinct look good. For example, they practice the simple expedient of "sitting-on" reported crimes until they can clear the report, i.e., bring a charge against someone for it; they often don't report those cases that they do not clear. This gives them a good ratio of crimes cleared to crimes reported, which helps their chances of advancement. (In Philadelphia, changes in reporting techniques in recent years, which involve more direct reporting to a central records division, have led to increases in the official crime rates of as much as 100 percent in one year.) The police can also produce sizeable increases in the serious crimes reported by campaigning to get more reports and by changing their recording policies so that felony charges reduced to misdemeanors (for "consideration" of guilty pleas, a standard practice in American criminal justice), get recorded as felonies rather than as misdemeanors. In 1967 the official crime rate of New York went up over 14 percent in six months, which led the police to make the following rare public explanation:

For one thing, the Police Department has been conducting an intensive campaign to encourage the public to report crimes. The establishment of a central number, 440-1234, and the installation of call boxes in the street that enable the public to call the police directly are part of this drive.

In addition, the Police Department has become increasingly conscientious in making certain that reports of crime are not buried or minimized as misdemeanors.

13. Arthur Niederhoffer, *Behind the Badge*, New York: Doubleday, 1967, pp. 14–15.

For example, when slum youths, strolling through a more prosperous neighborhood, force a youngster to surrender bicycle or money—even just a few cents—this is no longer a misdemeanor. It is robbery because there is a threat of force, if not actual force. Purse thefts that used to be considered misdemeanors are also robberies now.

Precincts now make daily reports to headquarters on complaints received. The statistical compilation is done by the Crime Analysis Units, not by precincts.

"We've reached the point," says Capt. James Meehan, in charge of the Crime Analysis Unit, "where if someone were to complain that a window was broken it could be listed as attempted burglary, not malicious mischief.[14]

Through a survey study of victimage, the President's Crime Commission found that people believed they have been victimized by crimes between three and ten times more often than the official statistics reveal. If crimes were reported more often, then we could have an increase in the official rates of crime anywhere from 300 to 1000 percent without having *any* change in what is actually happening. Indeed, there does seem to be a greater willingness to report crimes today than there used to be, partly because the police are seen more as the "experts" who should handle such things, and partly because people have become more afraid of crime. We are now experiencing a kind of national *crime-hysteria:* the rising official rates, which the people normally believe are true, lead to greater fear of crimes, which in turn leads to greater reporting of crime, which in turn leads to more fear of crime, and so on. On this basis alone, but also because it is to the advantage of officials who want more money and more power, *we can expect that the official rates will continue to rise steadily for many years to come. But it would be a mistake to believe this has anything*

14. *New York Times* (February 4, 1968), page 58.

to do with what criminals or other forms of deviants are doing.

The Problematic Nature of Social Categories of Deviance

Thus far we have been considering the nature of biases in the official statistics on deviance and the reasons for these biases. There is yet a more fundamental reason why sociologists must not use official information to try to decipher the social nature of deviance in our society. As I have already argued in Chapter 3, official organizations tend to create "information" about deviance that is very categorical, homogeneous, and non-problematic. But there is every reason to believe that the social categories of deviance actually made use of by members of our society—and by almost all officials in their *actual* operations, rather than in their officially recorded or *reconstructed accounts*—are fundamentally problematic. The social categories of deviance are problematic in two ways: they are abstractly or *essentially problematic* and they are *situationally problematic*.

A social category, such as "crime" or "suicide", can be said to be *socially problematic* when its meanings or uses by the members of the society involve disagreements, uncertainties, or conflicts. When, for example, individuals (or one individual at different times) disagree or express uncertainty about the appropriate use of a social category, then the meanings of the category can be said to be problematic for them. Social categories can be problematic for the observers (the sociologists), for the members, or for both. It is more likely that moral categories will be observed to be problematic by the outside observers than by the members, simply because it is normally assumed in our society that moral meanings are *absolute*, which means in part that moral meanings are non-problematic. Consequently, the members of our society (including the sociologists until very recently)

are apt to feel confused by moral disagreements, to believe
the other person is simply lying about his moral perceptions
("he *knows* what's right, but won't admit it"), and to feel
outraged that the other person has "intentionally" chosen
to do an "evil" thing. (When people do "recognize" the
existence of problematic meanings of moral categories, then
the level of the problem is very different—and far more
important, as I shall later argue.) Undoubtedly, this is sometimes true; it is possible to observe individuals involved in
disagreements later "admit" they were wrong, lying, kidding,
and so on. Equally apparent is that individuals more commonly have "sincere" disagreements about moral meanings
in our society, without "recognizing" there is a problem
in the moral meanings themselves; it is not at all uncommon
for individuals to fight, even to the death, over such moral
disagreements.

Social categories are *essentially problematic* when the
members disagree or experience uncertainty in using the
category in the abstract, that is, independently of the situation in which it is to be imputed to concrete events. (This
is not at all to say that the abstract use is not a social situation. It definitely is, and this social situation or context is,
presumably, an important determinant of the meanings of
the category; but the use or meaning of the category in a
situation that does not involve actual imputation of the category for the practical purposes at hand is quite different
from its use in a situation involving its practical use.) For
example, if members disagree about the meanings of the
category "suicide" or "crime" when they are trying to give
it an abstract definition, then that category is essentially
problematic: there is something about the shared category
itself *in any situation* which leads to disagreements or uncertainties in its uses. Social categories are *situationally
problematic* when there is disagreement or uncertainty in

their use in practical situations faced by the members of society. For example, even if two members agree on the abstract meaning of the category, such as "suicide" or "crime," they may still be found to argue intensely (and "sincerely") with each other over whether it should be imputed in a given instance.

Most morally meaningful social categories are both essentially and situationally problematic for members of our society. Recall that the formal definitions of "crimes," let alone the abstract definitions individuals carry around with them "in their heads", generally differ greatly from one state or locality to another in our society. In fact, the general category of "crime" itself has no commonly agreed upon definition, even among the legal experts, since it seems to cover a number of dimensions of meaning, with no one dimension found in all those concrete things called "crimes". It should be clear, then, that "laws" and "crimes" are *essentially problematic* social categories, and it follows that any uses of the terms in concrete situations will prove situationally problematic. This can be recognized from our discussions of police uses of "juvenile delinquents", as just one example. Probably a more important reason for the situationally problematic nature of laws and crimes is that their concrete uses are determined primarily, *and necessarily,* by the practical contingencies facing the officials seeking to use these social categories in concrete situations.

All of social life is so complex and changing that every social situation is to some degree situationally problematic for the members of society. Even when the abstract meanings of categories are not problematic for the members, the *situational uses* (or meaningful interpretations) of the categories are necessarily problematic; *the members of society must construct concrete interpretations of the meanings of the abstract ideas which they see as relevant to the situations they face.* While this construction of situational meanings is itself guided to some extent by various abstract social rules concerning "rationality" and so on, these rules themselves are abstract and must, accordingly, be given situational interpretations. They, then, cannot provide any completely determinant meanings for the situation-at-hand. *The situational contingencies, the situation-at-hand for the members of society, necessarily become a fundamental determinant of the meanings that the members will see as appropriate and binding for that situation. In this sense all human thought and action is necessarily existential: not only must we create our world of meaning (our essences) out of our existence, but we must also recreate some part of that world of meanings for every situation we face in everyday life.*

What we find in police work is that the police necessarily develop strategies and tactics of greatly varying degrees of abstraction and complexity to deal with the highly problematic situations they face on their daily patrols. These situational strategies are probably constrained to some degree by the abstract "laws" under which police work is supposed to operate, but this constraint is only piece-meal and episodic. The abstract "laws" and policies of the departments themselves become important only in so far as they are *used* by the police in constructing their situational meanings; the abstract meanings are important only as *resources for practical use.* This is precisely the way the police make use of the legal categories of crime: They use them to get the "job done adequately", as they define this, and they *see* the situational contingencies as defining the nature of the "job" and its "adequate" performance, hence, as necessarily defining how one should *use* the legal categories (such as whether one should see an event as a "crime" or look the other way). Bittner has described this aspect of police work brilliantly:

The virtual absence of disciplinary control and the demand for discretionary freedom are related to the idea that patrol work involves 'playing by ear.' For if it is true that peace keeping cannot be systematically generalized, then, of course, it cannot be organizationally constrained. What the seasoned patrolman means, however, in saying that he 'plays by ear' is that he is making his decisions while being attuned to the realities of complex situations about which he has immensely detailed knowledge. This studied aspect of peace keeping generally is not made explicit, nor is the tyro or the outsider made aware of it. Quite to the contrary, the ability to discharge the duties associated with keeping the peace is viewed as a reflection of an innate talent of 'getting along with people.' [15]

Bittner found that everyday police work is mainly concerned with maintaining the peace, rather than with enforcing the law, and that the laws are used only occasionally to get the job done:

Peace keeping procedure on skid-row consists of three elements. Patrolmen seek to acquire a rich body of concrete knowledge about people by cultivating personal acquaintance with as many residents as possible. They tend to proceed against persons mainly on the basis of perceived risk, rather than on the basis of culpability. And they are more interested in reducing the aggregate total of troubles in the area than in evaluating individual cases according to merit . . . .

Though our interest was focused initially on those police procedures that did not involve invoking the law, we found that the two cannot be separated. The reason for the connection is not given in the circumstance that the roles of the 'law officer' and of the 'peace officer' are enacted by the same person and thus are contiguous. According to our observations, patrolmen do not act alternatively as one or the other, with certain actions being determined by the intended objective of keeping the peace and others being determined by the duty to enforce the law. Instead,

15. Egon Bittner, "The Police on Skid Row," *American Sociological Review*, 32 (October, 1967), page 715.

we have found that *peace keeping occasionally acquires the external aspects of law enforcement*. This makes it specious to inquire whether or not police discretion in invoking the law conforms with the intention of some specific legal formula. The real reason behind an arrest is virtually always the actual state of particular social situations, or of the skid-row area in general.[16]

The same things are true of suicide: suicide is situationally problematic for the members of our society and, of course, for the coroners and medical examiners entrusted with officially categorizing suicide as a cause of death. Suicide is problematic in part because, as I have argued in *The Social Meanings of Suicide*, there are at least six dimensions of meanings found in the uses of "suicide" in our society:

1) the *initiation* of an act that leads to the death of the initiator;
2) the willing of an *act* that leads to the death of the willer;
3) the willing of self-destruction;
4) the loss of will;
5) the *motivation to be dead* (*or to die*) which leads to the initiation of an act that leads to the death of the initiator;
6) the knowledge of an actor that actions he initiates tend to produce the objective state of death.[17]

These six dimensions are combined in various ways by individuals, including coroners, in making their decisions concerning the abstract meanings of "suicide", so that a variety of specific formal definitions are possible.

The uses of the category of suicide are situationally problematic to an extreme degree, especially because so many different considerations are involved, even considerations

16. *Ibid.*, p. 714.
17. See *The Social Meanings of Suicide, op. cit.*, pp. 350–385.

such as whether classifying suicide "matters enough" to make it worth the pain it can cause individuals. When we look at the reports of officials we can find opposite conclusions concerning whether a given death is a suicide or something else, even when the observed and reported events appear to be extremely similar. The following two cases are good examples of this, even though they were made by individuals in the same organization who knew far more about suicide than any ordinary coroner or medical examiner.[18]

Case 1.

The victim was found comatose by his wife on his bed. She promptly called the family physician, who responded to the home and had the victim transported to the Hospital. The victim was pronounced dead at 6:00 P.M. with 1.9 mg. percent barbiturate and .09 percent Ethanol in the blood. Death was attributed to acute barbiturate intoxication.

The deceased's wife was interviewed in her home. The family physician was contacted on the telephone.

The wife reported that she had originally found her husband in bed at 2:00 P.M. but that she did not disturb him, since he frequently napped at this time on the weekends and had some difficulty sleeping during the nights. Both she and her married son were at home at this time. She stated that her husband had been an off-and-on heavy drinker for several years and that he had been drinking regularly during the week preceding his death. No pills or medication were found in the bedroom, but

18. It is important for purposes of maintaining the anonymity of my respondents and the organizations that helped me in this research that I not use real names here. However, note that the assistant coroners who were doing the studies from which this information was taken are far more highly trained in the area of suicide than the vast majority of coroners and medical examiners around the United States. In fact, the individuals who were doing this could well be considered to be among the best in the country.

two half empty bottles of whiskey were located in the dresser. No suicide note could be found.

The deceased had been retired from his grocery store business due primarily to poor circulation in his legs. He also had a heart condition. He was, however, making plans to purchase a small market in the near future. The wife and the family doctor concur that the deceased was restless but not depressed. He never spoke of suicide nor was there a previous overdose. He was probably experiencing some pain in his chest, but he rarely complained. He took cardiac medication regularly but disliked to take the Nembutal the doctor had prescribed. Both informants suspect that the deceased accidentally took an excess of sleeping pills while intoxicated. There is no evidence to the contrary.

On the basis of the investigation of the psychological aspects of this case, the recommendation of Probable-Accident is made.

Case 2.

Victim was a 42-year-old, Caucasian male. He was found by the apartment manager on April 7, badly decomposed. His room was locked from the inside. The manager smelled an odor from his room, called the police and they broke into the room. Victim died sometime between April 4th and 7th. Toxicology report indicates a barbiturate level of 9.1 mg. percent. Apparently, a test for alcohol was not done.

The following persons were contacted: the family physician; the manager of apartment; and the victim's employer. Victim's brother and fiancée could not be reached.

The doctor had treated victim for about a year. He last saw victim February. Victim was treated for gastritis and ulcers. Victim had eighty percent of his stomach removed. Victim was an alcoholic, belonged to Alcoholics Anonymous and had not been drinking for the past year. Victim was on the following medication: Ritalin, Adooyd, Entrazine and Noludar. There is no known history of depression or suicide attempts. According to the physician, victim was concerned about his health and careful in taking medication and did not take excessive amounts of pills.

Both the apartment manager and employer reported that victim had not drunk in over a year, did not appear to be under any stress, was a steady worker. Victim did not pick up his last pay check.

On the basis of the high barbiturate level, a recommendation of Probable-Suicide is made.

There is in fact a fundamental reason why all morally meaningful actions, and, indeed, all social actions, are fundamentally problematic, both essentially and situationally, for members of our society: *all social actions are seen as actions of the individual, actions for which he as a social person is responsible, only if he is believed to have intended to commit the actions and intention is highly essentially and situationally problematic for all members of our society.* Intention is so highly problematic for members of our society primarily because of the fundamental criteria of "reality" and "truth" shared and used by the members of our society. The externally observable phenomena (generally denoted by the social categories of "actions" or "deeds", "concrete realities", etc.) are imputed far more "reality value" or "truth value" than are the non-externally observable, "subjective" phenomena. (Presumably, this is related to the immediately "public" or "shareable" nature of the externally observable phenomena; they are more "objective" or object-like.) Those internal phenomena, such as "intention", "belief", "idea", "thought", "motive", and so on, are all considered to be far more "uncertain", "questionable", "doubtful", "illusive", more subject to "lying", "control", and so on. These subjective phenomena, then, are not only more problematic but are commonly recognized to be at least potentially so for most situations ("mere words", "actions, not words", "I'll believe it when I see it", "Don't believe anything you're told", etc.).

We have already seen that officials are in fact using the common-sense categories, such as the common-sense category of "suicide", and are trying to "correctly" apply these categories by using the common-sense means of determining the "truth" about what happened. While the categories of "crime", "suicide" and the other categories with moral meanings have a number of different dimensions of meanings, the dimension most commonly found is that of "intention". Unless the actor believed to have committed the action is believed to have "intended to commit the action", then the action cannot be considered to be a "crime" or "suicide". Instead, the action is seen as an "accident" (or as the intended action of someone else, such as a "homicide" rather than a "suicide").

When we consider the case of suicide, then, we find that most of the time coroners and medical examiners give common-sense definitions of suicide which involve the dimension of "intentional killing of oneself". The primary difficulty they face is that of "truthfully" determining whether the individual committing the act "intended to kill himself" by that act. If they conclude he did, then he is a "suicide"; if not, then the death is due to something else—a "natural death", a "homicide", or an "accident". In my study of coroners and medical examiners I found that some of them are quite aware of this necessarily problematic nature of suicide. Some of them made very clear statements to the effect that in almost all cases there was inevitably some "grey area" in which it was impossible to be certain whether death was due to the intended actions of the individual or to some such thing as "accidental consequences" of intended actions. At least a few of them had reflected upon this matter and seemed reasonably aware that the general implication of this conclusion was that the entire activity of classifying the cause of death must necessarily remain fundamentally problematic.

Operating common-sensically, coroners and medical examiners make use of a vastly complex set of strategies for *objectifying intention;* that is, they seek "evidence relevant to inferring intention" (or "non-intention"). There are many different kinds of evidence members of our society consider relevant to truthfully inferring intention, which are based, presumably, largely on their own "subjective" experience of the relations between their own experienced intentions and their own externally observable actions (even though this appears to undercut the whole idea that externally observable phenomena are the most reliable by making the "meanings" of these externally observable phenomena, which is what they are ultimately interested in, dependent upon subjective experience). The basic goal is to make the internal, subjective experience externally observable—to make the external an "index" or "sign" of the internal. While it is recognized that this *objectifying* of intention is always to some extent problematic in itself, it is felt to make intention less problematic. In this way objectifying intention becomes a basic means of "justifying" one's inference of intention: *by objectifying intention, or relating it to commonly accepted external signs of intention, the individual renders the most socially defensible accounting of his decision.*

Since, as we have seen earlier in this chapter, officials are most especially publicly accountable for their actions, it is officials who especially seek to objectify intention when they find an individual "guilty" of an immoral action. This is found most in cases of crime where one's decisions are so publicly accountable that a complex set of formal "rules of evidence" has been established to deal with this problem of accounting for the official decisions. But it is found as well among the officials classifying suicide as a cause of death.

Coroners and medical examiners make use of all the common-sense ideas about the relations of the nature of actions (e.g., the position of the wound) to intentions, the relations of the nature of persons (e.g., was he a "suicidal type", a "depressive type") to intentions, the relations of the situations (e.g., was anything wrong in her relations with her husband or lover) to intentions and so on. There are no set rules on how one should consider the relations of these various factors to the question of "the intention to kill oneself by the action committed", any more than there are in any such common-sense activities; one works in the situation-at-hand in terms of the contingencies *as they arise.* But there does seem to be a reasonably common pattern to such inference processes in the investigation of possible suicides, a pattern which we will probably find holds for the general common-sense inference of meaning in general.

The first thing considered, and generally the thing that leads to the whole process of "investigation", is the *consequences,* the "body". Is the person asleep, dead, etc.? What is the state of the body? Position? Wounds? How long dead? The next thing considered is how did the body get here, in this state? This immediately leads to the consideration of the *action* (e.g., shooting) and *instruments* (e.g., weapons) involved in its getting here in this state. Then the investigator looks at the *immediate situation,* both that leading to *discovery* and, most importantly, that at the time of the action producing the consequences, the *action situation.* Then the investigator seeks to determine the relations between the phenomena thus inferred (backward) to have taken place to produce the body and the intentions of the individuals involved. At this stage a crucial form of information is sought: the *expression of intention.* Even though members distrust words and believe that individuals may lie or hide intentions through what they say (e.g., it is believed by the students of suicide that individuals intending to use suicide as a gesture, rather than to die, may well leave notes around to make sure others get the idea), words are still the fundamental means by which members infer internal states such as intention. For this reason, investigators are more concerned with possible expressions of intentions in the action situation than with anything else. Did he say he was going to kill himself? Did he say he intended to do something else? Above all, did he leave a "suicide note", that is a note expressing his intention to kill himself? For officials the suicide note becomes the primary means of accounting for the decision that the death was a suicide. It is taken as *prima facie* evidence that it was a suicide and can determine the meaning imputed to any other aspect of the investigation. (In at least one major city only deaths with a suicide note are classified as suicides.) Most importantly, what was his immediate physical situation (e.g., alcohol) and social situation (e.g., argument with husband) preceding the action situation? Then the investigator considers the *long run situation* to see how these physical and social situations are related to the *type of person* (is he a "suicidal type"?) he is and the *types of actions* he has been known to commit in similar situations (has he committed suicidal actions before, threatened, gotten depressed in such situations, etc.?).

The tremendous complexity of such considerations comes primarily from the fact that, even given this rough order of procedure (which members are unaware of), *the meaning of any particular aspect of the investigative procedure, that is, its significance for inferring the intentions of the actor, is determined by its relations to all other parts or "findings" of the investigative procedure. The parts must all fit together into a plausible whole which will serve as an adequate (public) account for the inferred intentions and actions (e.g., suicide).* Consequently, one gets a great deal of jumping back and forth in the considerations. If one uncovered aspect doesn't fit with the inferences from earlier aspects, then the earlier aspects and, possibly, the inferences from them must be "revised" so that they fit with the new "discovery". This even means, for example, that once a plausible whole has been constructed to account for an official decision of "suicide", then any succeeding information that arises contrary to the suicide classification must be refitted into the plausible

whole by "finding" more aspects of the whole (or new interpretations of old parts) to show that this new evidence does
not "really" disprove the earlier decision. (This is especially
true of official classifications, since an official becomes publicly committed to a classification once it has been officially
recorded. There is, in fact, even a great deal of paper work,
and embarrassment, that must go into filing "amended death
certificates" in most states.)

An examination of one case for which there is more than
the usual amount of information will reveal many of these
aspects of the investigative procedure. This case will also
serve as an excellent example of some of the specific problems
of meanings that arise.

This case, like almost all cases of possible suicide, was first
investigated by a police officer who later filed a police report
which became the primary evidence on which the coroner's
decision to classify the death as a suicide was made. (Since
the police are partly responsible for deciding whether such
sudden and unattended deaths are homicides, they provide
the most complete reports available. In many cities these are
the only written sources of information made use of by
coroners in deciding that a death is caused by suicide. In
almost all cities the police first structure the situation by the
nature of their investigative procedures.)

On 6-30-60 reporting officer checked the inside of the premises
and viewed the body and at that time it was determined that no
foul play had occurred. A routine report was taken by the officer
and from all appearances it appeared to be a suicide.

Reporting officer bases that opinion on the cardboard placed at
the side of the bed, the position of the body along with the gun.
It is the common practice for persons when attempting suicide
to place newspapers or articles below their body in order to
absorb the blood and other messes created by the taking of their
life. The victim apparently took the 30-30 Winchester rifle which
was recently purchased from Sears by the victim as a purchase

slip from Sears was located on the premises. The victim took the gun from the box and apparently loaded it with one shell from a new box of shells (this was later determined by ID Technician as photographs of the scene were taken by him and also the gun and ammunition was brought to HQ by him for printing and further checking).

[It is important to note in this report that the primary focus of this first section and of the rest of it is on the scene or immediate situation and on the nature of the instrument, the gun. At no point in the report is there any significant consideration of the social and physical situation or the action situation which could be used commonsensically to infer likely intention. Instead, the police immediately jump from the nature of the instrument and the position of the gun and body to the conclusion that this is a suicide. The only accounting given of this inference is the idea that it is "the common practice for persons when attempting suicide to place newspapers or articles below their body in order to absorb the blood and other messes." This is an attempt to call on common-sense "knowledge" of the relations between such scenic devices and the "intention to kill oneself". Unfortunately for the reporting officers, there is no such common-sense understanding as this, at least outside of that small group of police where it might exist. This plus the failure to construct a plausible whole accounting for the inference of intention was probably much of the cause of the great argument that soon ensued over whether this was indeed a suicide.]

Approximately ten days later, without any further report by the coroner being included in the file (as is usual in this city), and, apparently, without an autopsy other than a toxicological report, this death was classified by the coroner's office as a suicide. According to a later record of an interview with the mother, this classification of the cause of death came as a tremendous shock:

She had spoken to the investigating police officers, to her son's employer, landlady and landlord, and formed an opinion from these conversations that the death was accidental. However, when the death certificate came and it said suicide it upset her tremendously. She is now trying to have the coroner's office reconsider this certification and change it.

She very quickly, and throughout the interview, attempted to put me in the position of proving that the boy shot himself, which was something that I could not do and kept pointing out to her that my purpose in talking to her was not to prove the point of suicide, but to gather some information on the boy's life-style so that we could evaluate psychologically whether there might have been a motive for suicide or the absence of a motive. She agreed to such a discussion but said that she only wanted herself interviewed, and that she wanted no other persons contacted as all of them now believe the death was an accident and my talking to them might start them thinking that it was a possible suicide.

[It is of some interest here to note both the official's understanding that he could not "prove" it was suicide and the mother's understanding that interviewing the others involved could "start them thinking" it was a suicide, that is, lead them to restructure the plausible whole they had constructed for the meanings of the events.]

Approximately three weeks after the official certification of the death as a suicide, and presumably at the time she received the death certificate in the mail, the mother wrote the coroner about her sense of shock:

Dear [Coroner]:

It was a great shock to me when I received the Certificate of Death stating that my son was a suicide.

His father, his landlady, and his employer have all said that he was in a happy mood and things were going well for him, when he came up to show me a new motorcycle he had bought.

[Here the mother is trying to show that his social situation was not one in which there was something "wrong", which is essential in common-sense understanding to provide an adequate account of the intention to kill oneself. She refers below to the ambiguity in the police report, something largely resulting from a lack of consideration of such factors.]

He had bought new clothes, and he had bought the death weapon —a Winchester repeater rifle. He liked guns and had owned rifles in the past, and fairly recently had a small revolver. Some months ago he drove with me to a Rifle Range. He told me then that he would like to come back and try target shooting there sometime. So his buying a new rifle was not extraordinary. Also, there was no note left.

[She is establishing here that buying the rifle in no way justifies the inference of an intention to kill himself with it. Then she further points out the crucial lack of any direct expression of intention to kill himself—a note, a further bit of evidence showing, presumably, that the inference of an intention to kill himself is not adequately accounted for or demonstrated.]

Having the cause of death changed on the Death Certificate will not give my son back to me. But a lot of people loved him and it is a further wound to our hearts to have him recorded as a suicide.

[It should be noted that "suicide" generally leads loved ones to feel intense guilt. They are the most important part of the social situation from which the intention to die is inferred: they are the most blameworthy thing in his situation. It is, therefore, vital that the death not really be a suicide. But all the rest of this record indicates that the mother was not acting "insincerely" or any such thing. She was constructing a perfectly plausible interpretation, one which others too saw as plausible; but one which the officials opposed with an opposite, and also plausible, interpretation.]

The coroner then asked a deputy coroner, who knew a great deal about suicide, to check into the case further. The deputy coroner then set out to provide the crucial information concerning the victim's long-run situation, especially his personality type and types of actions, especially any suicidal actions, and the social situation immediately preceding the death. He first talked on the phone to someone at the place where the dead man had worked for about a year. This person said several times that he didn't know much about the man, but he did have some ideas about his personality type and his types of emotional responses and actions. (This is a transcription of the taped conversation.)

Employee
He never did drink that I know of. Now he might have, but not to my knowledge. I don't think I have ever heard the owners mention the fact that they thought he drank anything.

Interviewer
Ok, so that was probably not a problem. Did he ever act as if he were depressed? Or despondent?

Employee
Yes, to me he did all the time.

Interviewer
That seemed to be his—

Employee
This was him.

Interviewer
That seemed to be his usual state?

Employee
Yes, I mean as far as ever laughing very much or anything like that—he always had to be serious and had a deep and far away look on his expression. On his face, as if his mind was somewhere else.

Interviewer
Ok. Was it your impression that there was anything wrong with him, or he was troubled or . . . ?

Employee
Well, my opinion is that he acted like he had something serious on his mind all the time. Something that was not connected with what he was doing at all.

Interviewer
I see.

Employee
As if he were really dwelling on something else, but he never talked or discussed anything with anyone else, that I know of.

[It is important to note here that the deputy coroner is specifically *searching for* information about personality, emotion, actions, etc., which are seen as relevant to inferring suicide. So, for example, he is interested in whether the victim had problems, not whether the victim had exultations. Since most people have both, and since we normally expect this, it might seem strange that there is this concentration in the investigative procedure on what is "wrong" or suicide-related. But it "makes good sense" when we remember that the official classification is already "suicide" and this search is probably implicitly directed at finding if there are "adequate grounds" to account for this as a "suicide", not adequate grounds to account for it as something else. We seem, then, to have a *primacy effect* here: once the classification is made of suicide, the rest of the investigation becomes a search for information that demonstrates that classification to be an adequate account.]

The deputy coroner next interviewed by phone the psychiatrist who had treated the dead man about a year before.

Doctor
Hello.

Interviewer
Hello. Dr. Jones, this is Phil Smith.

Doctor
Yes.

Interviewer
I'm calling you as a Deputy Coroner. We do some work for the Coroner's Office and I'm working on the case of Thomas Smith. He's a young man about 22 or 23 . . .

Doctor
Oh! My God! Yes. Jesus Christ!

Interviewer
He shot himself in the head June 30.

Doctor
Oh, oh.

Interviewer
And it was ruled a suicide by the coroner, but his mother has questioned that, asked the Coroner's Office to reopen it and restudy the situation. And what we do in a situation like that is call the survivors—people that knew him—to gather some history and see if there might have been some motive or what his life-style was. What kind of person he was. Had you not known . . .

Doctor
Yes. If it's the same one I know . . . yes.

Interviewer
No, I mean had you not known that he had taken his life?

Doctor
No, that's news to me.

Interviewer
Oh, I'm sorry . . . it's . . . Yes, it was June 30. Gunshot wound to the head.

Doctor
Oh. Oh.

Interviewer
It was a 30/30 rifle he had purchased the rifle shortly before the time of his death . . . it happened in his own apartment. And that was that . . .

[The deputy coroner has earlier stated that "he shot himself", which has clearly set the scene for the inference of suicide from the beginning. (Even at that, the doctor suggests below that it might have been homicide.) Then by this stage the deputy coroner simply provides a rough sketch and invites the doctor to fill in the rest with common-sense understandings of what would happen "in such a situation" by stating "And that was that . . ."]

Interviewer
Sometime in the past you had worked with him . . . treated him for about a year or so.

Doctor
It wasn't over that long time.

Interviewer
Yes. How long ago was it?

Doctor
I guess I last saw him over a year ago . . . I kinda lose track of the time . . . I would have to dig the notes out to be sure . . . but it was about a year ago. . . . I guess I last saw him well over a year ago.

Interviewer
I see.

Doctor
And he was essentially a . . . the closest diagnosis you could come to would be a . . . kind of a chronic schizoid character. He had a pattern of repetitive failure at almost everything . . . school, military service, occupations, far as I know he had few, if any friends, had had some when he was younger but gradually dropped away. Far as I know no overt psychosis of any kind, but

a lot of borderline kind of things. Let me see if there is anything else I can remember offhand.

Interviewer
Let's see. One person told me that he was involved sometime in glue sniffing and things of that sort. Was that . . .

Doctor
I didn't know of anything like that. He never mentioned anything like that to me.

Interviewer
All right. The mother mentioned he was in the Navy for just a month. Why did they not keep him?

Doctor
I don't know for sure. I think he got a psychiatric discharge, but you'd have to get that from the Navy. I think it was either for some kind of disorder type behavior or it was a psychiatric discharge, I'm not sure which and I suspect the reason I'm not sure is I don't think it matters too much which category they put him because he was just grossly unsuitable for military . . .

Interviewer
He was just in and out . . . actually.

Doctor
He may even have told them he was homosexual . . . I'm not sure now . . . he wanted to get out. And then was very sorry . . . that . . . that was it I think. He worked at getting out and then was very sorry that he succeeded. That would be it . . . a kind of a schizoid boy, lot of conflict with the mother, rather isolated, very few friends, a lot of borderline type ideations, a pattern of repetitive failure . . . that's about it.

Interviewer
Any history of violence or had he ever made any suicide attempts or threats . . . or . . . did that ever come up?

Doctor
Never did.

Interviewer
Never at all.

Doctor
Never did.
In fact I'm a little surprised to tell you the truth. It just doesn't
fit . . . He had gone through some . . . Again I'm having to
search my memory and I'm not sure. I think he may have had
some episodes of fighting when he was younger, but rather reason-
ing types of fights. Nothing special. And then he got, if anything,
rather withdrawn and introverted as he got older, and more and
more kind of schizoid, so that he didn't fight any more, tended
to be more . . . you couldn't really call it depressed . . . but
something like that. More apathetic if anything.

[Much of the earlier hesitancy and halting statements of the
doctor now are explained: he has not seen or heard of this
case for almost a year and is having trouble remembering it.
But the interviewer is "forced," by reason of the short time
available for this sort of practical activity, to take this sort
of testimony rather than seeking more "hard evidence" from
the doctor's files. This is the kind of thing that led Cicourel
to compare official information to "hearsay" or "gossip."
    It is very important to note that the doctor specifically
denies here that this man was the type who was likely to
commit suicide: "it just doesn't fit." Actually, this is the way
most individuals, including psychiatrists, seem to feel about
deaths they consider suicides. But this one is important because the doctor's ideas about schizoid type, etc., are later
used to help account for the classification of this as a suicide,
though his denial that this man was such a type is not then
mentioned.]

Interviewer
I see. The mother told me that there were periods of time that
he spent in — with the hippies, people in that area and that he had
sort of grown out of that.

Doctor
Yeah. He went through a lot of acting . . . a moderate amount of acting-out . . . that type. Had lived away from home and then come back, then he lived away from home again. Had a pattern of the mother of repeatedly putting himself in the position where he had to have help from her, and this kind of thing.

Interviewer
I note also that she sent him once to Europe, and once to Hawaii, I wasn't clear why . . . whether it was to get away from bad influences or whether it was to help him get over . . .

Doctor
I think it was probably both. A lot of guilt on her part, too. As I recall, very badly. She felt somehow it was her fault, that she hadn't been a good mother, and tried to make it up to him in material ways. This actually made him feel terribly guilty.

Interviewer
I see. And she is having a very difficult time with the certification of suicide. She's finding it extremely hard to accept that and is. . . .

[We seem to get some hint here that this investigation is intended to provide an account of this as suicide which she will accept.]

Doctor
I can understand that.

Interviewer
. . . . asking us to change it, to help change it.

Doctor
Well it would be in my mind to question it, whether he did it himself. He's been involved with some rather strange people to say the least.

Interviewer
The circumstances, he was in the apartment and the door was

locked so the police ruled-out foul play, and what remained would be the possibility of suicide or accident. But the scene was such that it looked more reminiscent of suicide . . . and I guess . . .

[It seems significant that the deputy coroner speaks of the scene as "reminiscent of suicide," that is, of calling to mind suicides for which there was "better" evidence in the past. He seems to be trying to convince the doctor, without wanting to seem to be doing so, and the doctor seems to be resisting, here cutting off his "guess" that it is suicide before he can make it.]

Doctor
There is one other thing . . . He was the kind of kid who might well experimented with LSD or something on that line. I think he may have used a little marijuana at times. He had at times in the past, he stopped that when I was seeing him and some excessive drinking. It is possible, in that kind of setting, he may have had a . . . I just don't know . . . It's all conjection on my part.

Interviewer
He wasn't drinking at the time of his death. He was sober and . . . of course we don't know whether he had taken any drugs or not.

Doctor
He was the kind of person that could have well been drawn into that. The pattern of withdrawal, and a lot of failure, and this kind of thing . . . but I really wouldn't know.

Interviewer
All right. Toward the very end for about a year or so he had worked in the laundromat. He used to . . . was the clean up boy and he would run errands and things of that kind. They felt that he was a pretty good employee, he would show up for work. He had limited responsibilities.

Doctor
Surprising, it sounds like, if anything, he was doing better.

Interviewer
It sounds like, if you look at his past life, he had stabilized; he had been in the same apartment for a year, he had worked about a year, he was not drinking . . .

[Here the interviewer agrees with the doctor that there is less reason to see the long-run and immediate situation as one in which the inference of suicide is justified. He then even provides some further information of this sort.]

Doctor
Anything anniversary type thing or . . . ?

[Here the doctor switches and searches for some evidence that might actually support a suicide inference. That is, he is asking if there was anything in the man's history which would lead him to associate suicide with June 30. He only has to refer briefly to this because it is commonly believed by suicide "experts", though probably not by the general population, that "anniversary suicides" are not uncommon.]

Interviewer
Not that I could find. I haven't talked . . .

Doctor
What was the date?

Interviewer
June 30.

Doctor
What's his birthday?

Interviewer
I don't know.

Doctor
I just wondered.

Interviewer
I don't know his birthdate.

Doctor
I was wondering about his discharge date from the Navy and I was wondering about his birthdate.

Interviewer
I can check back with his mother.

Doctor
Ok. That's about all I can think of . . . anything . . .

Interviewer
But the thing that I am particularly interested in, you don't have the impression of him as being a sort of depressed, suicidal individual?

Doctor
Not really. He was moving in that direction to some extent but it sort of surprises me, really.

Interviewer
Ok.

Doctor
Ok?

Interviewer
All right. Thank you very much Dr. Jones.

Doctor
I'm sorry to hear about it.

Interviewer
All right. I'm sorry too.

The deputy coroner later filed the following report.

Dear [Coroner]:
The following is the report of the investigation of the above mentioned case on which you requested a consultation.

A 23 year old man was found shot to death in his own apartment on June 30. Toxicology report indicated; Blood: Ethanol absent. . . .

Both parents strongly believed that the death was a probable accident. They pointed out that the deceased was a quiet young man who worked hard, lived alone, never got into any difficulties, saw the parents at intervals, was not despondent, nor had he any difficulty that might provide a motive for a suicidal death.

The boy was raised by his mother after the parents divorced when he was nine years of age. He was a quiet apathetic boy who did not get along well with his family or friends, did poorly at school and was a minor behavior problem. In late adolescence he used to keep company with undesirable individuals in the [hippie] area. He became interested in the hippie movement, experimented with marijuana and possibly other drugs. He dropped out of school and was a general disappointment to his mother and father. He seemed to fail at whatever he attempted. When he was 18 he was inducted into the Navy but after a month was discharged as unsuitable. Following that he had about a year of psychiatric treatment with Doctor Jones. Doctor Jones described him as a chronic schizoid character, a person with repetitive failure in school, military service and other activities. He seemed to always put himself in a position of having to be rescued and receiving help from his mother. Socially he was isolated. The few friends that he had had during adolescence seemed to drift away. More and more he spent time by himself. He had some interest in motors and in guns, and did own a rifle and a revolver. He would practice from time to time at shooting ranges. He was never in any difficulty with the police and he never made any suicide attempts or made any threats and was not known to have been depressed or despondent.

In the last two years of his life he seemed to be undergoing some change. He moved away from the hippie element and took an apartment in a better section. He worked for the last two years as mop-up boy and general handy man. There he was known as a good employee; he was reliable, did his work, kept to himself and never caused any trouble. . . .

The mother and the attorney made a strong point that in the absence of a note, and with the absence of a witness, and with a rather poor police report on this case, no one could say with 100 percent certainty that the death was a suicide rather than an accident.

On the basis of the information from the survivors there seemed to be an absence of a motive for suicide. While the deceased had had an early history of behavioral difficulties and adjustment problems he seemed to be making some progress toward a better life adjustment. He had worked for two years in one place and had remained in the same apartment for at least a year. He had no financial problems and was planning a job change. Because of the absence of a clear cut motive for suicide, and the absence of a suicide note, this investigator would recommend that the certification be changed from suicide to probable suicide.

Yours very truly,

[Just before reaching his conclusion the deputy coroner provides a list of justifications for classifying this as an "accident" or "homicide". His conclusion that it should be classified as a Probable Suicide comes almost as a shock, but, apparently, there would have to be far greater justification for changing the official classification to something else. It should also be noted that this "change" has no official significance, since Probable Suicides are still officially considered Suicides, as are other *ad hoc* categories, such as Accident-Suicide, Possible Suicide and so on. Moreover, the record contains no indication that this classification was even changed to Probable Suicide.]

Most officially classified cases of "suicide" are never subjected to such an extensive study or reporting, but every indication is that most other cases are subject to exactly the same kinds of problems of meanings. In many instances the problems are even greater. At times the emotional stakes are vastly greater. One coroner told me specifically that her life had been threatened in such a conflict over the classification of a death as a suicide.

Conclusion

We have seen that sociology became deeply committed to the use of official statistics on deviance because it arose largely in the context of the official agencies of control. Like all the officials, these sociologists were deeply concerned with using the most effective rhetoric for determining social policies to "solve" social problems. The officials in turn were committed to using the statistical approach to present and manage their affairs, not only because of its rhetorical power, but also because it provided the best form of *social accounting* for their activities (from their standpoint).

Not only did this statistical approach serve their purposes of official control—and does so even more today, but it also generated statistical rates which were quite stable in the short run. These stable rates are exactly what we would expect an organization functioning in a stable and probablistic fashion to produce. Indeed, even if the data composing these rates were entirely in error, we would expect such organizations to produce stable rates, since *error functions* are stable in precisely this way. This stability of the rates was misinterpreted by the early sociologists as an indication of the deterministic, hence lawful and scientific, nature of human action. They concluded that the rates must be non-accidental, hence truthful, representations of the social phenomena. This led to the development of the structural-functional and statistical-hypothetical approaches to man and society.

We have also seen that all available evidence shows that by any standard statistical criteria the official statistics on deviance are extremely unreliable. The essentially and situationally problematic social meanings of the social categories of deviance, which are themselves so problematic, are the ultimate reasons for these many unreliabilities. These problems of meanings make the notion of "quantifying" or "indexing" any moral meanings, and possibly any social meanings at all, suspect.

For the members of our society, including officials, any given act *may mean very different things at the same time.* While for some members a given act may be a "crime" or a "suicide", for others looking at exactly the same act it may be something entirely different, such as a "frame-up" or an "accident". Indeed, the same individual often experiences meanings as very problematic. For officials or sociologists to *impose* their own formal definitions upon such acts would be nothing more than the creation of an *ad hoc social reality* which contravenes the social realities of the members of society and, thereby, prevents our ever discovering the truth about such social phenomena. Such *ad hoc* realities may very well serve the purposes of officially controlling the members of society, of regimenting them to fit the policies of the officials; and, indeed, I believe this is precisely what they do. But *ad hoc* realities can never form the basis of a science of man and society. Only a recognition of the facts of the problematic nature of the social meanings, and of the far reaching implications of this for society and for the scientific study of society, can do this. Rather than putting society upon the rack, bending and distorting the fundamental nature of man and society to fit the narrow quantitative prejudices of officials and their supporters in the social sciences, we must begin by studying the fundamental nature of the phenomena, experiencing them as directly as possible, and then slowly constructing our formal methods of analysis to fit the experienced nature of those phenomena. This is the reason why only information gotten through participant-observation can be validly used to analyze the uses of social rules and the construction of social order. This, of course, is the only form of information used in our analyses in this book.

5. The Problematic Meanings of Social Rules

Abstract definitions and arguments have done little to advance our knowledge of social rules and their relations to social actions and social order. Our experience thus far shows *the need to develop our terms and their formal definitions in close conjunction with our empirical and theoretical investigations of social rules and their effects on social life.*

Durkheim and other sociologists have emphasized the need to *study* social rules scientifically. But, because they believed that, as members of the society, they knew what the social rules are and what they *mean* to all the members of society, they have rarely done empirical investigations of social rules. As we saw in Chapter 2, they assumed sociological omniscience in their understanding of social rules.

What is now needed is careful, systematic research on social rules *as used by the members of society in different situations.* We must do systematic studies of the everyday uses of rules by the police, judges, administrators, and individuals in all socially defined situations. Sociologists have barely begun this important task and it will be years before we have unraveled the important problems concerning the nature and effects of rules.

The Language of Social Rules

The most basic level of experience of concern to sociologists is the *intersubjective* (or mutually conscious) *experience* of members of society, much of which is unverbalized. However, the verbal level of our intersubjective experience has been the focus of most empirical attempts to study the nature of social rules, probably because spoken and written words seem more directly observable and recordable. This focus is only partially justified scientifically and is probably an artifact of the scholar's bias in favor of the articulated and written word. It seems likely that eventually research will use sound films to study the *silent language of morals*. At present the only extensive, systematic work we have concerning the nature and use of social rules has been done by the linguistic philosophers on *the language of morals*.[1] But the methods used by philosophers to analyze the language of morals are not the usual methods of empirical research. They do not make systematic observations and recordings of moral statements made by individuals in the conduct of their everyday lives. Instead, they rely on the kinds of statements which seem to them, the philosophers, to be "plausible" or "linguistically appropriate" moral statements. These are moral statements *made in the abstract,* rather than moral statements made by individuals *in the situations* of everyday life in

1. There are by now many works in the philosophical analysis of the language of morals. The classic works are, however, the following: G. E. Moore, *Principia Ethica,* Cambridge: Cambridge University Press, 1962; C. L. Stevenson, *Ethics and Language,* New Haven: Yale University Press, 1944; R. M. Hare, *The Language of Morals,* New York: Oxford University Press, 1964; Paul Ziff, *Semantic Analysis,* Ithaca: Cornell University Press, 1960. For an introductory treatment of the general problems and an excellent analysis of them, see C. Wellman, *The Language of Ethics,* Cambridge: Harvard University Press, 1961.

which they find themselves. As we have seen, *abstract meanings* are different in important ways from *situated meanings,* yet they are still important in determining what situated meanings are plausible, and are, therefore, important in determining the effectiveness of moral statements used in everyday situations. For this reason, sociologists must understand the nature of ethical or moral statements, even when made in the abstract.

The first problem is that of specifying the criteria by which one can distinguish "social rules," "morals," "ethics," from other phenomena and from each other. How can we tell when we are faced with a "rule"? How can we know that a rule is being invoked by a member of society? How can we know that a "rule" is a "moral rule," an "ethical rule," or some other form of "rule"?

The difficulty of answering such questions is obvious given the profusion of conflicting answers that have been proposed by philosophers of ethical language. Like many sociologists and anthropologists, many philosophers have tried to distinguish statements of rules ("ethical language") from other types of statements by arguing that certain words are distinctive of ethical statements. Thus, they focused their attention on words such as "good," "bad," "ought," "should," "right," and "wrong." But it did not take much investigation to discover that the attempt to define ethical statements as those involving the use of these words is inadequate for two opposite reasons: they both excluded too much and included too much. On the one hand, it was apparent from their understandings as members of the society that these rules are often communicated without the use of these special words. There are a large number of other words which also involve moral meanings, but which do not involve any direct or indirect use of these special words. "Repugnant," "filthy," "lousy," "wretched," "low," "sublime," "ideal," "pure," and "innocent" are only a few examples. On the other hand, it was equally apparent that these special words are often used to communicate meanings having little or nothing to do with what one common-sensically thinks of as ethical or moral meanings. For example, all of these terms are used in many different ways to evaluate or describe the *instrumental* worth of something. A word such as "good," for example, can be used meaningfully and appropriately in the following sentences: "That's good fun." "That's a good way to get yourself killed." In none of these instances would most people be likely to mean by "good" that they are "morally right" or "in accord with social rules."

In view of the inadequacy of this *linguistic approach* to analyzing ethical or moral statements, most philosophers have concentrated on the *semantic approach*. That is, they have made use of the following approach in some form

1) they have selected some set of (hopefully) representative statements which are generally agreed upon commonsensically (as the philosophers see common sense) to constitute ethical or moral statements;
2) they have then analyzed these statements to determine the *common* meanings they possess, which are then taken to be *the* necessary and sufficient meanings of ethical statements; and
3) they have then analyzed these meanings to reach more abstract generalizations about ethical statements.

The many philosophical analyses of moral statements have led to a number of positions regarding their general nature. Some philosophers have concluded that moral statements are entirely *expressive*, or emotional statements, communicating only what the speaker would *like* to see happen. Other philosophers have argued that statements are ethical or moral statements *only* if they prescribe action that is contrary to our desires.

Aside from the difficulties inherent in analyzing any such

complex phenomena, there may be a number of reasons for these conflicting conclusions. Philosophers have normally studied language non-empirically; they have relied on their own experience with language without making any systematic attempt to relate this to how people use the language in everyday life. Moreover, they have often assumed that there is some *absolutely right use* of language and that this is what should be studied rather than the ways common men use the language. Not being subject to empirical test, such conflicts are unresolved.

These conflicting conclusions have also been the result of the philosophers' failure to see how *problematic* it is for the members of society to know when a statement or gesture is moral or ethical in intent. In fact, people are often unable to agree over whether a given statement has moral or ethical meaning. There should be nothing surprising about this. Abstract terms, such as "moral," generally refer to several overlapping but partially independent dimensions of meaning; and in specific situations where they are used, the participants will choose to attend to whichever of the dimensions seem to them to best fit the situational context of the communication *and* their own intentions at the time. In every given situation the individuals involved must *construct* for themselves the meanings of things and, the more abstract the categories involved, the more likely are these constructions of meaning to be problematic.

The Phenomenological Analysis of The Language of Morals

Some of the basic problems of the philosophical analysis of morals can be overcome by studying moral meanings as they are actually imputed, communicated, and used in everyday life by the members of society. To do so is to make use of what is known as the phenomenological method in philosophy.

The moral experience of ordinary men—those who are not prophets or philosophers—is always situational. As we have already noted, abstract rules, moral statements, and other abstract meanings are of importance to men in everyday life because abstractions are an important part of the social substance they must use in constructing their specific meanings in specific situations. The specific meanings intended by the participants in any interaction are determined by the *situational context* in which the abstract idea is used. This *situational or contextual principle of meaning* is especially evident to the members of society when someone acts "out of context." Almost any behavior, such as taking one's clothes off, is appropriate or acceptable in some situational context, but not in most others. No abstract moral statement about nudity, such as "one should always be clothed," is likely to be valid for members of our society in all situations.

As a result of this situational determination of the meaning of moral statements, the only adequate analysis of the communication of moral meanings will be done in situations in which moral statements are actually used. That is, in order to get at the moral meanings the members are communicating, one will have to know *and understand* the situation in which they are doing the communicating, so the *very* idea of abstracting moral statements from their situational uses is absurd. This is a principle of the Wittgensteinian analysis of meaning that has been well-demonstrated by Alan Blum in his analysis of the meanings of "mental illness" or "insanity." [2] Using examples of the relations between the term "mental illness" and its situational usages, he has shown that there are many situations in which individuals might well think in the abstract that the term would be appropriately applied, until they learn about other aspects of the situation.

2. See Alan Blum, "The Sociology of Mental Illness," in Jack D. Douglas, ed., *Deviance and Respectability: The Social Construction of Moral Meanings, op. cit.*

For example, a woman observed on the streets of a city to be wailing might well be thought to be "mentally ill." Yet once we know that she has just been in an automobile accident in which a loved one has been killed, her behavior can be seen to be "normal grief" and not "mental illness." Only the situational context makes this clear to us.

Thus, one cannot deduce from abstract moral statements what the situational uses and, therefore, the specific meanings of moral statements will be. *There is no necessarily "logical" or "rational" relationship between our abstract moral statements and our situational uses of moral statements that would allow us to deduce the situational from the abstract or infer the abstract from the situational.* We must, therefore, concentrate on studying *rules in use* if we want to see what the rules mean to members in their everyday lives. Studying situational usages first, we can then try to determine those general dimensions of meaning shared by phenomena seen by members in situations to be "moral" phenomena; in this way we arrive at abstract analyses of the meanings of moral rules. We have no reason to believe or assume that the abstract dimensions of meaning arrived at by this analytical procedure will be the same as those we would arrive at by analyzing abstract moral statements in the way the philosophers of language have done.

While there have been many earlier phenomenological analyses of morality, probably the best recent analysis done by a philosopher is that by Maurice Mandelbaum.[3] Mandelbaum argued that there are three general dimensions of meaning involved in the moral communications of everyday life: (1) morality is seen by members of our society as being imposed upon them from outside, especially from God or society; (2) morality is seen by the members of our society as necessary, rather than as voluntary; (3) the members of

3. See Maurice Mandelbaum, *The Phenomenology of Moral Experience,* New York: The Free Press, 1957.

our society see morality as necessarily involving a feeling of "appropriateness."

Mandelbaum is obviously describing what we have previously called the *absolute morality*, though he has not considered some of its other important properties, especially those of timelessness, unchangingness, and necessary involvement in the structure of Being or God. His analysis of morality is, then, in agreement with our previous analyses of the absolute morality; but it is mistaken in its implication that this is the whole nature of moral experience in our society.

In one sense this identification of "morality" with "the absolute morality" is correct. The word "morality" is closely associated with this conception of "absolute morality." It is largely because of this that the word "morality" has been going out of use throughout most of our society as the belief in "absolute morality" has waned. Noteworthy here is that groups that still believe in absolute morality of any form (e.g. fundamentalist religions) still use the word "morality" a great deal. Words such as "ethics" are being used instead because these terms better convey the meaning of the more tentative and situational rules.[4]

But "morality" cannot be equated with "absolute morality." In common usage the former term has the connotative meaning of *rule-governed behavior* or *rule-related experience* of a special type. Morality is generally used to cover only those rules which are objectified. Objectified rules are those which, like absolute rules, are considered to be external to the individual and imposed on him, hence, independent of his will; unlike absolute rules, they are not necessarily considered to be part of Being, unchanging and timeless.

4. It now seems increasingly likely that the word "ethics" will eventually replace "morality" as the term most generally used to refer to rule-related experience in English-speaking societies, simply because there seems to be a general trend toward an increasingly situational view of rule-related experience. It is already becoming unfashionable and, thus, gives rise to a sense of uneasiness to use the term "morality."

Mandelbaum's analysis, then, is inadequate because it does not make the crucial distinctions between "moral experience" and the many other forms of rule-related experience. Rules may be seen as absolute or simply objectified (hence moral rules), but they may also be seen in other ways. Though the rules in simple societies tend to be absolute rules or, at least, objectified rules, the rules in more complex societies, such as America, are of many different kinds and tend to be less objectified.

In general *social rules are the criteria that normal members of the society are expected to make (sincere) use of in deciding what to do in any situation for which they are seen as relevant.* And *sanctioned rules* are criteria for which sanctions of some form are used to try to make actions *fit* these expectations. Sanctioned rules, then, involve "punishment" of someone for not *adequately* following social rules. Sanctioned rules are of many different kinds, being more or less situational, more or less formally defined (with "laws" being the most formally defined), officially sanctioned or not, physical in punishment or not, and so on.

Moral rules, as one special type of rule, also involve expectations of conformity and potential uses of sanctions. In fact, the potential sanctions for violating moral rules are far more important than those associated with other forms of rules. These are metaphysical sanctions: violations of rules grounded in Being are often subject to absolute sanctions, such as total ostracism, being eternally cut off from the grace of God, or even death. At the least, moral violations result in a *stigmatization of the violator's substantial self.*[5] That is, the substantial (timeless) self of the violator is transformed into an evil substantial self. The failure of Mandelbaum's analysis to include the role of potential sanctions in the social meanings of moral rules was due largely to his failure to see that

5. For a discussion of the "substantial self" see *The Social Meanings of Suicide, op. cit.,* pp. 280–283.

moral experience is necessarily *intersubjective*.[6] Even when no one else is actually involved in making moral judgments, *there is always implicit in the nature of moral considerations the assumption that judgment is being made or will be made, whether by other individuals or by Being*. This intersubjective judgment of oneself is so taken-for-granted that individuals can experience guilt when they believe they have violated a moral rule because guilt becomes a necessary part of the violation itself. That is, the experience of being judged in violation becomes identical with the violation itself; action and response become necessarily linked.

It follows that moral rules have situated social meanings, social responses, judgments, and sanctions. From the standpoint of any individual deciding whether something is moral or immoral, it is of crucial importance for him to consider the situational conditions under which the action will be judged as either. The important question for the sociologist or anyone concerned with the nature of morality, then, must be: what are the fundamental conditions under which anything can be judged morally?

The labelling theorists, especially Lemert,[7] Tannenbaum [8] and Becker,[9] were the first to see the significance of social response as a determinant of the *nature* of immorality. But their consideration did not go beyond recognizing that something is moral or immoral not because of any absolute morality, but because there is in fact a social response. The labelling theorists recognized the problematic nature of the categories of morality, but they took the imputation processes themselves as non-problematic. That is, they generally did

6. See my essay on "Deviance and Respectability", in Jack D. Douglas, ed., *Deviance and Respectability*, New York: Basic Books, 1970.

7. See especially Edwin Lemert, *Human Deviance, Social Problems, and Social Control*, Englewood Cliffs, N.J.: Prentice-Hall, 1967.

8. See Frank Tannenbaum, *Crime in the Community*, New York: McGraw-Hill Book Company, 1951.

9. See Howard Becker, *Outsiders, op. cit.*

not try to determine the conditions under which individuals impute categories of morality or immorality.

McHugh, following certain leads by Schwayder, has made an important beginning in the direction of determining these conditions in his work on "A Common-Sense Conception of Deviance." [10] He argued that an individual is imputed moral categories only if he is considered to be *responsible* for something. The individual is held to be responsible only if two conditions are met: (1) he must be considered to have *intended* to commit the actions being considered (including statements, thoughts, etc.) and *knows* the rules that are relevant for evaluating those actions; and (2) he must be considered to have chosen to commit those actions *freely,* or of his own accord, rather than as a result of some external constraint or force. To the degree that these conditions have been met, he will be considered responsible for the actions being judged and will, accordingly, be subject to moral judgment in terms of the categories of morality and immorality. Any action, then, will be considered by members of our society to be moral or immoral only to the extent that the individual committing them is believed to have been able to have done otherwise and to have known that they are moral or immoral. (If the moral rules are absolute, then they will certainly be assumed to have been known by the actor. For this reason, the consideration of "knowledge" of the rule is not particularly relevant to considerations of moral responsibility, but is quite important in considerations of responsibility for other forms of rule violations, especially legal violations in which the laws can be quite complex and obscure.)

McHugh's analysis leads directly to the conclusion that any action can be considered to be moral or immoral only

10. See Peter McHugh, "A Common-Sense Conception of Deviance," in *Deviance and Respectability: The Social Construction of Moral Meanings, op. cit.*

if it is arguable: "Moral rules not only permit, but create and require, the possibility of argument, denial and disconfirmation." [11] *That is, the imputations of categories of morality and immorality in our society are necessarily problematic because of the very nature of moral responsibility.* (They are also problematic because all internal states, especially "intention," are considered common-sensically to be less "real" or, at least, less subject to "objective knowledge" than externally perceivable states.)

The Problematic Nature of Moral Meanings

Labelling theory, we noted, made the first important break with the assumption of the traditional sociological perspective on social rules and social order that the social categories of deviance are absolute. It was rooted in the symbolic interactionist perspective of George Herbert Mead and other Chicago sociologists,[12] with perhaps the most important bridge to it being supplied by Lindesmith in his study *Opiate Addiction*.[13] Lindesmith's explanation made straightforward use of the central idea of the symbolic interactionist perspective, which is that social definitions of one's self and of actions are the major reasons why individuals perform actions. The social definitions provided by significant others thus become the primary determinant of any individual's definition of his self and his actions. He argued that an individual becomes an addict only when he learns from others, presumably "addicts" themselves, that taking the

11. *Ibid.*
12. The Chicago theory and research on deviance is all too commonly identified entirely with the so-called "ecological approach" to deviance. But, in fact, even the ecological works made significant use of some of the important ideas about language and meaning to be found in the other major stream of thought, that of symbolic interactionist thought, later to be identified as the primary Chicago approach to deviance.
13. See Alfred R. Lindesmith, *Opiate Addiction*, Bloomington, Indiana: Principia Press, 1947.

drug will prevent withdrawal symptoms. Also implicit in Lindesmith's argument is that an individual becomes an addict when others define him as one.

The symbolic interactionist approach to deviance focuses primarily on the situations within which an individual acts; consequently, it has little to say about structure. The early interactionist works on deviance were done within the context of the behavioral learning theory that was so often a part of Mead's own approach. As a result, they concentrated on determining the relationships between a social form of behavior and pleasure or pain. This is clear both in Lindesmith's and Becker's arguments that individuals tend to become marijuana users only when they learn socially to define the experience as pleasurable. Later, Becker put this earlier work into the theoretical context that has come to be identified as the labelling theory of deviance.

Because labelling theory draws upon a behavioral view of deviance, it tends to view social categories and their imputation as being largely unproblematic. There is a non-behavioral, phenomenological aspect of the theory, exemplified by Herbert Blumer in his analysis of Mead's argument that individuals must construct the meanings relevant for themselves in any given situation.[14] This phenomenological aspect has not been widely used by the labelling theorists.

Further, the basic model of society that labelling theory draws upon is what we might call *the conflict theory of society*. It posits conflict over values, especially the conflicts between values and laws, as arising primarily from ethnic pluralism. Conflict theorists such as Becker,[15] Horowitz,[16]

14. This aspect of Blumer's analysis of Mead's theory and its application to the study of deviance has been treated by John Lofland in *Deviance and Identity*, Englewood-Cliffs, N.J.: Prentice-Hall, 1969.

15. See Howard Becker, *Outsiders, op. cit.*

16. See Irving Louis Horowitz, and M. Liebowitz, "Social Deviance and Political Marginality: Toward a Redefinition of the Relation Between Sociology and Politics," *Social Problems*, 15(Winter, 1968), pp. 280–296.

Turk,[17] Quinney,[18] and Miller [19] have discussed the pluralism of classes in American society and the resulting conflicts over the imputations of the categories of deviance. Two questions prevail: (1) What will be considered deviance, especially, what will the laws be? and (2) To whom will be imputed the categories of deviance? Both labelling and conflict theorists see the important problems of the uses of categories in the society arising from conflicts among groups over these two questions. Both focus on the issue of power, i.e. identifying which group or class has more power to decide what the laws will be and to whom the categories of deviance will be imputed. Both also implicitly assume that the meanings of the categories themselves are understood in the same way and agreed upon by the different parties in the conflict. Their argument is that the parties to the conflict simply want to make very different use of the categories, notably through official actions intended to control the (lower-class) members of society.

To illustrate, for Becker the central question seems to be, first, whether marijuana use will be considered to be a form of illegal activity and, second, once it is so considered, to whom will be imputed the category of marijuana-user by the officials. He accepts the assumption made by the traditional perspective on deviance that the members of society share certain ideas about what constitutes deviance. His idea that there is "secret deviance," [20] and that one might seek to determine how much there is, presupposes that one knows what constitutes deviance, so that one might know how to

17. See Austin T. Turk, "Conflict and Criminality," *American Sociological Review, op. cit.*

18. See Richard Quinney, "A Conflict Theory of Crime," *op. cit.*

19. See Walter B. Miller, "Lower Class Culture as a Generating Milieu of Gang Delinquency," *Journal of Social Issues,* 14(1958), pp. 5–19.

20. For Becker's argument concerning "secret deviance" see *Outsiders, op. cit.* (The conflict between this idea of "secret deviance" and the assumption that moral meanings are problematic was pointed out to me in a private communication from Don Zimmerman.)

recognize it when he finds it. This is very different from arguing that deviance, or any other moral meanings, exist in situations only when individuals construct those meanings for that situation. It presupposes the existence of some structural, or quasi-absolute, social meanings which a sociologist can draw upon in deciding whether any given form of behavior is or is not a form of deviant behavior.

The more recent works done within the framework of labelling theory have continued this contradictory line of thought. On the one hand, they have insisted on the importance of social conflicts over moral meanings and the imputations of moral categories; on the other hand, rather than follow this argument to the conclusion that moral meanings are problematic, they have implicitly assumed the existence of some background moral meanings which are absolute, yet unseen by the structuralists. They then use this background structure to argue that the structuralists have not seen how much "real deviance" (or "secret deviance") there is, that the structuralists have not seen how the officials "falsely" (at least by implication) categorize people as deviants when "in fact" they are not, and so on. Hence, a "debunking" strain can be found in some of these works. For example, one implication of Scheff's work on *Being Mentally Ill* [21] is that people who are "not in fact mentally ill" get categorized as mentally ill because of the nature of official procedures. Although I would agree that it is legitimate for sociologists to examine critically the meanings and effects of social categories to see if we "should," in terms of some agreed upon ethical standards, use such social meanings in these ways, I believe it is also important that we recognize how we are then making an implicit moral judgment and that our doing so has covered up the fact of the problematic nature of moral meanings in our society.

21. See Thomas Scheff, *Being Mentally Ill*, Chicago: Aldine, 1965.

Other recent works in the area of deviance make moral arguments in society even more important to labelling theory, but they too fail to see the obvious implication of this. An example here is Kai Erikson's influential work on *Wayward Puritans*.[22] In many ways Erikson's work is an analysis of the attempt on the part of some members of society to reconstruct the basic moral meanings of their society; however, this theme was largely obscured by some of the social-systems vocabulary and ideas in the work. Erikson deals at some length with what he calls the "boundary-maintenance" activity of individuals. Boundary-maintenance is an idea derived from the kind of social systems analysis done by Talcott Parsons and others. Yet the nature of Erikson's information and argument are actually contrary to the basic assumptions of systems theory.

Erikson argued that some members of the society decided to try to change the social definitions of the "boundaries" of the society. He does not mean anything such as geographical boundaries or even "boundaries" of membership. What he has in mind is that the values and other shared meanings of the society in some way constitute a social unit that the members are seeking to maintain. Apparently, he is talking about the attempt by some members of the society to maintain the old moral meanings that are in conflict with the attempts of a new and growing group of people who are trying to change the meanings. When seen in this light the argument becomes far more important.

What Erikson argues is that in a number of very important ways the social situation of the American colonists, as they defined it, was changing drastically just before and during the great debates over witchcraft and related phenomena. As the social situation changed, the old purposes became less obtainable and new purposes were developing at the

22. See Kai Erikson, *Wayward Puritans*, New York: John Wiley, 1966.

same time. All of this led to some basic problems with their social and self-identities, to which they responded with various signs of anxiety. Most importantly, they also responded to it by carrying out a great social debate over the nature of society itself. This debate was the arena within which the members sought to reconstruct the moral meanings of their social lives and, although this debate was carried out in terms of the old vocabularies and beliefs of a theological and demonic nature, it led to some important reconstructions of the meanings of colonial society and even of the old theological ideas themselves. In time these debates and their outcomes became an important part of the increasingly secularized world view of the American colonists.

There is no justification for this continuing insistence on forcing the information that shows the problematic nature of moral meanings in society into the old mold of the structural-functional theories, which assume moral absolutism. Every form of evidence shows that the members of society experience uncertainties and conflicts over moral meanings in their lives, and that these problems of moral meanings are both abstract problems and situational problems (as we have called them in Chapter 4).

General Evidence of Problematic Meanings in American Society

The most obvious evidence showing the problems members of our society experience over moral meanings is derived from everyday life. Anyone who has lived in this society is aware that disagreements over moral ideas and decisions are common. Who in this society lives through a day without having some serious moral disagreements with others? Who lives through a day without having some important moral argument with himself? Certainly there are hermits, who do not have moral arguments with others;

there are fundamentalists and amoralists, who have no reason to examine their own morality; but these are rare types, and not representative of society.

If anyone in America is fortunate (?) enough to live in some state of moral bliss in which he is not in daily moral combat with others, and with himself, let him read newspapers, watch television or attend church services—or a revival, political rally or court hearing—or listen to a discussion between parents and children. Let him become a business executive or a professor on some idyllic campus—where SDS, YAF, YR, BSU, USMC, YMCA, ADA, and DAR struggle for what is left of the hearts and minds of students.

He will not find harmony over morals or over social rules. He will not find tribal rituals glorifying the ancient rules of the primal horde, though he may find these if he attends public rituals on Christmas, the Fourth of July, or on some other public occasion. If he looks with the eyes and ears of a member of the society, rather than those of a structural sociologist, he will not find happy citizens blithely "maintaining systemic boundaries," though he will find police and judges involved in deadly struggles with some "enemies of the state."

The whole idea of law itself in Western societies, especially in the Common Law societies, is based on the assumption that moral conflicts will arise and that these will in many instances lead to such intense conflicts between individuals, which cannot be resolved by their rationally trying to agree on the "one true moral solution," that measures must be taken by other members of society to protect themselves and the adversaries from such conflicts. The adversary system of our legal procedures assumes that individuals will at times have opposite views of the meanings of the same situation. The whole system of judicial appeals and checks and balances assumes that there will be disagreements among "experts." Our democratic form of government is based on the assumption that there will be reasonable disagreements among members over what is right and wrong. Freedom of expression is intended to allow all sides to conflicts to be heard so that individuals can then decide which side they prefer.

The *essentially political nature of American society* also assumes the existence of fundamental problems of morality. America, like most modern societies, is not generally *defined* by its members or by anyone else in terms of common morality or common goals. "America" is defined by almost everyone as a *political unit,* a political organization backed by the potential and actual use of power. Whereas everyone believes that America is many different things, everyone would agree that it is first and foremost a "government" or "state." And "politics" implicitly assumes the existence of problems or conflicts, since the purpose of politics is to find some way to *manage such conflicts.* It is quite true that these conflicts are commonly recognized to be of several different sorts and need not be based on moral conflicts. Certainly there are *conflicts of factual interpretation* and *conflicts of economic (and power) interests* which are partially independent of moral conflicts. But almost all such *conflicts also involve moral conflicts either as a cause or as an effect (or both).* In fact, these different forms of conflicts are so interdependent and their meanings so problematic that we often find individuals looking at the same kinds of conflicts, but seeing very different things. While looking at what some see as a "political contest," others will see conflicts of "class interests" and still others will see moral conflicts.

Even the ageless distinction between factual and moral conflicts fails. In his classical essay on "The Moral Basis of Political Conflicts" [23] Morris Ginsberg raised the question

23. See Morris Ginsberg, "The Moral Basis of Political Conflicts," in Morris Ginsberg, *On the Diversity of Morals,* London: Mercury Books, 1956.

of "how far and in what sense the political conflicts of the present time involve a fundamental divergence in moral outlook." He answered by arguing that what "appear" to be moral conflicts are often only conflicts over interpretations (or descriptions and explanations) of facts. At the same time, in his classical work on *The Genius of American Politics*, Daniel Boorstin has argued that in American society there is a tendency to draw the normative out of the descriptive, and has used the Civil War as an example:

The sectional character of the Civil War is as plain a feature of our history as the Mississippi River is of our geography. Yet its importance for the mode of our political thought has not been sufficiently noted. The fact that the conflict was along sectional lines, that each side purported to be fighting in defense of its institutions and way of life, made any elaborate philosophizing on the subject seem superfluous. The Civil War will thus provide an admirable illustration of our tendency to make sociology do for political theory, to merge the descriptive and the normative, to draw the "ought" out of the "is." Or, in a word, to confirm our belief in "givenness."

Neither North nor South was pursuing a new vision of society. Much of the polemical effort on either side took the form of describing its own institutions and those of its enemy. The upshot was both a stimulus to sociology and an incentive to make facts serve a normative purpose. Seldom has there been a stronger practical motive to lay bare the relationship among apparently diverse facts about a society: among the political system, economic structure, and labor practices of a region and its religion, morals, art, literature, and culture as a whole. The Mason and Dixon Line was thus a symbol not only of the regional nature of the conflict but also of the fact that, theoretically speaking, the conflict was to be waged on an empirical rather than a metaphysical battlefield.[24]

24. See Daniel Boorstin, *The Genius of American Politics*, Chicago: University of Chicago Press.

These different interpretations of the types of conflict involved in any argument are a direct result of the problematic nature of social meanings, as well as of the interdependency of the social meanings of factual descriptions, theoretical explanations, interest involvements, and moral involvements. Most important of all is the apparently necessary interdependency of "fact" and "evaluation." This interdependency is probably necessary because almost *all common-sense descriptions and explanations of social action implicitly assume some kind of evaluation and some social response, at least that of approval or disapproval.* For example, any given explanation of student protests involves an evaluation of that protest, an evaluation that will be accepted, approved, or disapproved by various groups and individuals in our society. An explanation of student protests in terms of childhood training practices necessarily leads individuals to approve or disapprove of what the radicals are saying and doing. Such arguments also have definite implications for social response. For example, explaining student protests in terms of childhood training practices involves a refusal to look at the messages being communicated by the students as being of importance in themselves, and this has the implication of not doing anything about the messages, whether favorable or unfavorable.

The same thing can be said of all social descriptions. One can never describe everything, even if one could see everything that is going on in any situation, so one must choose what to describe; such choices must be made in terms of what an individual considers to be valuable, relevant, and, most especially, what he considers to call for some kind of action.

The members of society not only find it necessary to do their explaining and describing in the context of some *background (or implicit) evaluation* and calls for action, but they also take it for granted that other individuals will understand this. They expect other individuals to interpret their descriptions and explanations, at least to some degree, in these background terms and they expect others to expect the same from them. (Parenthetically, it is because of this that all social research is assumed by members of society to have evaluational purposes and implications for social actions. This becomes part of their definition of the social research situation; consequently, when confronted with questionnaires or any other social research situation, they respond to it in the context of this assumption. Their responses, therefore, will be significantly affected by the evaluational and action purposes which they believe this particular research situation involves.)

It should be clear, then, that the common-sense assumption that ours is a political society means that there will necessarily be moral problems in society which must in some way be managed. In addition, even the common idea that the "genius of American politics" consists in finding a "compromise" to conflicts in no way denies the necessity of moral conflict. This view, which I believe is largely true and important for explaining how things happen in our society, assumes that there will be some common agreements, including some important agreements about compromise itself and about how compromises will be achieved. Yet it also involves the idea that conflicts, including basic conflicts, will inevitable arise in our society. Indeed, this view of American society (and of Anglo-Saxon society more generally) sees conflict and its resolution through compromise as so basic that it becomes the basic determinant of the nature of the society, of the politics of the society.

In spite of the fact that the dominant functional perspective in the social sciences has led social scientists to look for consensus rather than for conflict, there is abundant evidence of moral conflict in American society in their various studies, and even in their theories. Certainly this is true of the area of deviance. The sub-culture theories of functionalists, such as that by Cohen, recognize that there is moral conflict; nevertheless, they have simply tried to deny any great importance to this conflict by arguing that it grows out of a basic commitment to the values of American society (the mobility values) and that it results only in ambivalence (acceptance plus rejection at the same time) toward those values. This recognition has grown, so that by the time of Miller's work on lower class delinquency we find a strong emphasis on sub-cultural differences in values (or "focal concerns"). The argument has now intensified over the question of how much difference and conflict there are in values of various groups. (Valentine and Moynihan have reviewed many of these conflicting points of view and tried to show that they have serious practical implications, such as whether government welfare programs of any sort can be expected to produce great changes in the everyday lives of the poor.[25])

Some prominent functionalists show that they have been well aware of the existence of great moral complexity, conflict, and, hence, ambiguity in our society. Merton's work on bureaucracy,[26] while cast in a functionalist mold, was actually a study of the way in which ordinary members of our society view any rigid ("doctrinaire") application of rules as being "pathological." Merton's argument about "bureaucratic pathology" assumes that any attempt to directly, uncreatively (or unfreely) apply the rules, even the simple and rationally constructed rules of a formal organization set up to achieve relatively few goals, necessarily results in the "pathological," that is, impractical, wasteful, destructive, *and deviant in itself.* A lack of flexibility in the *use* of rules is, then, considered to be *immoral* by the members of our society (or, at least, by Merton).

25. See Valentine, *Culture and Poverty, op. cit.*
26. See Robert K. Merton, "Bureaucratic Structure and Personality," *op. cit.*

Talcott Parsons' work is an even better example. Certainly the overriding emphasis in Parsons' work as a whole is on "social system" and on value determinism, the ultimate expression of which is a totally ordered society. But even in *The Social System* there is recognition of the meaningful complexity, conflictfulness, and uncertainty of social action in our society. For example, immediately following his highly systemic analysis of "deviance" in our "social system," he then analyzes in detail some important problems with system analysis itself:

There is a second important range of problems concerning the difficulty of conformity with a normative pattern which focuses in the nature of the pattern itself. This concerns the question of how far the expectations of conformity are or are not specific and detailed. We have emphasized the importance of the fact that all normative patterns are to an important degree generalized relative to the particularity of the situations in which they apply. But there are enormous variations in the degree to which this is true. In proportion as the pattern becomes more generalized and hence "abstract" the problem of "interpretation" becomes accentuated. In other words, the actor faces the problem not only of living up to the expectations of his role, assuming that he knows exactly what they are, but of knowing just what is expected of him. In a society like our own there is an extensive proliferation of highly generalized rules and hence of difficulties in their interpretation. It may be noted that one of the primary functions of the legal profession is to advise clients on what their rights and obligations are. That the client should know them without expert advice is by no means to be taken for granted in a complex society, especially where certain aspects of the normative pattern system, those embodied in the formal law, are being continually changed by new legislation as well as by other processes. . . .

What has been outlined above takes account only of the most elementary beginnings of the complexities of the normative pattern system with which an actor may be confronted. A next step in complication is taken when in addition to the problem of interpretation of specific expectations there is introduced the problem of the applicability of alternative norms. This type of problem is most clearly seen in the case of a developed legal system, where quite clearly one of the most important functions of the courts is to determine which of a plurality of rules or precedents "governs" in a particular case. This possibility of "conflict of rules" is inherent in the nature of a system of generalized norms, and becomes a more acute problem in proportion to their generality and complexity. This is because generality implies abstractness, and abstractness means that one rule does not alone "cover" the concrete case, since the case will inevitably have a variety of aspects to which a corresponding variety of generalized norms is relevant. But if more than one norm is intrinsically applicable it is clear that there must be some order of precedence among them.[27]

Being unwilling to abandon the notion of an overarching social system, Parsons then proposes an interpretation of his idea of system which allows for the necessity of "interpretation" of meanings and which drastically modifies the assumption of value (or system) determinism:

It has been clear at many points that under certain conditions the interactive system operates to organize the motivational systems of the actors in such a way as to build up motivation to conformity with the expectations of a shared system of normative patterns, and that sanctions in such a "normal" case operate to reinforce this motivation. But the factors we have just discussed open the door to a range of variability on ego's part where within limits the question of conformity vs. deviance cannot be unequivocally settled. The question is whether alter's reactions are such as to tend to "bring ego back" toward the modal point in the range relative to the normative pattern structure, or to motivate him to diverge more widely toward one extreme of the

27. See Talcott Parsons, *The Social System*, Glencoe: The Free Press, 1951, p. 269, and pp. 271–272.

range, with the possibility of a vicious circle developing which carries him "over the line." [28]

This reinterpretation of the relationship between values and actions in our complex society, which might be called *modified value determinism,* seems very much like the idea of *constitutive rules* later proposed, and then partly abandoned, by Garfinkel [29] and others. Rules are seen in this sense as *heuristic devices* or criteria which can be used by the social actors to judge their actions in general, but they do not give detailed instructions as to how one would behave, or which rules are to be applied in any given situation. Although this is an important break with the simple system assumption of value determinism, it concentrates on trying to explain social order, which is assumed to exist, rather than being seen as something which members may or may not construct. It seeks to retain the idea of a social system even though this is contradicted by the idea that rules are heuristic devices. This approach ignores the fact that when rules are mere heuristic devices there must be something else *making use* of the criteria, something independent that either chooses to use the criteria or not and that chooses in which way to use them when they are seen as relevant. This independent factor, which we are arguing is the *constructive work* of individuals acting with some degree of freedom, becomes the crucial factor, with the heuristic devices (the rules) simply being used or not used in various ways.

Parsons' analysis does recognize the need for such an independent constructive factor, but he calls it "personality." However, he clearly argues elsewhere that personality is highly socialized by agents acting in accord with the values of society; hence he denies independence at the same time he appears to be arguing that it is necessary. Parsons' more

28. *Ibid.*
29. Garfinkel, *Studies in Ethnomethodology, op. cit.*

recent work, especially that on stratification, assumes the complexity of our society and the conflictful, uncertain nature of social meanings resulting from this.[30] Yet it is a mere truncated analysis set in the general context of his system theory which assumes value determinism.

Theoretical and empirical support for our analysis of the problematic nature of social meanings is to be found in the many works by the phenomenologists and existentialists, in the studies by sociologists directly influenced by these works, and in many participant-observer studies by sociologists, especially those on the uses of legal categories.[31] Unlike other philosophers, the phenomonologists and existentialists have been acutely aware of the fundamental problems of method and have sought above all else to "be true to the phenomena." Consequently they have provided much valuable evidence concerning social meanings in our everyday lives. However, most of this work has been done by Europeans. Because we are concerned primarily with American society, we shall forego a discussion of these works. In fact, there is no need to consider them directly, for many of their ideas have been well grounded in certain empirical studies by sociologists in the United States.

Some of the finest such studies are those by Egon Bittner, such as his works on the police and on radicalism.[32] Bittner has concentrated on the problems that any member would encounter in trying to devise an abstract method or formula for providing appropriate social meanings to concrete situations in our complex world, along with the ways that individuals go about deciding on the relevance of any one abstract rule for the concrete situations they face. He argues

30. See, especially, Talcott Parsons, *Politics and Social Structure*, New York: The Free Press, 1969.

31. See especially Egon Bittner, "The Police On Skid Row," *op. cit.* and "Radicalism and Radical Movements," *American Sociological Review*, 28 (Dec., 1963), pp. 928–940.

32. *Ibid.*

:hat individuals must reconstruct the meanings they impute to any situation when they find, as commonly happens, that the old meanings do not fit or satisfy their present purposes. His studies of the police have proven fruitful for discovering the ways in which individuals construct situated meanings (or, as he calls them, *ad hoc* meanings) to meet their new situations or their new purposes in old situations. (We shall be considering this evidence in Chapter 6 in our discussions of the details of situated constructions of meanings.)

Additional evidence of the problematic nature of social meanings in our society is found in the sociological studies of legal categories and the attempts to apply them in concrete situations. One of the more obvious examples would be the attempts to define "pornography" legally and to enforce the laws against it (whatever it is decided to be). Much has been written on the many different and conflicting definitions given the term by legislative bodies and courts in deciding on individual cases. Eventually the Supreme Court, one of the ultimate arbiters of fundamental problems of legal meanings in our society, decided that a work cannot be considered "pornography" unless, *taken as a whole*, it is "utterly without redeeming social importance." Yet this "definition" of "pornography" has not really solved any problems, since it merely shifts the problem from that of defining "pornography" to that of defining "social importance." In almost all cases *legal interpretations, like social interpretations or situational constructions of meanings, consist largely in providing alternative interpretations which the members will (hopefully) find less problematic to use in the situation-at-hand than they did the original one.* In the case of the court interpretations of "pornography" the problems of meaning are about the same when one shifts to the phrase "socially important." What appears to have happened, as in the case of almost all laws, especially the criminal laws, is that this new interpretation has been "accepted" by the great majority of the rest of society, but has then been provided with further interpretations for the kinds of purposes and situations shared by prosecuting attorneys, judges of lower courts, and so on. Specifically, situational meanings for the ruling have been constructed in such a way that material that looks "classy" because it is put into the context of "cultural" material is allowed, while non-classy looking works are forbidden. This is a good example of what I have previously called the *Playboy effect*. There is no reason to believe that the courts and most other members of our society believe that putting "naturalistic descriptions of sex" into a classy context actually eliminates its use to arouse sexual excitement, especially in conjunction with masturbation. Since these "social facts" are "known to everyone," there is no reason to believe that the members, such as court officials, do not know them. There is, then, no reason to believe that they are unaware that their "legal interpretations" allow these practices to go on. Because it is secret, I doubt that we shall ever be able to get hard evidence to "prove" the supposition that the courts and other officials are using the *Playboy effect* (and enforcement only against "non-respectable, lower-class types") to construct a situational interpretation that allows some *balanced observance* of the conflicting moral rules and social intentions involved in the whole situation. As Polsky has argued:

At the same time that society permits the dissemination of pornography, it officially denounces it. There is good reason for it to do both at once: from the desire to maintain a restrictive societal definition of "legitimate" sex, it naturally follows that pornography should be stigmatized and harassed yet tolerated as a safety-valve, in the same way that, as Davis demonstrates, society stigmatizes and otherwise harasses prostitution but never really abolishes it.

And just as Davis indicates for prostitution, the stigma attached to pornography is lessened when pornography is tied to some other socially valued end, such as art or science. One important result is this: when the "situation" being defined by society is a naturalistic depiction of sex, the most real consequence of a definition that labels it something other than pornographic is to increase its pornographic use in the society by reducing the inhibitions on acquiring it. This is obvious from the libraries of countless souls who avidly buy highly erotic works that society labels "art" or "literature" or "science" or "scholarship," but who take care not to buy "real" pornography.

And if the non-labelling of an erotic depiction as pornographic actually increases its pornographic use in the society, *de*-labelling increases such usefulness still more. As any publisher can tell you (I speak as a former publisher), it is much better for sales to have an erotic book that was once labelled pornographic and then got de-labelled than to have one that never got labelled at all. Thus such works as *Lady Chatterley's Lover* or *Tropic of Cancer* are, functionally, among our society's most pornographic books of all.[33]

In this way the legal definitions of "pornography" become *social fictions,* or meanings imputed to something that most of the members involved in doing the imputing recognize (either openly or, as in this case, secretly) to be "untrue," yet which they find *useful* to maintain, if for no other reason than that of maintaining the appearance of rational consistency or traditional legitimacy. There are, in fact, many explicit *legal fictions,* such as the one developed over centuries concerning the "king's two bodies" (his natural and spiritual body, the latter, being eternal, gave perpetual rights to property and so on). Another excellent example is the *factum valet laws,* by which it is maintained that there are legal sanctions for violating the laws when it is known that they will not in fact be imposed for any violation. The law

33. See Ned Polsky, *Hustlers, Beats, and Others,* New York: Doubleday, 1969.

is indeed complex, full of convolutions, and even contradictions intended to support consistency.

Another example of the problem in defining legal categories is the case of organizational "theft." It is common knowledge among working members of our society, and has been observed in many sociological studies of work and of organizations, that workers at all levels almost universally "appropriate" property for their own possession and use that was previously the property of the organization. In department stores, for example, this form of "taking" by employees probably constitutes the major component of what department store executives call "shrinkage" (because the quantity of goods just "shrinks"—inevitably). Anyone not knowing the complex nature of social meanings in these situations, would be tempted to see this as nothing but "theft." Certainly there are many times when the people involved choose to define it in precisely the same way and then fire the individuals involved for "theft." (Only rarely do employees get prosecuted for such "theft.") Liebow, for example, found that lower class Negroes, who were well known by their employees to be "taking" goods, were sometimes "fired" for this "theft." [34] The crucial point, however, is that there are well recognized choices involved in the definition of the activity. Employees generally see this form of "property appropriation" as a "right," and at least one sociological study found that a strike was called to protect that "right." Employers probably see it as a "necessary evil" and consider it to be a normal "cost" of operations, a form of what Garfinkel and others have called *normalized trouble*.[35] But there are situations in which employees do not see it as justified or in which employers take action. Which situations? There is no definite answer to this. The meanings of the situations and actions

34. See Elliot Liebow, *Tally's Corner, op. cit.,* pp. 37–41.
35. For an excellent treatment of "normalized trouble," see Sherri Cavan, *Liquor License,* Chicago: Aldine, 1967.

are fundamentally problematic, to be constructed for the situation-at-hand. Some properties of the construction processes can be specified.

In his excellent participant-observer study of *Men Who Manage,* Melville Dalton found wide-spread "appropriation" of organizational property among executives. Dalton found that these "appropriations" were treated by most people, though not all, as forms of informal "reward"; and he found that there was no abstract, clear way to distinguish between what was socially defined by the members of the organization as "theft" and what was defined as "reward":

Use of materials and services for personal ends, individual or group, is, of course, officially forbidden, for in both plant theory and popular usage this is *theft*. But our concern to pinpoint the informal phases of administration where possible requires scrutiny of this generally known but taboo subject.

Such practices are as delicate to discuss as they are to apply. For as long as rivalries can generate "reasons" there will be double talk around the concept of "reward," especially in organizations that stress "fair-dealing," "job evaluation," "merit-rated salaries," etc. The dynamics of individual and group action do not require that one agree fully with those who say that no word ever has the same meaning twice, but they do demand that one recognize the difficulties of assigning absolute meanings to terms describing the kinds of situations we are dealing with. What in some sense is theft, may, in the context of preserving the group and solving present problems, lose much or all of its odious overtones. We only need note the gradations of terms referring to theft to suspect this. As theft requires more ingenuity, becomes larger in amount, and is committed by more distinguished persons (whose power is often related to their importance in the operation of society), its character is correspondingly softened by such velvety terms as *misappropriation, embezzlement,* and *peculation,* which often require special libraries to define. To spare the living and some of the recent dead, and to ignore differences in time and place, we can point to Cellini—and remember Pope Paul III's judgment of him that "men like Benvenuto, unique in their profession, are not bound by the laws"— Aretino, Casanova, and even Voltaire. These men were all scoundrels of a kind who, nevertheless, were esteemed for their commendable contributions to society.

Always there are genuine transitional nuances, with debatable margins, between covert internal theft and tacit inducement or reward. Immemorially the esteemed personality who also performs unique services can move closer to "theft" than others without censure . . .

Between theft and informal reward is the gray-green practice of expense-accounting, which is also related to rank. "Theft" is softened to "abuse of privilege," but the feeling of some companies is clear in their demands for explanations. Others, however, including those sensitive to the tax factor, see large accounts as "part of the man's compensation," or as necessary to "attract and hold top men," or as a practice comparable to the "employee medical program." [36]

Dalton concluded that such "appropriations" for individual use of organizational property were supported by executives primarily because they believed that *practical situations* were so changing and complicated that no formal system could be set up to anticipate all situational needs. This led to a conscious demand for flexibility. These individual "appropriations" constituted a major form of organizational flexibility, but they were also subject to what the members in any situation might define as an "abuse" and then define as "theft":

Those who regard this chapter as merely a series of episodes on theft have missed the point. Our study of unofficial rewards is not an attempt to justify internal plunder or to say that theft by membership is inevitable. Both "theft" and "reward" derive their

36. See Melville Dalton, *Men Who Manage, op. cit.*

meaning from the social context. To insist that this context is constant—so that we can preserve the admitted convenience of fixed definitions—is to pervert meaning, block the issue, and deny that there are ethics in reward.

To repeat, the aim has been to show that however well defined official tasks may be, and however neatly we think we have fitted our personnel to these roles, the inescapably fluid daily situation distorts expected working conditions. Circumstances require various out-of-role and unplanned actions. Regardless of formal rankings, which are often only nominally based on potential for such action, some personnel more aptly do what is essential than do others. Tacitly or not, both they and their rewarders are aware of who solves problems and sustains the organization. Through time they are compensated as resources and situations allow. The process may seem to overlap with theft, or it may escape control and become theft, but able executives both utilize and contain unofficial rewards.[37]

Once we note that decisions concerning such things as "contributions," "problem solvers," and so on, are themselves very problematic and subject to different and conflicting decisions in different situations, we can see that there is no ultimate way of abstractly specifying what will be categorized as "theft" and what will be categorized as "reward." It is situationally problematic to a high degree.

Reasons for the Problematic Nature of Moral Meanings

Certain characteristics of American society, especially its pluralism, make moral meanings far more problematic than in most European societies. (We shall deal with these aspects in detail in Chapter 7.) There are also basic reasons for the problematic nature of moral meanings that are common to all societies and certain ones that are common to Western

37. *Ibid.*

societies. These form the background for all discussions of the problematic uses of moral meanings in our society and must be dealt with before proceeding further.

Probably the most basic reason for these problems is the *necessity of freedom* in all considerations of moral responsibility. This is revealed by the phenomenological analysis of the meanings of moral responsibility. It must be possible for an individual to have chosen to do other than he did do, or there can be no moral responsibility at all. Essentially, then, *moral meanings must be problematic* to be "moral" at all. They must be potentially arguable, and this potential is frequently realized in actuality. This is very likely the reason why even groups with highly homogeneous morality and social experience, such as families and groups of close friends, have serious moral arguments. In fact, the most intense moral disagreements probably are to be found only in such close relationships because there is a greater demand in such relationships for agreements on moral issues. (It is well known that most homicides are committed within such close groups; it seems likely that these homicides are most often the outcome of some serious moral disagreement.)

A second reason for the problematic nature of moral meanings in our society is that *all situations as defined by the members of society are necessarily complex and emergent.* Life itself is complex; that is, the relations between the basic needs of the human organism and the physical world are extremely complex. We can continue to exist only by developing very complex arrangements between our various needs and the world. There are always new enemies, new dangers, new experiences, new pleasures for which we must work out these relations not only for ourselves as individual organisms, but for ourselves in combination with other individuals. The human being is necessarily biologically dependent on other human beings. By their very biology, human beings are necessarily social and can exist in no other way. And as soon as we add a few human beings to our attempts to work out some kind of formulae by which we can relate ourselves to an already very complicated world, the world becomes immensely more complex. The problem of social order is far more complex than the problems of man's physical condition.

Our various social relations are also emergent, especially in the mass societies in which almost all human beings live today. New types of people are continually confronting us in our everyday lives with new ideas, new proposals, new possibilities, new dangers, new joys.

Furthermore, there are distinct limitations of our own ability to deal with that complexity. The human memory is able to store vast amounts of information and the human mind is able to analyze that information in myriad ways. Yet it is obvious that these capacities are far too limited to allow us to remember and to take cognizance of many of the things we encounter in even a limited period of time. Memory must be extremely selective and our analyses of our involvements in the world, which are constrained by the necessity that consciousness develops linearly (or in a single channel), makes it impossible for us to consider more than a tiny fraction of the information that we are able to remember. The complexity of the world in relation to our own limitations makes it impossible for us to in any way pre-program our responses to the world. In addition, the emergent nature of our own beings in combination with the emergent nature of the physical world makes it impossible for us to pre-program our responses to the world even if we were to have total knowledge of ourselves and the world in any given period of time.

Since it is impossible for us to pre-program our interpretations of the state of the world or our responses to those states of the world, it becomes necessary for us to create or construct our interpretations of and our responses to that world in specific and new ways. All situations and all of our responses to them must ultimately be new and distinct.

At the same time, and in opposition to this basic requirement of newness, we cannot achieve effective adaptations to the world if we treat all situations and all responses as completely new. If we had no memory and no other way of relating each new situation and potential response to previous ones, we would be faced with the task of learning for each situation all that was needed to respond in such a way that our basic needs would be met. We could certainly not long exist under such conditions. Memories are essential to our continued existence.

It is this necessity of bringing prior experience to bear effectively on new experience so that we can control the world to meet our basic needs that makes abstractions or symbolizations of experience necessary for human existence. However, the impossibility of creating any set of abstractions from our vast experience that will adequately fit new situations makes our meaningful relations to the world problematic. Even if we have complete agreement on abstract meanings, so that, for example, all individuals (or any given individual at different times) share exactly the same abstract meanings, there will necessarily be differences in the ways in which the abstract meanings are related to the specific situations. It is in this sense that situational meanings and actions are necessarily problematic for all individuals; and it is in this sense that human beings are necessarily free actors. Even the most tyrannical of societies must allow considerable freedom for its members to meet the complex, emergent situations of everyday life. (Because of this limitation on our ability to pre-program understandings and responses to the world, there is actually only a small difference of degree in the amounts of freedom and types of freedom between those societies we define as "tyrannical" and those we define as "free." But this does not mean such differences are unimportant: All life is concerned with small differences and small differences can be a matter of very great differences in value.)

The conflicting demands of freedom and constraint, and the resulting problems involved in constructing the meanings of rules and using them in everyday life, make the analysis of social rules and the explanation of social order far more complex than envisioned by the traditional sociologists. While we are probably a long way from solving, or even recognizing, all of the fundamental problems involved in doing this, we have made some important beginnings in this direction. As more social scientists become aware of the necessity for this new perspective on society and carry out the mass of empirical investigations of the uses of rules in everyday life that we so sorely need, our progress in understanding these constructions and uses should provide us with vital clues we can use in trying to solve the growing problems of social order in our society.

6. Constructing Meanings and Using Social Rules

Given the necessity faced by the members of society for constructing concrete meanings for the situations they face, it is clear that anyone concerned with understanding the relations between rules (or social meanings more generally) and social actions must take the analysis of the situational constructions of meanings and situated actions as his starting point. He must begin with the concrete uses of rules in everyday life. Only then can he move upward toward more abstract understandings and attempts to explain or predict the social uses of rules and social actions. This up-going approach, which is the opposite of the down-going approach of the absolutist sociologies, is necessary because, as we have seen, we have good reason to expect that the abstract expressions of rules will be quite independent of the situational uses of rules. Anyone who starts with the abstract rules and hypothesizes what the concrete, situational uses will be, or, what the social actions of those expressing the abstract rules will be, is almost certainly going to be wrong; yet this is precisely what those using the statistical-hypothetical and the structural-functional approaches have done. Both approaches take the abstract expression of abstract rules, such as a rule on universalism, assume it to hold (homogeneously) for the whole society, logically deduce hypotheses about concrete actions from this assumption, and seek to "verify" these hypotheses by "testing" them. It was precisely this that led students of "attitudes," which are abstract expressions of values or preferences given in interview situations (i.e., divorced from concrete, everyday situations), to believe that their thousands of "attitude" studies would allow them to explain and predict concrete actions. As Irwin Deutscher has shown so well, all evidence on the question shows that there is no significant relation between expressed attitudes and concrete actions. (Perhaps the only well-known instance in which attitude-takers are able with reasonable consistency to predict concrete actions, within about a 5 percent margin of error, is that of Presidential elections. The reason for this seems to be that polling attitudes is readily defined by the members of our society as a form of voting. In other words, the polling situation is so much like the actual voting situation, and the pollsters strive to make certain of this by their procedures, that one might well be able to get some close relations between an individual's expressed intention to vote and his vote a few days later. The more one can recreate the concrete, everyday situation for the individual, the more his abstract expressions will fit his concrete expressions and actions. Unfortunately for the attitude-takers and the personality testers, very few situations in everyday life can be so recreated in testing situations.)

We shall need many systematic descriptive studies (using participant-observation) of the situated uses of rules before we can be certain of the truth or falsity of any principles of the social construction of moral meanings which we might now propose.[1] But there are some principles that appear reasonably clear in the light of our common-sense experience and whatever good case-study material we do have. Each of these warrants careful consideration in itself.

Situational and Trans-situational Constructions of Meanings

The meanings of all communications are partially determined by the context of the communication, but the meanings of the context are partially determined by the meanings of the parts of the communication.

The principle of the contextual determination of meaning is the most general of our analysis. In fact, the idea of the necessity of situated constructions of meanings is simply the most important part of this more general idea of the contextual determination of meanings. But the contextual determination of meanings is only part of our principle. In a way it is simply an example of the ancient Platonic principle that one must know the forms of which any given individual thing is an example before he can understand that individual thing—the knowing or understanding consists largely in putting the particular under the "correct" general form. This *symbolist theory* of meaning has been represented

1. There are many social situations in which the actors involved articulate their ideas and feelings about social rules and which, therefore, are easily subject to social investigation. One example would be a study of the nature and use of rules in such standardized settings as traffic courts, family courts, and other forms of court activity. The basic problem involved in any such study, of course, is that some of the important meanings are so taken-for-granted by the members, even in those settings, that they have not articulated them very well. This demands participant-observation on the part of the researcher to enable him to come to share those taken-for-granted meanings. Some of these problems have been discussed in my essay on "Observing Deviance," in Jack D. Douglas, ed., *Observing Deviance,* New York: Random House, forthcoming.

in some form or other throughout the history of Western societies, and has been opposed at all stages of Western history by the *particularist theory* of meaning first stated clearly by Aristotle. This theory contends that the meaning of any communication can be given only by the parts and that the whole can mean only what is meant by some sum of the parts. I have previously referred to this as the *building-block theory of meaning*[2] because it assumes that the meaning of any communication is determined by putting together the pieces in the same way that one might put together a wall with the individual blocks (a wall without cement, presumably). Contrary to their own contention that the whole of society, the "social system", is greater than the sum of its parts, the functionalists have presumed that the building block or particularist theory of meanings is true. In their theories of value it is assumed that there is some basic set of social values that are somehow put together by individuals to give the value-meanings of any particular thing, situation, or action; it is assumed that by putting these basic values together a determinant value-meaning is given for that particular thing, situation or act.

In the early nineteenth century philosophers began to see the weaknesses of both these theories of meaning. Yet most of the emphasis has always been on the need to see the ways in which the whole (the context) determines the meanings of the parts, probably because there was a strong emphasis, especially in the fledgling social sciences, on breaking everything up into its parts and then analyzing them. This was the essence of the scientific method of experimentation, at least as conceived by the nineteenth-century positivists, and the prestige of science made this piece-meal analytical approach to meaning the "obvious" way to proceed.[3] This emphasis on the contextual determination of meaning (even

2. See *The Social Meanings of Suicide, op. cit.,* pp. 235–254.
3. *Ibid.*

of perceptions) became the basis of *Gestalt* psychology,[4] which in turn became so important in the development of the phenomenological tradition in which the fundamental data are always taken to be the natural experience.

Phenomenology, as developed by Alfred Schutz,[5] Maurice Natanson,[6] and many others,[7] has emphasized the ways in which the *immediate social context—the social (face to-face) situation*—determines the meanings of communications for the participants. At the same time, the linguists, notably those in the tradition of Wittgenstein, were developing their emphasis on the ways in which the *linguistic context of a verbal communication determines meanings* ("the meaning of language is its use," as it is often sloganized). These two traditions have recently been synthesized in various ways by the ethnomethodologists, though there remains a partial division between the *linguistic ethnomethodologists,* who emphasize the study of social usage of language, and the *situational ethnomethodologists,* who emphasize the more general social-contextual determination of meaning.

All too often in this tradition of thought we find that the contextual determination of meaning is stressed so strongly that the elements or particulars of communications are denied any significant independence from the

4. Probably the best discussion of the relevance of *Gestalt* psychology and the analysis of meaningful experience is that by Aron Gurwitch, *The Field of Consciousness,* Pittsburgh: Duquesne University Press, 1964, especially pages 85–154.

5. See Alfred Schutz, *Collected Papers,* vols. *1–3,* The Hague, Netherlands: Martinus Nijhoff, 1962.

6. See Maurice Natanson, *Literature, Philosophy, and the Social Sciences,* *op. cit.*

7. Both phenomenology and existentialism are highly relevant to the analysis of the situational or contextual determination of meaning. The vast majority of these works take a highly situational view of meanings and human actions, but there are some important conflicts arising from the failure of most of these theorists to deal directly with the issues of situationalism vs. structuralism. Many of these problems are obliquely revealed in Desan's analysis of the conflicts in Sartre's analysis of freedom and determinism. See Desan, *Marxism and Existentialism, op. cit.*

context in which they can be observed. Indeed, since observation itself necessarily involves situational communications of some kind, we find that some of these sociologists deny any independence of the observation from the situation in which it takes place. In this extreme form the idea of the contextual determination of meaning becomes a form of sociological *solipsism*: it makes all sociological (and all other scientific and non-scientific) observations and analyses completely dependent on the situation in which they occur, so that truth can no longer be communicated across situations, nor have any meaning independent of the situation in which it is constructed and communicated. The ultimate conclusion of this argument is that every man in a different situation must be taken to have a view of what is true that is equally valid to that of everyone else. Everyone, which certainly includes every scientist, "does his own thing," though this does necessarily include doing it with other people and, therefore, having to arrive at some situational agreement. Although this extreme situationalism may be tempting to some, it is not so grave a danger to all sociological thought as it might at first appear. For, in spite of its important elements of truth, it is self-destructive in the same way as the paradox in the ancient proposition that "All men are liars": Since extreme situationalism is itself subject to its own denial of situational independence, there is no reason for anyone to accept it unless he feels it fits his own practical needs in the situation at hand. Because it seems likely (at least to me in my present situation) that few of us will find it desirable, by using this pragmatic principle of truth,[8] to accept any kind of epistemological war of all against all, extreme situationalism is not really much of a threat.

Extreme situationalism is just as false as the positivists' extreme particularism. Each extreme fails to include the

8. See my essay on "The Relevance of Sociology," in Jack D. Douglas, ed., *The Relevance of Sociology*, New York: Appleton-Century-Crofts, 1970.

partial truth of its opposite, so each necessarily remains a partial truth. Hence, the meanings of any communication are determined both by the context in which the communication takes place and by the independent or *trans-situational meanings* of the elements of the communication. There is a "circular" relation between the meanings of the particulars and the contextual whole of any human communication, which has led some philosophers and literary critics to speak of a *circle of understanding* ("Zirkel im Verstehen"): One must understand the parts to understand the whole *and* one must understand the whole to understand the parts.

The truth of the principle is easily seen in the case of relatively simple verbal communications, though this is by no means its most important aspect. As is almost always the case when something is important in everyday life, common sense gives serious consideration to the contextual determination of meanings. There are many different *theoretical slogans* used in common sense discourse to deal with this truth: "It depends on what you *really* have in mind", "There are always exceptions." In America the importance of the situational context is enshrined in the distinction made between "theory and practice." For the most part though, common sense takes an analytical view of social meanings, and this is no doubt a reason why this approach was so uncritically accepted by social scientists. Take the *dictionary approach* to verbal communications, which is an obvious example of the building-block approach to social meanings. Dictionary "cataloguing" of meanings presumes that there are "appropriate" meanings that can be given to any word. Although it is recognized that the user will have to rely on the situation in which he finds or uses the word to know which meaning is intended, it is still presumed that words have discrete meanings that can be abstracted from their contexts.

All of us are aware of situations in which the dictionary approach fails. Most obvious is the case where a given word has two or more meanings. For example, a statement such as "Look how big his ear is" is indeterminant until we specify the context that will allow us to know whether the "ear" referred to is the "ear" on his head or something like an "ear of corn." Either meaning is equally plausible until we specify the context.

At the same time, this case shows us that the particulars do have meanings that are partially independent of the context in which they are communicated. After all, an "ear" may mean either a "human ear" or an "ear of corn", yet the number of possibilities is limited and known to anyone who has a normal understanding of the language. Any such person could tell us that there are these different possibilities, even though we have not told him anything else about the context in which it is used. This is what the dictionary relies on and this is why any worthwhile dictionary gives the major situational meanings of any word or phrase.

Clearly, then, the particulars do have meanings independent of the situations in which they occur, so that members of society who know the language can give the range of possible meanings with relative agreement; at the same time, the determinant meanings cannot be specified without identifying the situation or context in which these particulars have been used. Both the particulars and the context must be known to make the meanings determinant: each contributes independently to give the determinant meaning.

There are all degrees of contextual dependence and independence of the meanings of linguistic statements. It is easy to see that the social meanings of a statement such as "John Phillips Tobias Smith of Akron, Ohio, has no natural hair on his head" is largely independent of the context in which the statement might be made; any member of our society who knows the language could pretty well agree with others on what this means and could independently go about pointing at the same things others would point at as being the referents of this statement. On the other hand, there are many statements for which there is almost no clear meaning for the members of our society—that is, for which the meanings are extremely problematic—when they are not able to know the detailed context in which the statement is made. This would be true of such statements as "Don't do anything wrong" or "Be good."

Many linguistic philosophers in the twentieth century, such as Moore, Stevenson, Hare, and Ziff have written complex analyses of the many meanings of "good", yet they have not been able to reach agreement on what these common dimensions of meaning are or whether they exist. Yet, ordinary people in everyday practical affairs appear to use the term and its vast number of related terms ("excellent," "great," "virtuous," "pure," "splendid," "bad," "wicked," "evil," "terrible," "naughty," and so on) without the total breakdown in communication one would expect from observing the clashes of philosophers over the "question of good and evil." In everyday situations there is much *calling for clarification* (i.e., asking for more particulars on the situation of the usage), such as "What do you mean by 'doing good' here?" And there is often conflict over whether some specific object or act should be considered "good." But there is no wild confusion. People use this vast array of terms in some fashion that allows them to agree on the meanings of what they are saying. How? They are obviously "seeing" the "appropriate" meaning in the context—or situation—of the use: the contextual usage makes the meanings determinant for the participants in the everyday situation. The context makes it possible for the participants to reach some workable agreement between the *intended meaning* (the meaning given off by the person saying the statement) and the *realized meaning* (the meaning received or inferred by the person hearing the statement).

Without the context, even simple conversations about ob-

servable phenomena become indeterminant for the participants. Any member of the society hearing such a conversation would either supply his own context, and, thereby, be
mistaken in his interpretation of the meaning intended, or,
more likely, he would recognize that he did not "understand"
what was being said.

To the members of society the context is so crucial and so
omnipresent that it becomes *taken-for-granted,* that is, assumed for all practical purposes without having to discuss
it.

> *The meanings of any communication are partially
> determined by aspects of the situation (including
> the rules of communication themselves) which
> are taken-for-granted by the members involved in
> the communication.*

From his analyses of discussions, Garfinkel has shown that
many of the crucial aspects of any discussion are taken-for-
granted by the participants, including the crucial matter of
their understandings of the communicative processes in our
society. Specifically, he has concluded that

(a) There were many matters that the partners understood they
were talking about that they did not mention. (b) Many matters
that the partners understood were understood on the basis not
only of what was actually said but what was left unspoken. (c)
Many matters were understood through a process of attending
to the temporal series of utterances as documentary evidences of
a developing conversation rather than as a string of terms. (d)
Matters that the two understood in common were understood
only in and through a course of understanding work that consisted of treating an actual linguistic event as "the document of,"
as "pointing to," as standing on behalf of an underlying pattern
of matters that the person, by his speaking, could be telling the
other about. The underlying pattern was not only derived from
a course of individual documentary evidences but the docu-

mentary evidences in their turn were interpreted on the basis of "what was known" and anticipatorily knowable about the underlying pattern. Each was used to elaborate the other. (e) In attending to the utterances as events-in-the-conversation each party made reference to the biography and prospects of the present interaction which each used and attributed to the other as a common scheme of interpretation and expression. (f) Each waited for something more to be said in order to hear what had previously been talked about, and each seemed willing to wait.[9]

These taken-for granted features of conversations are what the phenomenologists and Gestalt psychologists have called the *background* meanings of social interaction. They are unspoken, and frequently only sensed by the members of society, rather than known explicitly, so that they are sometimes very difficult for members to formulate explicitly. Certain important rules of the society, such as those concerning communication, are *background rules,* or *deep rules.* These rules are so much a part of everyday life that they do not normally have to be expressed; they become so taken-for-granted that they are almost impossible to verbalize.

Deep rules are largely noticeable only when they are violated. This is especially clear in the case of violations concerning the appropriate social contexts for actions. The members of society take it for granted in practice that situations are relevant in determining the actual or practical meanings of rules; but they take it for granted that the particulars are also relevant in determining the meanings of rules. *These assumptions of situational primacy and individual (or particular) primacy are used independently and in combination in constructing concrete meanings.*

Probably the most important taken-for-granted aspect of situations in general is the situational nature of social meanings: *people generally take it for granted that all social rules*

9. Harold Garfinkel, "Studies of the Routine Grounds of Everyday Life," *Social Problems,* 11 (Winter, 1964), pp. 225–250.

must be interpreted in the context of (1) other relevant rules, etc., (2) the flow of communications, and (3) the situation-at-hand. They treat this situational nature of meanings as being the normal and appropriate state of affairs. To do otherwise is to "act out of situation" and the consequences can range from a sense of insult to categorization of the offender as insane.

This *assumption of situationalness* is evident in the more specific *assumption of the primacy of the situation-at-hand,* which is the primary reality for those communicating at any given time—it is more "real" than any unseen, past or prospective situation, and is of value in itself to those involved in it. Situational primacy can be seen in the visual encounter, which is *the* basic encounter of human beings. Being unseen (being alone) and being seen (being *with* someone else) are the basic dichotomous states of our exisf-ence, as Sartre and many others have argued. Being seen and seeing others is the heart of the face-to-face situation, which almost all human beings value and fear for its own sake. Seeing is the heart of intimacy, and the heart of shame. The fact of being seen gives the sense of "reality" to things and that not being seen makes them "unreal" is evident in the physical distinction made between *front regions* and *back regions* of situations. The flimsiest physical barrier makes the back region an area where *dirty work* can go on without affecting our sensibilities, regardless of how well we know it is going on.

Situational primacy is further evident in the taken-for-granted rules concerning the *integrity of situations and persons* in situations. In any face-to-face situation, individuals are expected to work to maintain the integrity of others with whom he is involved. This means that he must take note of them, show proper deference or respect, and so on. To ignore them, turn his back on them, break off the encounter without first preparing the end and appropriately making his exit, and so on, is immoral, unexpected, and categorized as "rude," "discourteous," "gruff," "short." These many rules and the complex constructions of meanings that can be made with them have been analyzed in detail by Erving Goffman and his students, who have made these everyday situations, especially the consequences of the assumption of situational primacy, the basis for the dramaturgical school of sociological thought.[10]

More general operations of situational primacy have been dealt with in a number of important sociological studies, most notably in studies of "insanity" or "mental illness." As Thomas Scheff has argued,[11] an individual is most apt to be categorized as mentally ill when his behavior violates those social rules which are so deep that the members would rarely think of stating them, except, perhaps, in teaching a child or foreigner to be a "normal adult." But what makes these actions violations in the first place is that they are committed *out of situation,* which is, in fact, the term commonly used by psychiatrists to characterize the nature of these "violations." If the individual who can be presumed to "know" what the rules are has acted in such a way as to violate the integrity of the situation, that is, if he has acted as if it were not in itself a valued reality or, more likely, has said things that do not *make sense* in the situation-at-hand, then he has shown a lack of his "grasp of reality."

Another example of "acting out of situation," and one which involves a global insistence on doing precisely that, is "prophecy," as Weber called it, or "radicalism," as it is more commonly known today. Egon Bittner has concluded that the unifying characteristic of radicalism is its dedication

10. See, for example, Erving Gottman, *The Presentation of Self in Everyday Life,* Garden City: Doubleday, 1959.

11. Thomas Scheff, *Being Mentally Ill, op. cit.*

to the subjugation of all of everyday life to "a unified and internally consistent-interpretation of the meaning of the world." [12] The "radical" is trying to abolish all of the usual, taken-for-granted situationalness of social meanings and actions; he is trying to make all situations non-problematic, consistent, and logical. Since he is acting contrary to the nature of reality, he is doomed to failure.

But "radicalism" fails as well for other reasons. It fails in our society because its basic pre-condition—of achieving power sufficient to "bend" all situations to fit its principles—is never allowed to be met. The insistence on totality is usually expressed by "radicals" today as the "need to change the entire system"; the need for power to do this is almost always recognized by their insistence on the need to "repress the repressors," to "suppress suppressive tolerance." Most members of our society are *in practice,* that is, in most of the concrete situations of everyday life, completely opposed to any attempt to subjugate all of life to any one principle. Most especially, they are opposed to any attempt to subjugate the realm of everyday life that they call the realm of *practicality* (or *practical affairs*) to any such universal principles. Most people make a distinction between "theory and practice" or between the realms of "ideals" and "practice." Although in ritual situations they may allow and even praise the support of "ideals," such as "universal brotherhood" or "universal equality," they are opposed to attempts to apply such principles *in practice.* The attempt to do so, the denial of the primacy of the situation-at-hand in the practical realm, is denounced as "utopianism," "idealism," "radicalism," "fundamentalism," "impracticality," "foolishness," and so on. In recent years, for example, such attacks have been made innumerable times against the "radical protests" of "student radicals." In this way ideas categorized as "radical" are not

12. See Egon Bittner, "Radicalism and the Organization of Radical Movements," *op. cit.*

only attacked, but are socially defined as irrelevant for any practical purposes, though any "holy-roller" who wants to can "preach" all he wants and may well be given considerable expressive support on Sundays.

The insistence on maintaining the primacy of the situation-at-hand, is, then, reasonably universal in our society, yet it is counterbalanced in practice by the opposite insistence on the *primacy of personal factors.* An excellent example of this is found in the social constructions of meanings for suicidal actions. In any given case of suicidal action, those involved can choose to impute causality for the action to the nature of the situation, to the nature of the individual committing the actions, or to some combination of these. This is well-illustrated through a transcribed discussion I had with a young woman concerning her suicidal actions.

V. had attempted suicide at least two times in one year. Her last attempt had occurred about two weeks prior to this discussion. Upon discovery the morning following her consumption of numerous sleeping pills, she was rushed to a hospital, examined for signs of life while still in the ambulance, declared Dead-On-Arrival, and sent to the morgue. A morgue attendant noticed some faint signs of life and began to revive her. At the time of the discussion she had been released from the hospital, was very willing to discuss the event, and, while able to talk only in a high whisper because the tracheotomy performed to allow breathing had not yet been closed, she was extremely articulate. Because she was so obviously concerned with getting at the "truth," and because the external events of her story checked out with accounts given by friends and acquaintances, her account as a whole constitutes one of very few excellent personal documents concerning suicidal actions.

D. As far as you see it, what were you doing?
V. Well, the main thing that I was doing was just escaping. I've been depressed many, many times and usually can handle it.

I've learned *how* to handle it. I've learned that certain things will help me feel better and I know that what I had planned to do that night—my original plans—would help me feel better. But I didn't want to go through with that. I didn't want to feel better. I was tired—very, very tired. Because I knew that if I felt better that night, that the same pain would come again another time. And I'd have to go through it all over again. And so primarily I just said I'm finished fighting this thing. I just want out.

In this initial account of what she was doing, she is emphasizing the primacy of personal factors, that is, the way in which she, the acting and responsible subject, was choosing and controlling what she did. As she says below, she was doing it all very "rationally." But she also introduces the element of "depression," which she shortly comes to treat as an external, situational factor.

D. Did you—uh—you know—these—these depressions. Um—they just come at certain times? You are—you don't normally feel terribly depressed?

[Brief interruption while V. answered telephone.]

D. Uh, you know, you don't have a continual kind of depression.
V. No. In fact—my depressions were getting very few and far between. I think I was as surprised as anyone when I went that far down and all of a sudden it happened in a matter of hours.

Depression is now more clearly treated as outside of the self. It is something that the self *becomes conscious of,* something the self is "surprised" by, rather than something that is part of the conscious, choosing self.

D. Uh-huh.
V. I was fine Tuesday morning . . .
D. You mean you—you were surprised as anyone by your becoming so depressed? Uh-huh.
V. Yeah, by the intensity of it, I guess. Even though I felt it

before, I just had—had not experienced it in several months really.

D. Uh huh, um, did you feel that, uh, because of the depression you couldn't control yourself—or do you feel you (V. No.) were—were conscious of where you were, what you were doing?

V. Oh. I was very conscious and felt very much in control. I simply didn't have the willpower to do what I knew I could.

D. Uh, how do you mean—the willpower? to do what—what did you do . . . ?

V. Oh, when I get really depressed I see it as, as a thing of will power. I have to force myself to do the healthy thing instead of taking pills, like, like I did . . .

We can see here a reassertion of the personal factor—the self in control of what is happening. But, at the same time, there is a shift to consideration of "will power," which is seen as somehow both a part of the self and not a part of the self. It is something that is created by the self, in that the self can increase it by willing more of it, but it is also partly outside of the self, affected by external things such as depression, so that the self cannot just create however much of this will-power it wishes to create. It is both controllable and uncontrollable, whereas the essence of the self is controllability or willing—it *is* the controlling. This ambiguity in conception of the place of "willpower" seems to lie behind the ensuing uncertainty concerning how to treat it.

D. Uh huh.

V. And usually I manage to force myself to do the thing.

D. Uh huh. How do you force yourself, by the way, is it just a matter of sheer will power?

V. I—uh—it's partly that, but it's also—that, well, I'm not sure really. It depends on *how* deep that depression is and it reaches a point where death takes over from my will power.

D. Uh huh.

v. But I still don't feel that I was out of control, really. I almost turned around and came home. You know I . . . I certainly was very rational.

We now see that the external factor of "depression" can overcome the "willing" self. The situational factor is seen to assume primacy in explaining what happened. But, at the same time, she was still in some way "in control," still "rational." At this stage we get the combination of external and internal, of situational and personal factors. Yet this is necessarily a problematic combination, so that one can swing from one to the other.

d. Um hum, what exactly happened by the way? Uh, I mean, what did you do, this somehow . . .

v. Well. I was expected at some friends' house. I called and told them I'd be a little late, that I was having car trouble or something.

d. Were you having car trouble or . . . ?

v. No.

d. This was—to—to put them off?

v. Just to put them off a little bit. I—took all the sleeping pills I had, which was about 30, plus another bunch of dramamine and stuff like that—that I had around the house. Took a thermos bottle of water and got in the car and drove, and I just drove and drove and drove until I found a very lonely looking country road. I just kept taking smaller and smaller country roads. Sort of drove around until it was good and dark. Then I sat in the car for a long time, thinking that I kind of wanted to go back home. And then I was really late for where I was going and I was embarrassed for that moment as much as anything. I didn't . . . the closer not to taking the pills the less I felt like doing it, in a way. Because I had my help, which you know was right there in my lap. I didn't feel quite so desperate but somehow I went ahead and did it anyway. I was still tired and still afraid of coming back, and have it start all over again—so I just took them all. But uh—the newspapers said they found a little bottle of pills with one pill left in it in the car you know—I'm not sure because I distinctly think I remember throwing it out the window and being very disturbed because it wasn't hidden in the bushes—I knew somebody would find it—and see the label on it, and so forth, which meant they might be able to save me. So, I don't know, there's a discrepancy there and maybe I'm not as really as sure as I thought and it gives me pause for it.

In this last part, the description of what she remembers from the situation in which she committed the suicidal action, we find the emphasis on the relations between the concrete, situational factors and other, trans-situational factors. Even such apparently "inconsequential" factors (inconsequential only from the standpoint of someone abstractly viewing her situation) as embarrassment at the thought of having to face people whose party she was to attend become of great importance in going ahead with the planned action. Yet, when she thinks that she no longer feels as desperate in that situation, she remembers that she will have to return to her everyday situation in which she does feel very desperate; and this becomes an important reason for going ahead with the action.

Throughout V's discussion we find statements about the relations between situations, especially about the ways in which the meanings of some given action in a given situation change or develop as she experiences new events and situations which she sees as relevant to the meanings of the earlier action and situation. For example, we shall see below that her ideas about her original intentions changed as other people gave her their ideas about her original intentions.

The relation between meanings, situations and actions are developmental.

These developmental relations are very complex, as we saw in our discussion of officials' inferrences of meanings in Chapter 4, and, although we cannot yet specify very clearly what most of them are, we should note a few of the most important ones. First, it is not always the case that symbolic meanings, which involve both linguistic categorizations of the situation-at-hand and conscious consideration of one's intentions in that situation, precede action. For example, there are situations in which the individual acts "out of anger," "blindly," "sense-lessly," "without a thought for the consequences." Such non-symbolically mediated actions can produce a sense of shock in the individual himself (such as, "My God! What have I done?") after he has time and composure enough to think about it.

More commonly, symbolically considered actions frequently change their meanings as we consider other meaningful factors. This can come about through our simply "reconsidering" the event or through our learning of other meaningful factors we did not previously know, but in terms of which we must now "weigh" our earlier constructions of meanings. In this event, changes in one part of the meanings will generally result in changes in other parts in line with the principle of the contextual determination of meanings. The nature and determinants of these complex relations will take a long time to clarify. One guide here is Kenneth Burke's argument in *The Rhetoric of Motives* that there exist *ratio relations* between the meanings of acts, actors, situations, agents, and events, such that a change in one means the others must be changed to produce the overall meaning.

Freedom and Constraint in Constructing Meanings

Man is free to construct his social world and constrained by that social world: Man is both the creator of society and created by society.

The preference of the social scientist for the simple over the complex and the uni-directional over the multi-directional has been apparent in our many criticisms throughout this chapter. Nowhere has this preference for the simple and uni-directional been more apparent than in the theories of the relations between the individual and society, especially the question of whether the individual causes society (or is society) or whether the society causes the individual. This question of causal priority is, of course, precisely the question of individual freedom versus social constraint, which are the common-sense terms in which the argument was pursued for the first hundred years or so of the existence of the social sciences (though the terms have now been displaced by more specialized ones, such as "social causality.")

One question that greatly concerned the early social scientists, especially the moral statisticians, was individual freedom. These analysts believed that science was possible only if there existed deterministic causal relations. If individuals were free, then there could not be deterministic causal relations existing in the realm of human affairs. They took the view of man as free to be that of common-sense and saw science as in complete opposition to it. Therefore, the first step that must be taken by anyone concerned with establishing a science of society was to prove that there were deterministic relations in human society, and that, consequently, there could not be the kind of individual freedom that men believed in.

As we saw in Chapter 3, these social scientists thought they had been successful when they showed that there exist stable rates of social behavior, including *moral phenomena,* which had previously been taken to be the prime realm of free will. Since there were stable rates of behavior for any given society for reasonably long periods of time, it was argued that there must be something external to individuals causing these, something other than free will. Argument raged throughout the nineteenth century, but an increasing number of those involved in social analysis professed themselves to be convinced by the evidence against free will.

The belief that man is not free became an implicit part of social science theory and research in the guise of *social determinism*. In the second half of the nineteenth century, social scientists had come to believe that society, the "social system," was the most important determinant of individual human actions. Morselli, for example, while believing in the multiple causality of human actions, held that the social factor was the most important one.[13] By the latter part of the nineteenth century, as seen in the work of Durkheim, society was not only held to be the most important cause of social action, but was, in fact, considered to be an independently existing phenomenon *causing* human actions. The issues, of course, remained very complex. Durkheim and almost all succeeding sociologists accepted that individual factors did enter into the causation of human action,[14] but belief in society as an independent level of existence and *the* cause of actions continued to grow. (Eventually sociologists created slogans for expressing this idea, such as "the social must be explained socially.") The social scientists had so moved from the earlier common-sense belief in man's free will to the opposite extreme of a belief in complete social determinism that there was no longer any significant discussion of the matter.[15]

13. See Henry Morselli, *Suicide*, New York: Appleton-Century-Crofts, 1867.

14. For a discussion of the difficult question of the ways in which Durkheim believed individual factors are involved in the causation of human action, see "Durkheim's Theory of the Relations Between the Individual and Society and Suicide," Appendix I of *The Social Meanings of Suicide, op. cit.*, pp. 341–349.

15. David Matza has previously argued (in *Delinquency and Drift, op. cit.*) that social scientists no longer assume the extreme form of social determinism that they once did. I believe, however, he has simply failed

The evidence never justified such a conclusion. In the first place, as we have seen in Chapters 3 and 4, the official information used by the nineteenth century social scientists to prove social determinism could certainly not be used to prove anything of the sort, since the information itself was so highly biased. Second, even the most thorough-going and valid form of statistical analysis of social data could not possibly show that human actions are unfree or "caused" by the nature of society. This is true for several reasons:

1) No statistical study can hope to explain more than a small part of the variation in data. Given the complexity of human behavior, all statistical explanations are only very partial.

2) One justification given for the use of a statistical approach to human phenomena is that the phenomena are so complex that one cannot hope to explain all of them, or, perhaps, *any* of them in complete detail. The argument is that one can only hope to explain basic patterns of behavior, such as a social rate of suicide, rather than individual choices of action. As was seen so clearly by Quetelet in the early nineteenth century, the point is to eliminate those factors which are predominantly individually determined, to get at the *commonality* in the actions of individuals in a given society. The statistical approach, therefore, presupposes that one is eliminating the kind of phenomena in which the freedom of human action will be most apparent.

3) Even if one were able to construct very determinant theories that could adequately predict patterns of social behavior (which, of course, has not been done

to see that the assumption of social determinism has become so complete that it is taken for granted. It is this that explains their no longer considering it in their works rather than their having lost faith in it.

by the social determinists) there would not be reason to believe that human behavior is totally determined. The only conclusion in that case is that for some reason human individuals are acting in the same way. We could not be able to show that they are not freely choosing to act in such a patterned way.

Just as the social scientists were unjustified in concluding from their evidence that human beings are not free, so were those who asserted the freedom of human action equally unjustified in their conclusion. They were similarly guilty of making an assertion that is far too simple to explain what can be observed about human beings.

Much of the disagreement regarding the issue of individual freedom and social determinism has resulted from a confusion over the meanings of "freedom." Freedom is one of those terms in the Western societies that are essentially problematic; that is, the term has many different meanings, even in the abstract. This is apparent in the works of philosophers, scholars, and other writers. There are fundamental arguments over the meaning of freedom, so much so that even the scholars are forced to make use of terms such as "freedom from" and "freedom to" as distinctions between the basically different "types" of freedom. This centuries-old confusion has been the source of many arguments in the Western world, resulting in a vast metaphysical and philosophical polemic.

The proponents of free will theory and of human freedom have certainly never believed that the human beings they observed were in any way *completely* free, unconstrained or unpredictable. On the contrary, metaphysicians themselves have been aware of the patterning that exists in human behavior. For example, in *Enchirdion* Saint Augustine made a basic distinction between *libertas* and *libertad* in order to distinguish between the "absolute freedom" of man before the fall and the kind of "relative free choice" that man had after the fall. This relatively free choice after the fall was constrained by the evil passions of human beings resulting from that notable event. Philosophers, historians, and most other men of the Western world have long been aware of the existence of social customs, or the "cake of customs" as Bagehot called it. They have noted since Herodotus that there are patterned differences in human beliefs and actions between different societies; they have certainly recognized that there are some similarities in basic needs and feelings. It is equally apparent that there is some general social order among most groups of human beings and in the everyday lives of most people. It is perfectly apparent that the world is not a random event, so that anyone who ever thought that a theory of freedom or free will meant that the world would be disordered, or completely random, was simply missing the point.

The issue concerning human freedom is twofold. First, there is the question of whether human beings choose what they do *because* something previously existing and *external* to them has made them what they are in such a way that they will choose to respond to the order they find in the world in the way in which they do. Second, there is the issue of whether human beings are able to alter the nature of their world (and possibly themselves) in order to fulfill their own desires and beliefs, regardless of where those desires and beliefs originally came from.

Clearly no one has been able to demonstrate that human actions are entirely or even predominantly the result of what has been put into them. No one has yet been able to predict in detail what human beings will do in specific situations. In its extreme form, this belief must remain nothing more than an article of faith until such demonstrations through prediction are provided. It is also clear, however, that the number of things that go into any individual human being and into any specific situation facing him are so exceedingly complex that it would be almost impossible to expect to get highly specific predictability. It is likely that human consciousness is a special factor in any given human being which acts to some degree independently of external phenomena to bring order and to structure decisions from the mass of complex factors interacting within himself and between him and the situation he faces. To the degree both that he does not control the inputs from the situation, and to which he himself has been socialized to have certain feelings and beliefs, without being able to change those feelings and beliefs, he is not free. But to the degree that he acts as an independent factor in ordering those internal and external phenomena, he is free. To this degree one would expect to find some irreducible element of unpredictability in human events. But it is the second issue, that of whether individuals *can* alter situations, that is the most relevant for our purposes.

As I argued in Chapter 2, there are some very simple societies in which individuals normally take the social rules, social beliefs, and so on, to be absolute. There are also true believers or fundamentalists in our own society, though very few, who are, apparently, innocent of any doubts concerning their own social rules and beliefs. In our pluralistic society individuals have been subject to all kinds of conflicts and changes in social rules and beliefs, so it is very difficult for them not to come to see social rules and beliefs as at least partially relativistic, and not be "cynical," "skeptical," "hypocritical," or "sophisticated." This is especially true of individuals living in a highly technological society as our own, in which so many share a generalized rational orientation toward things. It is even more difficult for those living in a rapidly changing and democratic society, in which they are frequently remaking the rules, to view the rules and beliefs as absolute. Anyone involved in remaking rules and introducing new rules is aware that the rules are not a necessary part of the structure of reality. If he can make the rules, then anyone else could do so too. Living in an age of mass education and mass communication, he knows that others have arrived at very different rules and beliefs.

In a complex and rapidly changing society, then, we would have to expect on *prima facie* grounds that individuals would not take an absolutist view of social rules and social beliefs. But we must not conclude that this relativistic attitude is universal in our society or that, even if we were to grant that it is a dominant attitude, that there would be no social constraint on the individual's construction of social rules and beliefs.

We have already argued that the complex nature of the physical and social world, combined with the nature of man and the nature of social meanings themselves, makes it clear that the individual *must* rely upon his own constructions of unique interpretations to fit the inevitably unique situations that he encounters in everyday life. In this sense, then, man is necessarily free. But we have not yet investigated the question of whether he is free in the sense of being able to affect the inputs into his constructions: Do individuals have any control over what goes into their own constructions or are these inputs (i.e., beliefs, rules, immediate situations, biographical details, social position, and so on) quite beyond his control, provided for him, whether he realizes it or not, by the society in which he lives? These are the crucial *conditions* under which choices are made and these determine how significant and effective any freedom in decision-making can be.

All men are probably free to some degree to affect the conditions of their choices and, thence, their acts and the consequences of their acts. All men with reasonably normal physical capacities can rearrange the immediate physical situation as they find it, and in this sense they are free (unless, as rarely happens, there is someone acting to constrain their immediate physical actions). But there is far more question concerning the ability of men to affect the other conditions of their choices and actions. There are two issues in this problem: (1) are individuals free to determine the inputs of symbolic resources into their constructions of the meanings of situations at hand? and (2) are individuals free to determine the social nature of the situations for which they are constructing such meanings? In both cases I believe that the answer is clearly that men are both free and constrained, but that the degrees of each vary greatly across societies and for individuals within any one society. The most obvious aspect of freedom is the first, which is essentially the ability of individuals to control the meanings of things for themselves. We shall investigate this first and return in the next chapter to consider the second aspect, the control over the situations in which the constructions of meanings occur.

Unless we assume the programming of man by the gods or the fates, it is clear that man has created culture over the eons, that man is the *culture (shared symbol) creator*. Symbol creation and transmission is what distinguishes man from all other animals. Unless we are to deny all of the evidence of the transmission of culture and of cultural relativity, we must recognize as well that men are constrained by culture, that they are not free to construct just anything, that they are themselves creatures of culture. As Berger and Luckmann have put it so well, man and society are necessarily involved in a dialectical process, each one creating the other and each being created by the other, each one cause and effect of the other.[16]

The evidence of great individual freedom in our pluralistic society in constructing situational meanings is everywhere at hand. The great majority of individuals have available to

16. See Peter Berger and Thomas Luckmann, *Social Construction of Reality*, Garden City, New York: Doubleday, 1966, pp. 57–58.

them a wide variety of abstract meanings, which they can make use of in constructing the meanings they choose for the situation they face. For example, taking a traditional, Puritanical view of sex one might expect that a member of American society faced with a non-marital sexual possibility would apply the general rule "no sex outside of marriage," meaning that he would have to do all of his activity within such a constraining rule—and would no doubt find that he couldn't get much done with it. (This has, in fact, been the assumption of all too many of the early sociological works on "deviance".) But this is certainly not so today. Any reasonably sophisticated young American would come to such a situation well-equipped with a barrage of resources from which he would hope to construct a fine legitimization for whatever he intends to do: Freudian theory, Kinsey data, glorifications of love, hip lingo, Eastern glorifications of communication with the inner being—and birth control manuals. The fact that he might, depending on his social group and his particular date, have to make use of such rhetorical devices would indicate that the old rule may still have some constraining effect; but the acceptance of this would not deny that the other meanings have force as well (nor would it deny that the old rule has no effect until an individual makes use of it to construct the meanings for the situation-at-hand).

On the whole, individuals in our society today have great freedom in constructing legitimate and plausible meanings from the meaningful resources available to them. In addition, because most people have come to accept and value change, openness, and creativity for their own sake, even to the point in some of the arts of disowning all standards, it is sometimes possible for individuals to create or impart very new ideas and seek to build their lives around them. Artists are able—and encouraged by many—to develop "bizarre" art forms from the sounds of automobile engines, from wires, from tin-cans, and so on almost endlessly. Millions become involved in seeking their own forms of mysticism, nirvana, mystical transcendence, mind-freeing (and clothes-freeing) group relations ("T-group sensitivity training"), and so on. This insistence on the "totally new" and the "totally individual" has grown steadily in Western societies for at least a century and has become a generalized attack on all shared abstractions, on all "forms," as Simmel argued almost fifty years ago.[17]

However, even in a pluralistic society in which so many people come to see the rules and beliefs as relativistic and to recognize their problematic nature, this understanding is by no means consistent or universal. The same individuals who explicitly recognize that "there is no arguing about tastes" or that "there are always exceptions to any rule" may well forget all about this in other situations, both because such constructions of the general meanings of rules and beliefs are themselves situational, and because he may consciously use the presumption of the absolutism of rules and beliefs as a strategy for controlling others. The same man who feels no guilt about theft might well feel guilt about sexual matters because he has very different feelings about the rules governing each realm.

More important than the constraint exercised by individuals' situational views of rules as absolute is the constraint resulting from the shared abstract meanings. As we have already seen, the fact that individuals must construct concrete meanings for the situation-at-hand does not at all mean that "anything goes." On the contrary, the particulars have meanings themselves, which are simply (partially) indeterminate for the actors until they are provided concrete mean-

17. See George Simmel, "The Conflict in Modern Culture," in *George Simmel: The Conflict in Modern Culture and Other Essays*, tr. and ed., by K. Peter Etzkorn, New York: Teachers College Press, 1968, pp. 11–26.

ings. It is very possible through the constructions of situated meanings, and the cutting off (or compartmentalization) of the situation from other situations, to construct meanings that might well be seen as very much in conflict with the more abstract rules if they were to be compared; but this in no way denies the independent importance of the particular, which in this instance is the abstract meanings or rules.

It is, in fact, only because individuals do share particular abstract meanings that are partially independent of the situations-at-hand that they are able to communicate at all. If they came to situations without trans-situational shared meanings, then they would have to begin by developing some shared meanings for things before they could communicate.

The abstract meanings serve as the basic resources from which concrete meanings must be constructed for the situation-at-hand.

Although there is a great deal of freedom involved in the construction of such situated meanings, the abstract meanings that must be used as common resources by those who want to communicate in the situation-at-hand act as a definite constraint. Abstract rules and beliefs act as a constraint on concrete, situational constructions simply because they have meanings that are partially independent of the situational interpretations that might be provided them; but their primary constraining influence comes from the fact that situational constructions of meanings for the concrete situations become routinized for any group with reasonably stable patterns of interaction.

There are many interpretations of both the relevance and the relatively concrete meanings of the abstract rules and beliefs for the situations individuals *typically* face in everyday life. For example, in our society the shared abstract value on equality ("All men are created equal . . .") is associated with specific and different interpretations for the realms of "justice" and "economics." These interpretations are, in fact, normally expressed in slogans: "Equal justice before the law" and "Equality of opportunity." These slogans are then further associated with various more specific interpretations widely shared in the society (equal justice meaning that status will not be considered in weighing guilt). In line with our previous arguments it should be clear that the more specific we get, the more problematic the meanings will be. But these widely shared situational constructions constrain individual constructions of meanings for the situation-at-hand more than the shared abstract rules and beliefs.

It would be mistaken to conclude that individuals look at such *routinized meanings,* or *typifications,* as Schutz has called them,[18] primarily as constraints. This is true partially because, as should be apparent from our discussion, their constraining effect, while greater than that of abstract meaning, is still not very great. But it is equally true because most people do not look at their social lives primarily in terms of their constraining effects. It is taken-for-granted by most people that their lives are necessarily social and that social interaction itself is of fundamental value. *They can only fulfill their human selves through society.* In addition, because meaningful differences and problems are taken-for-granted by the vast majority of people, individuals come to assume that compromises are necessary in their everyday lives. Although the necessity of compromise constrains the individual, it also allows him to fulfill himself by acting *with* other human beings toward some common goals. But, whether cooperating with others or fighting with them, an individual's constructions of meanings are normally interdependent with the constructive work of others.

18. Certainly one of the best uses of Schutz's idea of "typifications" is the essay by David Sudnow, on "Normal Crimes," in *Social Problems,* 12(1965), pp. 225–276.

Social Interaction and Constructing the Meanings of Rules

> *The most important factor for situational con-*
> *structions of meanings is the actual and potential*
> *interactions with other individuals. That is, the*
> *constructions of situational meanings are primar-*
> *ily the result of social constructions, of meaning-*
> *ful interactions (actually in the situation, or*
> *potentially); but the individual's own construc-*
> *tions are also independent of this interaction and*
> *may be contrary to it.*

This principle of *interdependency in the constructions o[f]*
situational meanings is most commonly associated with th[e]
symbolic interactionist tradition of thought in sociology, a[s]
represented in the works of George Herbert Mead, Herbe[r]
Blumer, Howard Becker and the many other "Chicag[o]
School" sociologists. There is though an important differenc[e]
between the symbolic interactionist theory, as it is mos[t]
commonly presented, and this general principle.

It is apparent why meanings must at some point be th[e]
result of social interdependencies. Communication is funda[-]
mentally social: without social interaction there is no com[-]
munication and no need for communication. What is com[-]
municated is "meanings." The "meanings given off" (a[s]
Goffman has called them)[19] by individuals in social inte[r]
action may or may not be shared. For example, when i[n]
dividuals impute "dishonesty," or "nastiness" to someone els[e]
they are not normally sharing these meanings of the pers[on]
with the person to whom they impute them. But even "give[n]
off meanings" that are not shared have meanings, becau[se]
at some point in the histories of the individuals involv[ed]
there has been some reason to share such imputed meaning[s]

19. See Erving Goffman, *The Presentation of Self in Everyday Li[fe]*
op. cit.

We have, in fact, already seen that moral meanings involve the idea of social judgment, of judgment by someone of someone else.

The symbolic interactionists have almost always emphasized the social imputations of meanings, and assumed the acceptance of these social definitions by social actors in their research. This *asymmetric bias*, or the overemphasis on the way in which social meanings are "imposed" on any given social actor by those around him, comes close to the assumption of the functionalists that the meanings are universally shared and would be the same for anyone, so that one does not have to consider any construction process. The asymmetric bias can, for example, be seen in Becker's explanation of "becoming a marihuana user." [20] Becker argues that there are three crucial stages in the process. In the first stage the individual must learn how to smoke the marihuana so that it will have some effect on him. Since this method of smoking is different from the method used to smoke any ordinary cigarette, most individuals will not know how to do this without being taught by people who already know how. But learning how to do it is not enough. The individual who tries marihuana will only continue to use it if he goes on to the next two stages. Having learned how to do it, he must then identify the symptoms; he learns this from other users who already know how to "recognize" the effects. The individual must then define these effects as pleasurable and this definition is primarily the result of having users impute the meanings of "pleasure" to the effects for him. In this sequence there is little consideration of the possibility that the individual who is having the use of marihuana defined for him by users would act as an independent agent in the construction of the meanings of use for himself. This asymmetric bias in the treatment of imputed meanings is found

20. Howard Becker, *Outsiders, op. cit.*

also in Becker's analysis of jazz musicians and in his more general argument that "deviants" are defined by the members of society, usually the middle class part of society and their official representatives.[21] There is little consideration of the ways in which individuals might fight such definitions of themselves, reject them, reinterpret them, convince society that they are wrong, and so on.

This asymmetric bias is probably more the result of certain methodological factors than of any theoretical convictions on the part of the symbolic interactionists. For one thing, Becker and others have concentrated on studying *groups;* this concern has led them to concentrate even more in other works on what they call "perspectives," which are the shared social meanings that operate to focus group activities.[22] Perhaps without their realizing it, this has resulted in a concentration on *group routines,* or the routinized aspects of social meanings made use of by individuals to get through their everyday lives. They have not taken equal note of the ways in which routines themselves must be *made use of* in concrete situations by the members of the group to construct acceptable (shareable) meanings for the situation-at-hand. In addition, the use of the participant-observer method can very easily involve a "taking of sides," as Becker has more recently called it.[23] By taking the side of the group one is studying, one may look at their imputations of meanings very asymmetrically, rather than looking at the way in which the meanings must compete with and conflict with the meanings of the same things imputed by other groups or individuals.

But the general theory of the symbolic interactionists, especially that presented by Herbert Blumer and others, tends far more to see the constructions of meanings as coming

21. See, especially, *Ibid.,* pp. 1–18, and 121–164.
22. See for example, Howard Becker, Blanche Geer, and Everett C. Hughes, *Making the Grade,* New York: John Wiley, 1968.
23. See Howard Becker, "Whose Side Are We On?" *Social Problems,* 14(1967), pp. 239–248.

about through a *symmetric process,* one in which all the individuals involved work with and against each other to construct meanings for the situation. This is clear in a paper by Norman Denzin [24] in which he argues that the symbolic interactionists make a fundamental distinction between *routinized activities,* in which individuals already share meanings and can count on having their imputed meanings accepted by others, and *non-routinized activities,* in which the individuals involved must undertake far more *negotiation* with the others involved to reach any agreements in meanings for their activities.

However, the extensive research work done by the symbolic interactionists provides us with little evidence concerning the construction processes by which interacting individuals do reach agreements and disagreements about the meanings of things. The asymmetric bias involved in their methods has prevented this, so relevant evidence must be sought elsewhere. Fortunately, it is not hard to find such evidence in any careful transcription of communications or in descriptive studies of activities in our society. There is far too much "disagreement," "non-conformity," and "bull-headness" for it to be hard to find.

A fine example is, in fact, already at hand. In the last part of the material from the case of suicidal action we were considering in the last section we can see that V. had a disagreement with newspaper accounts of her actions. They defined the facts in one way and she in another, producing what she called a "discrepancy." It is clear, however, that she did move in the direction of the newspaper's account of the events. She has come to have "pause" over her own interpretation. A similar sequence of development is appar-

24. See Norman K. Denzin, "Symbolic Interactionism and Ethnomethodology: A Convergence of Perspective?" in Jack D. Douglas, ed., *Understanding Everyday Life,* Chicago: Aldine, 1970.

ent in that part of this transcription which picks up immediately where we left off in the last section.

D. Uh—your intention was clearly—uh—you know, you had definitely made up your mind to kill yourself actually?

V. I tried this once before and the analysis after the first time was that I hadn't really been that serious about it. And I'll tell you about it if you like, but . . . this one was quite different, and nobody had any question that I really meant business.

D. Uh huh. Why—uh—what do you mean the analysis was that you didn't really intend it the first time? I mean . . .

V. Well I talked it over, was over with my psychiatrist afterwards and also by the second psychiatrist and some psychiatric nurses, and none of them seemed to think that I really wanted to be dead at the end of it all.

D. What did you think though? Was your . . . ?

V. At the time I thought I did but afterwards I agreed that certainly a lot of the things that I had done weren't very conclusive.

D. You mean that the things you had done were not really (V. Yes . . . I . . . I) very effective (V. Yeah) in doing it, so you began to suspect that, uh, maybe you hadn't really intended it?

V. The first time I gave myself only 2 hours leeway—before people started looking, and I told them exactly where I'd be and I was right there.

D. Uh huh, Uh huh.

V. You know . . .

This section bears very directly on our discussions in Chapter 4 of the necessarily problematic nature of the meanings of "intention." V. first thought that she had definitely "intended" to kill herself, but others, especially her analyst and her nurses, disagreed. This disagreement made her question her own imputation of "intention" to herself, but, very importantly, it did not make her simply reject her own previous imputation of meaning to her own action. The fact that she came to question her own "intention" is of greater interest because it is probably unusual. Most of us are quite resistant to others' telling us what we intended or thought, since we alone directly experience our intentions and thoughts; but the effect of others' imputations of meanings to our actions is so important to us that, if we are generally prone to accept their ideas, and see them as friendly toward us, rather than acting against our best interest, then their imputations may lead us to doubt our own minds—while generally not convincing us that we were completely wrong. In the case of V. this reinterpreting effect was probably so great precisely because she was very prone to agree with the views of the psychiatrist and to trust him. Her former husband, for whom she still apparently had great respect and regard, had been a psychiatrist; her boyfriend was a psychiatrist; some of her old friends were psychiatrists; and she had a high regard for her own psychiatrist's views, while maintaining a clear distinction between his views and her own.

But this effect of others' imputations of meaning to her actions was not simply the result of her trusting their views. It was partly the result of her having to partially rely on other people for interpretations of reality, in the same way everyone does. All of us to some degree take it for granted that our perceptions of reality and our interpretations of our perceptions are subject in some situations to "distortions" resulting from "personal bias," "drunkenness," "ignorance," and so on. We all use others to "correct" such perceptions and interpretations: "Do you see something up there or am I seeing things?" "Did you hear what I heard?" "Are you thinking what I'm thinking?" "Don't you think I'm right?"

But her "change of mind" was also partly the result of the "evidence" others used to show her that they were "right" and she was "wrong" about her own intentions. They *objectified* intention: that is, they pointed out various kinds of externally perceivable phenomena—her movements following the ingestion of pills, etc.—which they interpreted as having certain "demonstrated" or "obvious" relations to "intention" or "non-intention" to die. Since she shared some of these routinized ideas about the relations between actions and intentions, she became doubtful about the meanings she had previously imputed to her actions and then apparently came more to agree with their imputations. But she did not completely agree. Her own imputation of meaning remained partially independent in spite of it all. She then gave support to her imputation of "intention to kill herself" the second time by referring to an external source, the newspaper.

D. Um. The second time, uh, this time they—uh—what did happen? Uh. Somebody found you—uh—undoubtedly—uh—you only know about this from the—uh—what people have told you as well, of course.

v. Oh, I've read the newspapers too.

D. They found you the next day or something wasn't it?

v. Yeah.

D. Uh huh. What was your impression of the newspaper accounts? Uh—What was your . . . how did you feel about them?

v. I felt that . . . well, I suppose if they have to be in the paper at all I felt they were not too bad about it—they didn't bring my kids into it, for example. They didn't list me as a university student, which left the university out. They didn't really bring any other people in my family and things of that sort that depends on how you feel about it. I feel, however, that it's nobody's business but mine and the people intimately concerned with me who found out through other media, certainly not through the public mass media, and then I'm very cynical about the whole thing—they just latched onto something rather morbid.

D. Yeah, how did . . .

V. And I'm very bitter.

D. They always do this. Um . . .

V. The last time when I tried this very few people knew what I'd done. Now the whole town knows what I've done, and there's no getting out of it.

D. Yeah. What is the, uh—we're talking about this, what has . . . uh—what's been your impression of how you felt about your neighbors or—how have your relations been with other people?

V. Well, they've been very nosy (laugh) very curious. Some of them I know have spread some stories around. But really this is something I don't have to conquer too much. I kind of notice it but it doesn't bother me much. I know I have much more important things to conquer than what they think of me.

Here we see V.'s reaction to the stigmatizing effect of the mass media. While seriously questioning the motive of the mass media in giving such extensive coverage to her case, which, as I have noted above, involved treatment of her as the "Woman Who Returned From The Dead," she does not here question their presentation of the facts of the case. She apparently believed some people, including some of her neighbors, interpreted the facts as presented in the mass media in such a way as to think very badly of her— perhaps to see her as "strange," or "insane," or "immoral." But certainly she has no intention of letting this affect her own ideas about herself. She sees such interpretations of her actions as simply something that one might "conquer," and, indeed, she says she is not even so "bothered" by what they have to say as to have to conquer it; she has more important things to do and what they say is largely treated as irrelevant.

Throughout this discussion by V. of her actions and thoughts we can see the interdependent relations between the imputations of meanings by others and the imputations of meanings by V. herself. At times she and others are in definite agreement from the beginning (as in her acceptance of the criteria of evidence being used implicitly by those who argued that she didn't "really intend" to kill herself the first time); at times she comes to largely, if not entirely, agree with others, whereas she had apparently disagreed to begin with (as in her eventual agreement that she probably didn't "really intend" to kill herself the first time); at times she is in definite disagreement with the views of others, maintains this view steadfastly, and tries to conquer any effect of their views on her own and to change their minds (as when she opposes their interpretations of the meanings of her suicidal actions for evaluating her self—her substantial self); and she herself in many places recognizes that there are many problems (e.g., doubts) in trying to get at the "real" meanings of her actions and that others have very different views about the meanings of her actions, all of which she must strive in different ways to manage effectively.

There is obvious support for the fundamental emphasis in symbolic interactionism on the effects that others' definitions of one's self and one's actions have on the individual. But there is equally obvious evidence contradicting the asymmetric assumption found in so much of the symbolic interactionist work. Moreover, there is definite reason to doubt the effect of others' views of the self on one's own views of one's self. We see that specific constructions of meanings are far more affected by others' imputations of meanings than are V.'s imputations of meanings to her self. Her conception of her self seems to remain pretty stable, though it might have been affected more by the views of others at an earlier age (which is generally what Mead and others seemed to have in mind when dealing with the question of the social formation of the self). We find that the individual is very active in trying to construct the meanings for herself and for others of her actions in the construction of her "self." The relations between meanings imputed by others and the meanings imputed by her are very interdependent. (This interdependency, and certainly the active part played by the individual in controlling the meanings imputed to her actions and her self by others is even more obvious when we consider the ways in which others are deeply affected by the suicidal actions which she has chosen in part precisely to affect the meanings of her self to them. I have previously discussed the ways in which suicidal individuals are doing this in *The Social Meanings of Suicide.*[25])

We can see that the nature of the meanings imputed by others makes it necessary for the individual to take a primary part in constructing the meanings of things for himself. Any individual who relied upon the input of messages from a world in which everyone finds the meanings of things so problematic to provide him with some stable, rational meanings and plans for actions would be in an impossible quandry. *If there is to be any order in his world, any reason, then he himself must construct it by his own efforts.* As Sartre has said, "Man is condemned to freedom." Only the illusion of absolutism, all too frequently abetted by an absolutist social science, hides this basic truth from us.

But man is also constrained by his need to live in society. It is this which leads him to cooperate most of the time in his interdependent constructions of meanings with others.

Negotiating the Meanings of Rules

> *In most situations in daily life individuals intentionally try to construct working agreements with the other individuals involved to manage the situation-at-hand.*

We are born into a world in which there is a considerable degree of order, regardless of how problematic the construc-

25. See especially *The Social Meanings of Suicide, op. cit.,* pp. 271–319.

tion of that order is; and most situations we enter in life involve some pre-established order or routinized meanings (typifications) given to the situation by those already involved. When we enter a work situation that is new for us but not for others, we know and take it for granted that there will be "ways of doing things around here" to which we will have to "catch on" before we can be accepted as a complete, competent member of the work group. We know that any "new man" will make mistakes until he learns; we know there is much he must "learn" if he is to do it "right."

Whenever we have constructed (or accepted previously constructed) routinized meanings for situations we face, we tend to continue using them in that situation until their use creates a problem. The problem may arise either because our purposes change or because the situation is believed to have changed. Hence, all routines are taken as tentative, to be used "until further notice." [26]

When we do encounter a "problem" in our everyday lives, we do not then throw out all of our routines. Rather, we make use of these previously established routines to construct a *practical solution* to it. Only if we are unable to do this will we seek to construct a very new interpretation by creating new meanings; and, failing this, we may then categorize the whole thing as "crazy," "impossible," and so on. Berger and Luckmann have illustrated this process well:

The others with whom I work are unproblematic to me as long as they perform their familiar, taken-for-granted routines—say, typing away at desks next to mine in my office. They become problematic if they interrupt these routines—say, huddling together in a corner and talking in whispers. As I inquire about the meaning of this unusual activity, there is a variety of possibilities that my common sense knowledge is capable of reintegrating into the unproblematic routines of everyday life: they may be

26. See Egon Bittner, "Radicalism and the Organization of Radical Movements," *op. cit.*

consulting on how to fix a broken typewriter, or one of them may have some urgent instructions from the boss, and so on. On the other hand, I may find that they are discussing a union directive to go on strike, something as yet outside my experience but still well within the range of problems with which my common sense knowledge can deal. It will deal with it, though, *as* a problem, rather than simply reintegrating it into the unproblematic sector of everyday life. If, however, I come to the conclusion that my colleagues have gone collectively mad, the problem that presents itself is of yet another kind. I am now faced with a problem that transcends the boundaries of the reality of everyday life and points to an altogether different reality. Indeed, my conclusion that my colleagues have gone mad implies *ipso facto* that they have gone off into a world that is no longer the common world of everyday life.[27]

Berger and Luckmann's analysis does not tell how the individuals would decide which other routinized meanings are applicable to the problematic situation. As we have argued before, it is not true that "anything goes," yet this is what their analysis might lead one to suspect. In fact, individuals apply only those routinized meanings that appear *relevant*. While it is not clear just how individuals do this, there seem to be two factors involved in constructing the new situational meaning from routinized meanings. First, the individuals proceed by a *process of analogizing*. The relevance of any routinized meanings is decided on the basis of their *similarity* in applications to those routinely applied in this situation. In the case of law, for example, this process is very clear in the *use of precedents*, as Vaughan and Sjoberg have shown in their analysis of the way in which Israeli judges constructed (new) legal interpretations to fit the unusual case of Adolph Eichmann.[28] Second, the general rules

27. See Peter Berger and Thomas Luckmann, *The Social Construction of Reality, op. cit.*, p. 24.
28. See T. Vaughan and Gideon Sjoberg, "The Social Construction of Legal Doctrine," in *Deviance and Respectability, op. cit.*

of "truth," "rationality," and "reality" are used in complex non-routinized ways to test the *plausibility* of the emergent meanings for the new situation.

The use of *rules of plausibility* involves the same problems as the use of any rules in constructing situational meanings for problematic situations. The most serious problem here is caused by the ostensible universal applicability, or absolutism, of rules. If a rule is relevant at all, then it must be used in the routinized fashion—applied to all to whom it is relevant in the same way. And yet this is precisely what is impossible in a problematic situation, in which the previously established routines have produced a problem for the participants.

The abstract assumption that the rules are absolute in this sense as opposed to the reality of the use of rules, that is, that the rules are *used* (selectively) by the actors to achieve their purposes at hand, can be seen in the case of contracts and police work. The case of contracts is of some particular interest in sociology because of its historical importance in the origins of sociological thought. Many social scientists in the nineteenth century, as well as in our own day, firmly believed that human behavior is basically "rational," and by "rational" they meant the kinds of thought one finds in the sciences. They applied this form of rationalism to morality and law and developed their theories of the *contractual nature of human society,* which are the direct antecedents of the many rationalistic exchange theories of our own day. They believed that moral rules either were of the nature of a contract between the members of society or, in the case of the extremely popular "ethical positivism," they believed that moral rules should be made in this way by "rationalizing" them through the use of scientific method. To prove their point they noted the growing practice of making and using legal contracts in business. After all, this was *the* form of the contract. Durkheim chose to attack this theory. He argued that any contract in fact relies on many unspoken and unwritten (taken-for-granted) rules and other meanings in society, both to be correctly understood and to have the intended effects. More recent studies by American students of law have shown that this is not only true but that the businessmen who make use of the contracts understand this, and make use of complex ideas about the nature and uses of contracts in their contractual and extra-contractual relations with each other.

Most situations in which contracts could be used, so that the legal rules applicable to contracts would become applicable to to these situations, are purposefully not covered by contracts. The businessmen *choose not to apply the rules of contracts* to their relations in these situations. There are numerous reasons, some of which have been identified by Stewart Macauley:

Why are relatively non-contractual practices so common? In most situations contract is not needed. Often its functions are served by other devices. Most problems are avoided without resort to detailed planning or legal sanctions because usually there is little room for honest misunderstandings or good faith differences of opinion about the nature and quality of a seller's performance. Although the parties fail to cover all foreseeable contingencies, they will exercise care to see that both understand the primary obligation to each side. Either products are standardized with an accepted description or specifications are written calling for production to certain tolerances or results. Those who write and read specifications are experienced professionals who will know the customs of their industry and those of the industries with which they deal. Consequently, these customs can fill gaps in the express agreements of the parties. Finally, most products can be tested to see if they are what was ordered; typically in manufacturing industry we are not dealing with questions of taste or judgment where people can differ in good faith.

When defaults occur they are not likely to be disastrous because of techniques of risk avoidance or risk spreading. One can deal with firms of good reputation or he may be able to get some form of security to guarantee performance. One can insure against many breaches of contract where the risks justify the costs. Sellers set up reserves for bad debts on their books and can sell some of their accounts receivable. Buyers can place orders with two or more suppliers of the same item so that a default by one will not stop the buyer's assembly lines.

Moreover, contract and contract law are often thought unnecessary because there are many effective non-legal sanctions. Two norms are widely accepted. (1) Commitments are to be honored in almost all situations; one does not welsh on a deal. (2) One ought to produce a good product and stand behind it. Then, too, business units are organized to perform commitments, and internal sanctions will induce performance. For example, sales personnel must face angry customers when there has been a late or defective performance. The salesmen do not enjoy this and will put pressure on the production personnel responsible for the default. If the production personnel default too often, they will be fired. At all levels of the two business units personal relationships across the boundaries of the organizations exert pressures for conformity to expectations. Salesmen often know purchasing agents well . . .[29]

We can see, then, that there are many reasons for choosing not to use the legal rules of contracts to govern one's relations, including the very important "rational" understanding of the contextual (contingent) nature of future decision-making and action. That is, it is rationally expected that one cannot correctly expect all that will happen, so that one must remain "flexible" (which is undoubtedly one of the favorite words of businessmen in America); one must expect that the situation at hand will change, that there will be

29. See Stewart Macaulay, "Non-Contractual Relations in Business," *American Sociological Review*, 28 (February, 1963), pp. 55–67.

"further notice" in one's relations (sometimes called "acts of God" for extreme contingencies), even though one obviously cannot predict and, thence, plan what that further notice will be. (This is the kind of thing astronauts have in mind when they say they have confidence in getting back from the moon because there are no "known uncertainties," which means about the same as "known contingencies").

But it is more important to our argument to note that, even when business relations are covered by contracts, and even when the businessmen believe that the contract has been violated to their injury, they normally do not bring legal suit against the offender. This raises the whole question of why they choose to make use of contracts at all and, once made, why they do sometimes choose to bring suit to attempt to enforce the legal terms. Again, Macaulay argues that there are many complex considerations involved, including their use as communication devices within a large corporation.[30] In general, businessmen make use of contract rules and choose not to make use of them on the basis of the usefulness of the legal rules of contract to themselves in the situations they face. This is made even more apparent by Macaulay's finding that different men in different organizational situations within the same organization systematically make different choices regarding the use and enforcement of contractual rules.[31]

Lemert has marshalled an impressive variety of evidence to show that administrative and judicial bodies in our society have come increasingly to use rules very selectively and that jurists, such as Pound, have come to recognize the general significance of this for the nature of legal rules:

Even when the scene changes from administrative agencies to traditional courts, the nonsubstantive nature of legal norms remains clear. The vicissitudes in the interpretation of our anti-

30. *Ibid.*
31. *Ibid.*

trust laws are a record of shifting value dominance, in which court judgments have been taken, or frequently modified, by the perception of intolerable costs which literal enforcement of the laws would impose on socially important or strategic industries. Furthermore, it has had to be recognized that literal application of the laws may have effects opposite to those intended by regulators, so that increasingly, policy or values guide court decisions rather than deviation per se. Unmistakable signs that this is true are seen in a recent anti-trust decision.

"While it must be admitted that not all of these acts are prohibited, nevertheless we must view them in the broad panorama of other acts and their associations with each other to note, not only the effect but to pierce the veil of intent . . . it is clear that the . . . result of the conspiracy was to restrict competitors, which is illegal."

It is significant not only that courts are empirically moving toward an ends orientation, but that students of jurisprudence have consciously recognized this development, which places formalistic law in a broader setting of social control. Thus Pound speaks of the important, new directions of juristic thought:

"One is the insistence on function rather than on content; the tendency to ask how do precepts work, to ask whether they can be made to bring about just results rather than whether their abstract content is abstractly just. The moment we ask such questions, we are driven to inquire as to the end of law. For function means function toward some end. Thus for a generation philosophical discussion of the legal order has taken a continually larger place in jurisprudence." [32]

Police activities are subject to precisely the same kinds of highly selective situational uses of legal rules to achieve the purposes at hand, in spite of the moralistic rhetoric about the "moral foundations of society" that we often hear from the

---

32. See Edwin M. Lemert, "Social Structures, Social Control, and Deviation," in Edwin M. Lemert, *Human Deviance, Social Problems, and Social Control, op. cit.,* pp. 3–30.

official representatives of the police departments. The lowliest police officer knows how intentionally selective he must be in enforcing laws.[33]

It is of fundamental importance, however, to see that this situational choice to invoke and enforce rules, or not to invoke and enforce rules, is not merely the result of the changes in our society producing more complex and problematic situations that must be effectively dealt with by officials and all men involved in practical activities. It is certainly true that this increasing change and complexity is producing an increase in the problematic nature of social meanings and their uses, including the meanings and uses of rules, in our society. This is exactly what we would expect in the light of our previous discussions of the relations between social change and complexity and the problems of social meaning. But it is of fundamental importance to see that this decrease in the absolutist view of rules and in the absolutist applications of rules is only a matter of degree. *The selective use of rules has always been necessary because social situations have always been so complex that the members of society have experienced important problems in relating the rules to the situation; and there has always been some recognition by some members of society, especially those entrusted with interpreting and enforcing rules, that situational choices to invoke and enforce, or not to invoke and enforce, and how to do these things must be made.* This is the very nature of rules and of all social meanings. (It is very important to keep in mind that the general failure to recognize this as a fact of life has been due both to the relatively simple nature of rural life in Western societies for centuries and to the use of the *idea of absolutism as a rhetorical device,* especially by officials seeking to enforce their own morality upon the rest of the society.

33. See Egon Bittner, "The Police on Skid Row," *op. cit.*

If the enforcer can convince others that the rules are absolute, that neither he nor the victim of enforcement "has any choice" in the matter, then he has a powerful weapon in the conflict. The source of this power will be discussed in more detail in the next chapter.)

But, if rules are necessarily invoked, interpreted, and enforced selectively and flexibly for the situation-at-hand, then what are the determinants of this contingent choice? Because the choice is contingent on the situation-at-hand, and because the situation that will be at hand when the choice is made is partially unpredictable, *it is impossible to say exactly what the determinants of these uses of rules (and other meanings) are and what the resulting choice will be.* This, as we have seen, is the basic way in which man is condemned to freedom, a freedom that only the total fanatic can deny in practice—and only then until our Don Quixote gets killed by one of his windmills. For us to pretend to make realistic choices totally predictable would be to commit the absurdity of denying that necessary freedom; we would commit the basic mistake of the rat-psychologist: believing that man is like a bred and trained rat living in a simple and static maze. (In fact, of course, even these idealized rats are not that predictable, much to the continuing chagrin of the psychologists.) However, this is not to say that we cannot specify many of the factors that go into such considerations and, thence, decrease the unpredictability.

> *The members of our society make use of rules to
> adequately achieve their purposes at hand.*

This vague generalization covers many different but standardized ways in which rules are used, some of which we have just dealt with in our analyses of contracts and police work. Most importantly, this generalization is not like the rationalistic generalizations often made about human decisions. On the surface it might seem that we are saying that human beings seek to optimize their gains in any given situation, in which the use or non-use of a rule would be determined entirely by the "cost" or "gain" "rationally expected" from the use or non-use. But this is contrary to our theory thus far. The wording is intended to communicate a very different idea.

In the first place, the rule itself is sometimes part of the purpose of the individual in the situation. That is, living by the rule, or imposing it on others, may be important in itself, especially if the individual has an absolutist view of it. (At the extreme apparently not rare in centuries past, the individual may fear for his immortal soul if he thinks of violating God's rule.) In such cases, the individual must weigh the invocation and enforcement of the rule against other factors; yet it seems likely that in most situations the use of rules is done in a very mixed way: there is some consideration of the long-run effects of invoking the rule, of how important the rule and its observance are in themselves, or some immediate response without such a careful weighing of factors. In fact, in most situations there is little consciousness of this weighing of "practical" considerations against the importance of invoking and enforcing the rule, since the actors have probably already developed some *situational routines that involve such compromise solutions to problems they normally face.* Given such routines, most of the compromises and situational constructions of meanings for the various rules will be taken-for-granted.

Both these routines and the more immediate constructions of meanings that the participants must make to meet the situation-at-hand will be evaluated by the participants in terms of their "adequacy": Do they get this particular job done? Do they meet the purposes immediately at hand? For almost all practical activities, except, perhaps, the activities of judges and high-level administrators who must be concerned with the long-run or precedent effects of any given situational choice, the determining criteria in the use of rules seem to be that of achieving the purposes at hand. A very good example is given by Bittner in his discussion of the reasons police give for not invoking rules in a skid-row area:

A man in a relatively mild state of intoxication (by skid-row standards) approached a patrolman to tell him that he had a room in a hotel, to which the officer responded by urging him to go to bed instead of getting drunk. As the man walked off, the officer related the following thoughts: Here is a completely lost soul. Though he probably is no more than thirty-five years old, he looks to be in his fifties. He never works and he hardly ever has a place to stay. He has been on the street for several years and is known as "Dakota." During the past few days, "Dakota" has been seen in the company of "Big Jim." The latter is an invalid living on some sort of pension with which he pays for a room in the hotel to which "Dakota" referred and for four weekly meal tickets in one of the restaurants on the street. Whatever is left he spends on wine and beer. Occasionally, "Big Jim" goes on drinking sprees in the company of someone like "Dakota." Leaving aside the consideration that there is probably a homosexual background to the association, and that it is not right that "Big Jim" should have to support the drinking habit of someone else, there is the more important risk that if "Dakota" moves in with "Big Jim" he will very likely walk off with whatever the latter keeps in his room. "Big Jim" would never dream of reporting the theft; he would just beat the hell out of "Dakota" after he sobered up. When asked what could be done to prevent the theft and the subsequent recriminations, the patrolman proposed that in this particular case he would throw "Big Jim" into jail if he found him tonight and then tell the hotel clerk to throw "Dakota" out of the room. When asked why he did not arrest "Dakota" who was, after all, drunk enough to warrant an arrest, the officer explained that this would not solve anything. While "Dakota" was in jail "Big Jim" would continue drinking and would either strike up another liaison or embrace his old buddy after he had been released. The only thing to do was to get "Big Jim" to sober up, and the only sure way of doing this was to arrest him.

As it turned out, "Big Jim" was not located that evening. But had he been located and arrested on a drunk charge, the fact that he was intoxicated would not have been the real reason for proceeding against him, but merely the pretext. The point of the example is not that it illustrates the tendency of skid-row patrolmen to arrest persons who would not be arrested under conditions of full respect for their legal rights. To be sure, this too happens. In the majority of minor arrest cases, however, the criteria the law specifies are met. But it is the rare exception that the law is invoked merely because the specifications of the law are met. That is, compliance with the law is merely the outward appearance of an intervention that is actually based on altogether different considerations. Thus, it could be said that patrolmen do not really enforce the law, even when they do invoke it, but merely use it as a resource to solve certain pressing practical problems in keeping the peace. This observation goes beyond the conclusion that many of the lesser norms of the criminal law are treated as defeasible in police work. It is patently not the case that skid-row patrolmen apply the legal norms without recognizing many exceptions to their applicability. Instead, the observation leads to the conclusion that in keeping the peace on skid-row, patrolmen encounter certain matters they attend to by means of coercive action, e. g., arrests. In doing this, they invoke legal norms that are available, and with some regard for substantive appropriateness. Hence, the problem patrolmen confront is not which drunks, beggars, or disturbers of the peace should be arrested and which can be let go as exceptions to the rule. Rather, the problem is whether, when someone "needs" to be arrested, he should be charged with drunkenness, begging, or disturbing the peace. Speculating further, one is almost compelled to infer that virtually any set of norms could be used in this manner, provided that they sanction relatively common forms of behavior.[34]

34. *Ibid.*

The use of the rules to achieve the purposes-at-hand must be done in interaction with the others involved in the situation. Some of an individual's constructions of meanings can be done secretly, even to the point of saying nothing about them. But rules are different. As we saw in Chapter 3, *rules are for social use; without at least potential communication or social use, rules are useless, irrelevant.* This essentially social nature of rules has important consequences for anyone using them to achieve his purposes in any situation. Because few situations in our society involve anyone's having the power that would be needed to invoke and enforce his own rules arbitrarily, and because there are so many potential conflicts over rules in our society, most situational constructions of the meanings of rules involve taken-for-granted *negotiation.* If the members of an egalitarian, complex, and pluralistic society are to work together in situations outside of the groups in which there is a high degree of agreement on the situational meanings of rules, then they will have to negotiate the situational uses of rules. *They will have to reach some agreement on what constitutes an adequate use of rules for the purposes at hand.*

In reaching such agreements certain strategies will prove most effective and will, consequently, tend to become routinized for use across different kinds of situations. Some strategies of compromise involving the use of rules are completely standardized in our society. "Copping a plea," or pleading guilty to a criminal charge for a lesser sentence (a "consideration"), is one example. About 80 percent of all sentences are the result of such compromises between prosecuting attorneys and defending attorneys.[35] They "get the job done" in an acceptable manner for both sides.

Many other strategies remain problematic, though still reasonably clear to those involved. One is the "piece-meal

35. Probably the best study of "bargain justice" is that by A. Blumberg, *Criminal Justice,* Chicago: Quadrangle Books, 1967.

strategy," or what social planners have called a *strategy of incrementalism*. It begins with the fact that individuals are normally willing to compromise. Understanding this, individuals can try to take advantage of it by approaching situations *sequentially*. They may make their demands for the present situation with the idea of compromising, but also with the idea of continuing to escalate the demands to get further compromises in future situations, until they can get their way by completely transforming the situational meanings. This kind of activity is found in the work of *moral provocateurs* who try to change public enforcement of rules. Individuals involved in selling nudity to the public, for example, seem to make a sequential use of the *Playboy effect* to wear down the rules against public nudity: they increase the amount of nudity relative to the "socially redeeming qualities" of their product in stages, to let the public (and the district attorneys) get used to each new stage before proceeding to the next, meanwhile always hoping they will not cross the "line" that precipitates arrest.

Another device for reaching agreements acceptable to most members of the society is based on the distinction between *public situations* and *private situations*.

Using Rules in Public and Private Situations

> *Individuals in our society distinguish between public and private situations and take it for granted that rules will not be invoked or enforced across the boundaries of private situations unless what happens in these situations is believed to affect the public realm adversely.*

We might call this a *rule of relevance:* it specifies what situations are subject to the invocation and enforcement of rules by those not normally involved. In public situations "outsiders" are legitimate enforcers, while in private ones they are not. This is an ancient distinction in Western societies, being intimately related to the pluralistic nature of these societies. Its meanings and feudal origins are obvious in such slogans as "A man's home is his castle." The small group—family, commune of farmers, fief, city—was originally a society unto itself in every way and, at least at the level of the fief in the Middle Ages, was a state in itself. Each of these social units has maintained its autonomy over the centuries. Their independence has become a basic assumption of law and is supported by the government structures which have partially superseded them. This independence is, in fact, an important part of what is meant by *individual freedom from the state* in our society. Invasions of the privacy of these units by the state is seen as a violation of fundamental rights, except in those cases in which the activities going on in private situations are believed to be detrimental to the common interest of the other independent units in the society. Protection from invasion of privacy is guaranteed by the Bill of Rights, and the distinctions between private and public situations runs throughout our laws. Stinchcombe has analyzed the legal rationale for the distinction and shown how it profoundly affects the nature of police work in our society:

Most of our daily life is lived in a number of small, bounded social systems, such as families, schools, factories, clubs, etc., that have their own norms, goals, and facilities. The maintenance of the boundaries of these systems is necessary to their free and autonomous development. If agents of the state or strange private citizens could enter these systems arbitrarily and interfere with interaction within them, they cannot develop freely.

The central practical boundaries are such mundane things as walls, doors, window shades, and locks. But in modern society few of these are made to withstand a concerted effort by a group of men to breach them (in contrast to feudal societies, for example). Yet these fragile doors and windows effectively prevent police or private citizens from interfering with our sleep, our classrooms, our toolbenches, or our bars, at least most of the time. This is because a door is a legal entity of great importance: legitimate concerted social efforts to break down a door may only take place on legally defined occasions. These occasions are defined in the law of arrest and the law of search and seizure, and therefore, derivatively, in the criminal law.

The legal defense of doors and walls and windows means that small social systems which have legal possession of a place can maintain *continuous, discretionary* control over who crosses their boundaries. And this discretion may be enforced against agents of the state unless they have legal cause to penetrate the system or are invited in. Whenever such continuous discretionary control is maintained, the law speaks of "private places." The legal existence of "private places," then, is the main source of the capacity of small social systems to maintain their boundaries and determine their own interaction without interference from the outside. The distinctive feature of a modern *liberal* state is that it uses the monopoly of violence (which all modern industrial states have) to guarantee the boundaries of small, autonomous social systems.[36]

In everyday life the rules against invasions of privacy by private citizens are as strongly expressed and enforced as the rules against invasions of privacy by public officials. These rules are sharply stated in terms such as "Don't be nosy," "Don't go butting in where you aren't wanted," "Don't go butting into other people's business," "Mind your own business," and so on.

This distinction becomes a support for the situational construction of meanings for rules that are at variance with those in other situations and that would probably be seen as immoral were they to come to light in those other situations.

36. See Arthur Stinchcombe, "Institutions of Privacy in the Determination of Police Administrative Practice," *American Journal of Sociology,* LXIX (September, 1963), pp. 150–160.

These distinctions and rules, then, become meaningful resources which can be purposefully used to get done whatever an individual or group wants to do. *They provide the means for cutting off the rest of society and the rest of the social meanings, making them irrelevant, so that they do not become a hindrance to what one wishes to do.*

Physical segregation is the easiest. It is done by the use of walls to cut off private property and by other devices, including simply signs saying "Private Property—No Trespassing." An excellent example of this is found in the nudist camp. Few things are less comprehensible to most Americans than a group of strangers of both sexes carrying on their daily lives without clothes. "Private parts" of the body are on public display. As long as the nudists remain behind fences to prevent any genuinely public display, which, presumably, might "corrupt public morality," they are free to do so. This *physical situating* of activities makes them *secrets* from the public, either actually or fictionally. ("Out of sight, out of mind".) In a mobile society such as ours this kind of secreting of activities by physical separation becomes relatively easy because individuals can so readily go where they are anonymous. Because they go to some trouble to physically separate their nudism from their "normal" lives, the majority of nudists are not known to be so by their non-nudist neighbors and friends.[37]

The *meaningful situating* of activities, which has often been called "compartmentalizing" or "segmenting" ideas and feelings, is more difficult, but can be achieved to a greater extent than most people might imagine, especially when combined with the use of the physical situating. Nudism again provides us with an example. Most members of our society

37. For a discussion of the situational nature of nudist activity see Martin S. Weinberg, "Nudist Management of Respectability: Strategy For, and Consequences Of, The Construction of a Situated Morality," in Jack D. Douglas, ed. *Deviance and Respectability, op. cit.*

probably find it hard to believe that an individual could "walk around in the nude" in a mixed company of strangers without feeling "embarrassed," "sexual excitement," and the other things one might expect to feel if he were to take off his clothes in a more "normal" situation, such as at work. But, in fact, nudists do not have such feelings as long as they are only in the presence of other nudists. Through their careful, systematic construction of situated meanings that separate nudity from sex, their socializing of all new members into this meaning of nudity, and their physical situating of their nudist activities, they are able to maintain a special set of meanings for their activities. Only when they get their nudist life mixed up with their non-nudist life in some way, such as having their nudist life revealed in non-nudist circles, do they experience "embarrassment" or feelings of "unnaturalness." [38] Numerous examples of the same ability of individuals to meaningfully situate their activities can be found in Goffman's analyses of the ways in which members of our society segment *front regions* from *back regions.*[39] Even the flimsiest physical barrier can be used to meaningfully situate the "dirtiest work" from "clean work" as long as the members are willing to maintain the pretense of separation by not invading the back region situation.

In our society it is very probable that most people potentially could be seen as "deviant" from the standpoint of many others. Indeed, most of us are involved with so many groups having different rules and beliefs that we must in some way become "other directed" if we are to continue our effective involvements with each of these groups. That is, we must be "tuned in" to their beliefs and rules and avoid doing things that would upset them or even that would indicate that we

38. *Ibid.*
39. See Erving Goffman, *The Presentation of Self in Everyday Life, op. cit.*

have contrary feelings and beliefs. We must have "tact" and "sophistication" to get through our normal set of social involvements. And maintaining the distinctions between public and private are extremely important, especially if we are to avoid "losing ourselves" by coming to confuse ourselves with our many different involvements. In fact, we often have to manage a number of different public and private involvements, in such a way so as to maintain in our own minds the distinction between the "real me" and the various public "masks" we use to get through our potentially conflicting involvements.

We can see these problems and the great capacities of individuals to deal with them in the statement of a male homosexual studied by Carol Warren:

J.   I started kind of late in life . . . (laugh) . . . that actually started, I started rather late in life as far as leading—uh—exclusively—homosexual—uh—well, not homosexual—leading the gay life with a particular set of people that I knew where just about everyone *was* gay.

c. w.   Um Hmm.

J.   Prior to that time, even though I *was* a homosexual I—my life was strictly based on—the straight people—per se.

c. w.   How do you think this has changed you personally—in any way, or not at all?

J.   I don't know—I really don't—*I'm* much more relaxed—as I've said before, it's,—you're not living a double standard of life, which—to me, can—can get very complicated. However, I think so many people in this particular life are very well adjusted it it *because* of the fact that they have to lead two entirely different—social standards, and generally they can adapt themselves to it. You've got to be able to make instant changes—you can be flitting around in one instant and just absolutely have to stop dead in the next. Uh—it's just like putting on a mask and taking it off and you have have to do it instantaneously—you—and—and literally you have to change your—your method of speech and everything else—your vocabulary changes—there's a lot of things that you would say in one instance that you would not say in the next—and you have to be able to turn it on and off just like you would light a switch. Uh—most people *in* this particular situation *do* it very well—uh—Mentally I think they *adapt* themselves better than—straight people do, because they have to contend with it.

c. w.   Do you think they're adapting mentally, or just in what they say?

    j.   I think they're adapting mentally because it can be very much of a mental strain, I think, on a lot of people, because a lot of people—have not adjusted, or *do not* adjust themselves—to this life—uh—mentally, because they—they *still* have a feeling, you know, that it's wrong, or they're *doing* something wrong. And it's hard for them to—to *cope* with a situation such as this, where you're obviously *trying* to live, to your ability, a *comfortable* situation in life, and yet you're an extreme minority in a group of people that *obviously* disapprove of you, which can become a very uncomfortable situation because you run into people that—uh—that their actions don't contend with yours and you're uncomfortable. Uh—it's very difficult to carry it off—in a lot of cases. You do that when you run into them in restaurants or run into them in street—on the street corner or something. And you may be with business acquaintances. Eventually—I think—uh—the majority of people just get where they carry it off and don't really get *too* upset about it. Uh—some people I know just almost have a paranoia complex—they're out on the street and they run into a—a gay person that they know and they just absolutely will ignore them—they may be friends of very good standing. These people, I don't think, have adjusted themselves quite properly yet to the two standards of life. Uh—however, like I say, most people in this life *are* going a double standard —and if they see friends on the street, and in a lot of cases they *will* not talk to them, or in the most cases, they *will,* and there's no embarrassment on either people's part—or at least there shouldn't be, but it—it's hard to switch on and off.

Probably the extreme case of the ability of people to totally situate the meanings of their activities is that of the Nazi exterminations of the Jews. As Hughes has argued so persuasively, the normal or "good" Germans knew a great deal about the people "going up the chimneys," yet they were apparently able to not think about it, both during and after the events.[40] In the case of the Germans, as Hughes argues, there was an important element of physically situating the activities, of secreting them as much as possible from most Germans at the time they were being done.

There are also carefully reported cases in which the meaningful situating is achieved with almost no physical situating of the activities. For example, Reiss reported in his study of "queers and peers" that male delinquents were able to "hustle" adult "queers" as "fellators" without developing any conception of themselves as "queers." [41] They did this by totally separating, meaningfully and in action, any actual sexual involvement from the sex act and by refusing to perform any sex act other than passive oral-genital fellation.

The prevention of the invasion of privacy and its consequent (even if unintended) abetting of highly situated constructions of meanings and activities is found even more in the common practices of cooperating to maintain the *public fiction* of morality *and normalcy*. The public fiction of normalcy and morality is even sanctioned by the many *rules of discretion* and *rules of tact*, which proscribe communications

40. See Everett C. Hughes, "Good People and Dirty Work," in Howard S. Becker, ed., *The Other Side: Perspectives on Deviance*, New York: The Free Press, 1964, pp. 23–36.

41. See Albert J. Reiss, Jr., "The Social Integration of Queers and Peers," in *ibid*.

about certain rule violations. Maintaining these public fictions is common partly because it is an effective strategy for achieving working agreements on the meanings of rules. It avoids conflict by denying that there are any deviations, as long as these deviations are not important to achieving the purposes of the individuals involved in the situation-at-hand, as they see it. Again, individuals will often "violate" rules for the specific purpose of avoiding conflicts with other individuals who share those rules; then all involved will commonly act as if there were no violation. An example of such *altruistic deviance* is reported by John Johnson in his study of "Practical Reasons for Gundecking" on a destroyer. While the meanings of the category are problematic for the sailors, "gundecking" generally involves some form of fictitious construction of official records required by naval rules. Gundecking of records is almost universally understood by the members and at least some forms are generally accepted in specific situations. Some of the "practical reasons" are found in Johnson's analysis of gundecking the records on the sonar noise level:

. . . accomplishing the task of measuring the ship's sonar performance, if taken to mean "to the letter" of the various rules and procedures, entailed stopping the "normal working day" of nearly all of the personnel on the ship whether or not they were actually involved in the many complex processes of the measurement itself, which most of them were not, in order to reduce to the very minimum the noise on the ship. Given the knowledge of the "disruption" of the practical tasks of so many others, as those others saw it, in the literal application of this procedure, then, the ASW personnel considered that the measurement task could be accomplished in a sufficient-for-all-practical-purposes manner without the necessity of requesting so many of their fellow shipmates to bring to a halt their practical affairs for a period of several hours. Also, although "the letter" of the formal procedures called for the shutting-off of all the electrical equipment in the ship's kitchens and galleys, the ASW personnel considered this unnecessary in order to accomplish their task in a sufficient-for-all-practical-purposes manner. Also, there were other occasions when either the operational commitments of the ship precluded the possibility of making the sonar performance measurements at those speeds which required greater and greater amounts of fuel which might be needed for another occasion, or the requirement for the engineers to "bring all four boilers on the line" would entail a great deal of inconvenience for them, possibly causing serious delays in their everyday maintenance routines, and this meant that the measurements were only accomplished for the lesser speeds, with the ASW personnel "sketching in" the measurements for the higher speeds using a commonsense extrapolation based on the measurements taken at the lower speeds. That these practical exigencies of the situation called for relatively minor modifications of "the letter" of the formal procedures reflected the practical interests of the ASW personnel in maintaining a social environment in which they didn't "catch flack" from their shipmates for an "inappropriate" disruption of the normal working routines, and reflected their knowledge that this was indeed an important consideration given "what anyone knows" about sustaining a cooperative atmosphere for social relationships in such a physically confining setting.[42]

One of the most obvious forms of public fiction is found in *fictitious rules*. Most segments of our society have many rules which those involved almost never invoke or live by, and which they all understand to be normally violated, but which they also know they are supposed to support in their public statements. A cab company, for example, may have a definite rule against the cabdrivers ever giving the passengers advice on what hotel or restaurants to patronize. (The idea of such a rule might be to avoid display of favoritism

42. See John Johnson," Gundecking," unpublished paper.

on the part of an employee of a publicly licensed company, which often has a monopoly.) Of course, no cabdriver in his right mind would obey the rule; and the company would probably be upset by all the unhappy customers if they did. But they do maintain it as a fictitious rule and the uninitiated are sometimes taken in. Again, most organizations "pay lip-service" to efficiency and cost-cutting by maintaining a rule that employees never use the phone for "private calls"; but this too is generally a fictitious rule maintained for public purposes and privately reconstructed by all those "in the know."

One of the best examples of cooperation in maintaining the public fictions of morality and normalcy is to be found in Fred Davis' classic analysis of "deviance disavowal." [43] Making use of the experiences of the physically handicapped, Davis was able to show how the handicapped and those interacting with them cooperate to maintain a public image of the handicapped individual as "normal" for all purposes in the situation at hand. There were at least three major stages in the sequential development of this "deviance disavowal." The first constitutes a "fictional acceptance" of the handicapped as normal by the non-handicapped. The second phase in the sequence consists of coming to treat the handicapped as normal. But in the third phase, called "breaking through," various "amendments and special considerations" to this normalized public image are made to allow the handicapped individual to actually interact effectively with the normal persons in everyday situations. The important point here is that we have a movement from the public front of normalcy to a certain willingness to recognize the existence of the physical handicap. This movement away from the cooperatively maintained front of normalcy takes place pre-

43. See Fred Davis, "Deviance Disavowal: The Management of Strained Interaction by the Visibly Handicapped," in *ibid.*

cisely because the individuals have moved increasingly from a public relationship to a more private relationship. We would expect that only those relationships in which there is this move toward the private relationship will there be this move away from the front.

The essence of the public situation is strangeness and a resulting untrustworthiness; the essence of the private situation is personal knowledge and a resulting trustworthiness. The distinction between the public and the private situation is of basic and growing importance in our society because it is so complex and pluralistic. Only in such a society is one commonly performing for strangers, that is, individuals of whom one has little personal knowledge, so that one has little reason to know if they can be trusted. Because we all know and take it for granted that there are many conflicting values and beliefs in our complex society, we all know that strangers may be completely against what we "really" think and feel, that we must be on guard against them, and that we must use *publicly acceptable* fronts whenever we might be observed by strangers.

In any society in which there is so much disagreement over values and beliefs, all individuals have potential enemies in any public situation who are ready to make use of any information from which they can construct damaging interpretations. For this reason we find the highly formalized development of Machiavelianism in Renaissance Italy, the obsession with interpersonal strategies among courtiers (Castiglione) and diplomats (Lord Chesterfield), and the mass interest in self-presentation strategies—"how to win friends and influence enemies"—in our own society today. In such a society we also find that various forms of *public rules*, rules recognized as relevant only to the public realm of life, are developed to facilitate the achievement of the purposes-at-hand in public situations.

In our complex society public rules have become
of increasing importance in adequately achieving
one's purposes in public situations; the public
level of existence becomes increasingly important
in itself, so that actions come to have a publicity
effect largely independent of their private effects.

The most obvious public rules are those concerned with
tolerance, public order, courtesy, decency, respectability,
presentability, and so on. All are of value in making it possible for disparate populations from very different kinds of
private worlds to work together in public situations where
they remain relative strangers to each other. All of these
rules help to produce an homogenization of public life in
American society.

Probably the most crucial public rule for a pluralistic
society is that of tolerance. As actually used in everyday
situations, and as extolled endlessly in high school composi-
tions and oratory, the tolerance rule specifically bans consideration of all differences in values, beliefs, private lives,
skin color, and so on that are not relevant to the situation
at hand, as the members see it. As work situations in the
giant technological organizations have become increasingly
public and impersonal, the criteria considered relevant to
evaluations of workers have become ever more specific,
formalized and limited in number. Social movements have
sprung up to ban all considerations of sexual differences, age
differences, racial differences, and even linguistic differences
in some instances from consideration in all hiring and pro-
motion practices. The same drive toward non-distinction (or
indiscriminateness) has taken place in voting, education,
recreation, and just about all other public situations—generally called "public facilities" in the legal battles.

Insofar as these homogenizing tendencies have in fact
further segmented public from private situations, they have

probably led to less conflict over the differences in values and beliefs of the different groups. (They may also be producing more conflicts over status striving on the part of those sharing status goals.) But some of the tendencies have served to *break down* previous boundaries between public and private lives among some groups in our society and this has led to more conflicts. Consider, for example, changes in the residence patterns and the laws helping to control such patterns.

This has been compounded by the fact that there are real differences over the meanings constructed for "public situations" and "private situations." Such a conflict was especially apparent in a group of gang boys studied by Werthman and Piliavin. The boys defined their "turf" as private, while the police defined it as public and this led to many conflicts:

The police are the most despised and least accommodating threat to a gang's conception of a hangout. Like gang members, the police have a vested interest in imposing a set of normative claims on the people who use the streets. The very places that are defended like homes by gang members also constitute places of work or "beats" to the police, and the home-like uses to which gang members put the streets are often perceived as threats to the patrolman's task of maintaining the conventional rules that ordinarily govern behavior on them. Although the boys attempt either subtly or violently to convince outsiders that their behavior at the hangout is a strictly private affair, the police tend to insist with equal conviction that all behavior on public property is their legitimate concern. The relationship between gang members and policemen thus has its roots in an ecological conflict over claims to final authority in the same setting. The Chicago police apparently have a phrase that expresses this relationship. When they are annoyed at a gang for their behavior at a hangout, they will say "Gi'me that corner!" [44]

44. See Carl Werthman, and Irving Piliavin, "Gang Members and the Police," in David J. Bordua, *The Police*, New York: John Wiley, 1967, pp. 56–98.

The same kind of conflict over the meanings of public and private have been relevant in the racial conflicts in recent decades. In the South the public realm is far more sharply distinguished from the private and far more broadly defined than is true in the Northeast. In the South we get the same kind of emphasis on public manners and the same fear of "outsiders" that we find in France, where "ils" is often a term of contempt for outsiders. Again, much of the conflict between the young and the old in our society today seems to be due to the young's *publicizing* a much broader gamut of life than the old do.

Tolerance is the foremost example of public rules that facilitate working relations in public situations. Combined with the various rules of courtesy, decency, respectability, and so on, it constitutes a complex of rules specifically relevant only to behavior in public places. These rules enable any individual who knows them and knows how to act in accord with them to "fit in" in any public situation (providing he also understands the more specific nature of the situation), regardless of how very different his private life might be from those of the other individuals involved.[45]

The role of "fitting in," of not "making a scene," of "getting along with others," of being "nice," of not being "gauche," and of being "correct" in a complex society is so apparent that these behaviors are a major basis for judging the "character" of a person and they become an explicit part of informal and formal socialization in the society. This is the first part of what we can call the *publicity effect*, the effect on the meanings of things of their being public rather than private.

Another part of the publicity effect has become ever more important in our age of electronic mass-communication, an age in which one's activities may be observed not only by

45. See Erving Goffman, *Behavior in Public Places, op. cit.*

millions of total strangers, but even without our own knowledge at times. The simplest form of this aspect of the effect
consists of being concerned .h the nature of the public
appearances for their own sake, independently of what one
knows or suspects about the private person, and even in contrast to what one might think about the private person. This
is apparent whenever people wish to "maintain appearances"
even though they know that everyone knows what is going
on: Being seen to take "public appearances" seriously and
giving them their "due" is itself important. To illustrate,
Warriner found that the people in a small Kansas town voted
for Prohibition and publicly opposed drinking. Yet they
drank as part of their social lives in much the way other
people in our society do, except that they lowered the blinds
first so that they could not be observed doing so by the
public outside. The public, of course, would generally know
what they were doing. Hence the expression of support for
public rules becomes important in itself. To do otherwise
in this case, as in so many other situations in our society,
would be condemned as "flaunting" one's wrong-doing,
which would be seen as "adding insult to injury" by those
who agree with the rule for private and public life and as
simply insulting or immoral by those who only think of it
as "wise" to uphold it in public.

There is yet another feature of the publicity effect. This
is the *response to the abstract public,* that is, the effect on
what people think of something that results from what they
think "the public" response will be.[46] It is now common for
individuals in everyday life to talk about the "public effect"
of something, something which is quite independent of what
they themselves might think of it. In discussing political

46. Again, see my discussion of the "publicity effect" in Jack D. Douglas,
Youth In Turmoil, Washington, D.C.: U.S. Government Printing Office,
1970. Also see Joseph R. Gusfield and Michael Schwartz, "The Meanings
of Occupational Prestige: Reconsideration of the NORC Scale," *American
Sociological Review,* 28(April, 1963), pp. 265–271.

matters, for example, journalists will ask people if they think something will have an adverse effect on what the public thinks of a politician; those questioned will then evaluate the possible responses, often saying that they don't agree with the public view but, since that is the public view, then they think he should resign and so on. What happens here is that the generalized conception of the public and of the nature of the public morality, ideas, feelings, tendencies to action, and so on lead an individual to respond in a different way from the way he would respond if thinking only of what he and the people he knows directly would think and do.

This kind of publicity effect becomes all the more important in the age of mass communications because people giving their views in the mass media face a situation of maximum conflict of rules and beliefs. They are exposed to the *whole* complex society in immediate detail and "on the record." The effect is to force them toward a *least-common-denominator morality which is the public morality—* a communicative strategy aimed at offending the fewest possible people. Public representatives who are publicly visible, are often in a situation in which they must anticipate the abstract "public" response to their statements and in which the "public" is the most diverse of all possible audiences (short only of the international audience that is becoming common through TV-satellite hook-ups). We are moving toward a form of *public communication* with its own special vocabulary and a minimum of specific commitments to anything other than a celebration of the least-common-denominator public morality and beliefs.

The move toward a reliance on least-common-denominator public rules and beliefs for public activities is not solely the result of such publicity effects. There is more reason to it. The public realm of our society is that part in which the members from the many private realms interact. As the public realm has become ever more complex because of the growth of many different kinds of private realms, the members of our society have felt a need for some means of bringing order into that public realm. The device they have created to do this regulating, this ordering of the potentially chaotic, complex society, is the official agency of control. These official agencies have grown massively in size and power over the last century and have increasingly used power to try to regulate the growing "public sector" of our society. These official agents of control have greatly changed the nature of social rules and their relations to actions in our society. They have especially made it wise for individuals to appear to be acting in accord with the public morality, regardless of what they are in fact doing.

7. Constructing Order in American Society

The simpler description or explanation is always more alluring. Ockham's razor in philosophy is complemented in common sense by the preference for the simple, the unitary, the uni-directional, over the complex, the pluralistic, the multi-directional. By its natural bent the mind prefers an "either-or" to a "both this and that," a "system" to a "conglomerate," a "cause-and-effect" to a "both a cause and an effect." Considering the need we have for simplifying a vastly complex world, especially in view of our limited memory and analytical capacities, we can see the value of such a preference. But this bent can become dangerous whenever we distort the nature of reality for the sake of simplicity.

In theories of society this preference for the simple over the complex and for the uni-directional over the multi-directional is seductive and dangerous. It is seductive because social theories, at least those of common sense, are preeminently intended to be useful. They are intended to help us achieve our goals and our intentions in society—to maintain our status, make our wealth, win our loves, derogate our competitors, disprove our enemies, exalt our friends. And what could possibly be more useful than imposing our "useful" social theories on the world? If the world accepts our social theories, then our interests will be best served (or so we think). This is one reason for the preeminence of absolutism in men's theories of society, moral rules, and so on. The assumption of absolutism means that all others must see the world in the same way we see it: There can be no other legitimate view of the world. The assumption of absolutism in beliefs or morality, then, is a form of *mental imperialism* which, if successful, constrains others to act so as to best serve our own interests. The acceptance of our absolutist theory would order the world in complete accord with our own best interests (as we see them). It is little wonder, then, that men seek to impose their absolutist theories on the world.

As a kind of Gresham's law of society, we can say that *absolutism tends to drive out relativism.* Absolutism gives one a strategic advantage over someone using a relativistic or situational theory, because anyone who accepts your view as being possibly as valid as his own view, while you insist on your own view as being exclusively true, has already been beaten halfway. It's like getting your opponent to negotiate on the basis of "what's mine is mine and what's yours is negotiable." Such a strategy fails only when the opponent refuses to accept your basis for the negotiation. In this case it means he remains absolutist. This, presumably is a basic reason why individuals who become involved in conflicts tend to polarize. In any situation in which some individuals have more power than others, they will tend to enforce their absolutist views of the world; and generally only in a world made up of many powers roughly equal to each other will there be a tendency toward relativistic views of the world, which is the situation producing the relativism or situationalism of democracy.[1]

1. There is a vast literature concerning the relation of feudal pluralism to the development of group and personal freedoms and to democracy in

The tendency toward absolutism has been all too apparent in Western social thought in the last century, and has been very clear in dominant streams of American sociological thought in the last few decades. It is not that some group of conspiratorial functionalists has snuffed out all opposition to their simplistic models of society, for that itself would be too absolute a position. Although the functionalist "systemic" model of society has dominated, it has been well opposed by other models of society, such as conflict models. Rather, the problem has been that both the functionalists and their main opposition have been too absolutist in their positions. Each has insisted on maintaining one relatively simple view of the nature of society, the one a simple-system model and the other a conflict model. The result has been that the one has concentrated almost exclusively on explaining social order, the prime symbol of functionalism, while the other has concentrated on explaining social disorder or conflict, the prime symbol of the conflict theorists. *Yet the obvious truth about society, especially our society, is that there is an abundance of both order and disorder, of both consensus and dissensus.*

There is no prima facie reason to reject such fundamentally different theories of society. One might argue that they are each trying to explain very different things and that we simply must have independent and conflicting theories to explain independent and conflicting aspects of reality. Certainly there is precedent for such an approach to theory in the other sciences, the most obvious case being the complimentarity principle in physics by which both the wave and particle theories of light are accepted as true—yet independent. But I believe this would be another of those seemingly

the Western world. Some of this literature will be referred to later in this chapter. One of the more brief, recent discussions can be found in Randall Collins, "A Comparative Approach to Political Sociology," in Reinhard Bendix, *State and Society*, Boston: Little, Brown, and Co., pp. 42–67.

endless false analogies with the natural sciences. The important point is that in sociology the phenomena to be explained by conflicting theories are not independent, nor, most importantly, are the practical consequences of the theories. It makes a real difference whether one seeks to explain social order, stratification, and so on in terms of a consensus of values or in terms of conflicting interests combined with the use of power. The very conception of "social order," of what "social order" is, is very different in the two different perspectives, and any policy decisions concerning what to do (or not to do) about poverty, education, protest movements, and an endless number of other things is fundamentally affected by accepting one of these views over the other. The issue is not one that can be resolved by making use of some simple pragmatic division of function among theories. At the same time, I do not believe the issue is one that demands an either-or choice.

From the ground level, that of "the man in the streets" in America, the everyday lives of most of us are variegated and protean, with few sharp lines and many diffuse shadings. *American society is one of great contrasts; and it is certainly so with respect to consensus and dissensus, order and disorder.* Some areas of our lives are highly routinized and display considerable consensus among those involved, at least in the short-run; other areas are very disordered and display great dissensus among those involved, demanding continual negotiation and reordering simply to get through the day. Some areas of life are so routinized and homogenized that they "bore us to death," while others are so disordered and jumbled that they "drive us out of our minds." In some common settings we can so easily predict the essentials of what people are going to do, and find them so uninteresting, that we find it difficult to simulate any polite interest, to avoid the tactless yawn in many others; equally or more commonly, we find our relations with others so trying that we find it difficult, if not impossible, to "keep our cool." Nevertheless, to all settings, however peaceful at one moment, there do eventually come the crises, the arguments, the fights, and, sometimes, the killings.

The crucial task of sociological theory, one thus far unaccomplished, must be to deal with this contrasting character of the everyday realities: the dissensus within consensus, the disorder within order, the freedom within constraint, the change within stability. But we must do far more than this. We must discover what specific kinds of order and disorder, dissensus and consensus, change and stability exist; and we must learn how each of these is related to the important aspects of our society. Only then will we have an adequate factual and theoretical understanding of our society.

America as a Pluralistic Society

It is strange that the social-systems view of society should have reached its zenith in America. For, in terms of "what anyone knows," American society is one of the most complex in the history of the world. From its beginnings American society has been highly pluralistic—yet there is hardly an adequate vocabulary for discussing this pluralism. This verbal inadequacy should not be surprising, at least not once we understand the largely rhetorical purposes of common-sensical vocabularies and theories of social phenomena. Almost all of the major Western societies were at one time quite pluralistic. Diverse tribes lived side by side, fought intermittently, were invaded and sometimes overwhelmed by waves of conquering nomads—Celts, Romans, Norsemen, Magyars, Mongols, Germans and many lesser groups. At some time or other all of these nation states had severe "nationalities" problems. All of them had to be welded together by unscrupulous barbarian conquerors—or scrupulous

Christian conquerors acting with Divine Right—who would do *whatever* seemed necessary to construct a political order out of this chaos of warring peoples. So intense was this problem, so recurrent, so costly, so entwined with international conflicts, that over the centuries the European rulers—the entrepreneurs of social order—developed the theory of *Machiavellism*, which enthroned the *raison d'état*, the right of the would-be rulers to do *whatever* was necessary to maintain and develop the State.

The state, the nation, the society, was so vitally important that it was increasingly treated as a separate level of existence, as a "thing" in itself. Having all of the human characteristics, plus the divine characteristic of eternal existence, the "myth of the state", as Ernst Cassirer has called it, grew over several hundred years to be one of the most important ideas in Western society. The rulers and their supporters developed many social theories, or ideologies, that supported the independent and supreme existence of the State as the *core* of each society. In conjunction with the development of these theories, a special vocabulary was developed to communicate most effectively the ideas within them. Because of its purposes, the vocabulary was preeminently rhetorical (or mythical). The very words used "justified" the State, the Nation, the Society and the most crucial element of all was the name that treated the State as *the* Society. The name provided a basis for the mystique of the homogeneous society. France, Germany, Italy, and all of the other societies that had been so torn by internal warfare came to be called by one name; and calling them one name became an important element in helping to hold them together as one group. Once the idea of France, or Germany, or Italy as a unit category had been developed and accepted, it affected the thinking of Western men who were trying to decide exactly what the essence of each of these categories was, and the development of theories of national character, national personality, national race, and so on. All of this was not simply the result of any Machiavellian manipulation, of course, nor was it the result of an insistence on using one name. Because of the homogenizing effects of the centralized political and economic power, the societies did become more integrated, more unitary. The remaining differences, conflicts, and heterogeneity were then covered up by the use of one name for all of the different groups and interests involved. The rhetorical use of one name to help construct social order was, at least partially, an intentional, self-fulfilling prophecy.

In the case of "America" the issue is clearer, for there was no such thing in the beginning. There were distinct and conflicting colonies, each jealously preserving its independence and forwarding its own interests against those of the others. There were similarities, because most of the members of the colonies came from England. Yet the common elements were never important enough to enable anyone to weld the society together; and by the eighteenth century many of the common elements were even beginning to disappear. Catholics and various nationalities had been added to the original English populations. The regional contrasts between the South and the Northeast had become established, as were those between the Frontier and the more developed Eastern Seaboard.

Only the development of the common enemy, one who could only be defeated by a combination of colonial efforts, made it possible to supersede these growing differences. Perhaps because there developed a coalition of interest of the dominant social groups in the South, notably the Tidewater groups, with the merchants of the Northeast, it was possible to create a reasonably strong central government after the common enemy had been defeated. Whatever the reason, it is very hard to believe that there was not an element of both historical accident *and* rational calculation of self-interest on the part of very small groups of elites that led to the creation of a single government; yet this government itself was permeated by the assumption that this was to be a pluralistic society, one in which the many differences would be not only recognized but enshrined for all time in the structure of the government.

This pluralism was essential to the idea of a federal system with three conflicting branches, each one intended to check the other and to prevent too much accumulation of power in any one segment of the society. Almost all of the men involved in the construction of the American Constitution and the American government were convinced that the only way in which they could agree on any centralized government was to keep it to a bare minimum and to allow all of the local differences to be as free as possible under the constraints of a very few fragmented central powers. Indeed, for the most part the central government was restricted to fighting any common external enemies and to forwarding the common economic interests of the states, all of which continued to see themselves as separate and independent nations for the first hundred years of the existence of the central government.

The result, of course, was that the central government remained weak. The differences among the various parts of this "one society" continued to grow. In less than one hundred years the society was torn apart by one of the most bloody wars in the history of man. Only through brute force was the nation held together at all.

The Civil War was fought over one of the earliest great divisions in America, the sectional division between North and South, which includes within itself very important differences in language, values, beliefs, history, and so on. Force settled this sectional division and force has continued to make secession impossible. The enforced unification of the different groups, combined with the systematic socialization of the young in the values and beliefs of nationalism, of "the Nation," have led to a decrease in the social significance of these once fundamental differences. But this has in no way produced a generally homogeneous society. There are probably still millions of Southerners who would like to "rise again" and, presumably, secede again. There are even many Westerners who would like to secede from New York.

At the same time that some of these earlier differences were decreasing in importance, new ones were arising and creating new conflicts of interest, values, and beliefs; some of these new differences coalesced around old ones. Doubtless the most important new source of pluralism throughout the nineteenth century was the growing racial and ethnic heterogeneity.

By the end of the first quarter of the nineteenth century the black population of the South equalled or surpassed that of the white population. While this largest racial minority in the United States began to decline steadily in its proportion of the entire population, it remains somewhere around ten to twelve percent of our population today. No other Western society has ever included such a large racial minority. Wherever there are large racial minorities, there are social differences that produce important conflicts.

The fact of the black population in the United States has obviously been the source of fundamental differences and conflicts throughout our history. Though most social scientists were long loath to admit or even to see it, the black population has for the most part created and transmitted a very different culture from that of the other groups in this country. Not only do they have many different values, beliefs, daily customs, and so on, but they also have one of the most distinct dialects of the English language. As long as this distinct cultural group was isolated in the rural South, the conflicts were mainly among white groups over what should be done *about* the black culture. As the blacks have dispersed throughout the rest of the society, and as they have been integrated into the schools, work situations and political groups, the conflicts between the black group and the others have intensified—and the demands for isolationism have grown on both sides.

Whereas the other racial groups constitute a smaller part of the whole population, making up only about five percent of the national population, they have long been quite important in some areas of the country. There are approximately five million Mexican-Americans in the Southwest who are defined by many as a separate racial ("raza") group, not to ignore the several million Indians and Asiatic Americans.

While the cultural pluralism related to racial differences in the United States is more apparent, the cultural pluralism related to ethnic differences has been more important until recent years. (Indeed, as many people have pointed out, the differences and conflicts between the racial groups in recent years have increasingly resembled the much earlier differences and conflicts among ethnic groups.) The migration of thirty-five million Europeans to the United States from 1820 to 1920 had far-reaching consequences for American society that have continued up to the present. The sheer size of the migration alone was significant, and, as Oscar Handlin has noted: "Contemporaries often found it difficult to judge the migration of Europeans to America because the numbers involved were of such a magnitude and the forces at work of such broad scope as to stagger imagination."[2] The most important effect of the great waves of immigration was to transform the Northern states and some of the Middle Western states from ethnically homogeneous into ethnically heterogeneous societies. Whereas most of the earlier population had come from England and Scotland, most of the new immigrant population came from other

2. Oscar Handlin, *Immigration*, Englewood Cliffs, N.J.: Prentice-Hall, 1959, p. 5.

nations and were Catholic. America's large Northern cities and many areas of the Middle West typically became polyglot societies which were so pluralistic as to make communication difficult. The Little Italys, Little Polands, China Towns, and centers of other ethnic groups still exist as testimony to this period. In one hundred years the partially federal United States had been transformed from predominantly Anglo-Saxon, Scotch-Irish and Protestant societies into a sprawling nation of polygot cities, in which the Anglo-Saxon groups had become a minority. The Catholic population constituted approximately two-fifths of the population; the Jews numbered nearly five million; many non-believers entered. By the early twentieth century the American nation no longer had a dominant ethnic or religious group. In these respects the nation was more pluralistic than almost any other major nation.

Certainly there is not as much ethnic pluralism in America today as there was in the 1920s; but it would be mistaken to believe it has been superseded by an era of ethnic homogeneity. Ethnic studies have been out of vogue with social scientists for several decades, but there are a few important recent studies of ethnicity in American life.

One of the most important of these is *Beyond the Melting Pot* by Nathan Glazer and Daniel Moynihan. This work is primarily about New York, which is more ethnically heterogeneous than most American cities, but which is also important because of its great dominance in the mass media, publishing, finance, commerce, art, advertising, and other vital areas of American life. Glazer and Moynihan believe that all evidence shows conclusively that the "melting pot" thesis has not yet come true in New York and, by implication, in most of the United States:

In 1660 William Kieft, the Dutch governor of New Netherland, remarked to the French Jesuit Isaac Jogues that there were eighteen languages spoken at or near Fort Amsterdam at the tip of Manhattan Island. There still are: not necessarily the same languages, but at least as many; nor has the number ever declined in the intervening three centuries. This is an essential fact of New York: a merchant metropolis with an extraordinarily heterogeneous population. The first shipload of settlers sent out by the Dutch was made up largely of French-speaking Protestants. British, Germans, Finns, Jews, Swedes, Africans, Italians, Irish followed, beginning a stream that has never yet stopped . . .

The census of 1960 showed that 19 percent of the population of the city were still foreign-born whites, 28 percent were children of foreign-born whites, another 14 percent were Negro, 8 percent were of Puerto Rican birth or parentage. Unquestionably, a great majority of the rest (31 percent) were the grandchildren and great-grandchildren of immigrants, and still thought of themselves, on some occasions and for some purposes, as German, Irish, Italian, Jewish, or whatnot, as well as of course Americans.

Of the foreign-stock population (immigrants and their children), 859,000 were born in Italy or were the children of Italian immigrants; 564,000 were from the U.S.S.R. (these are mostly Jews); 389,000 from Poland (these too are mostly Jews); 324,000 from Germany; 312,000 from Ireland; 220,00 from Austria; 175,000 from Great Britain; almost 100,000 from Hungary; more than 50,000 from Greece, Czechoslovakia, Rumania, and Canada; more than 25,000 from Yugoslavia, around 10,000 from the Netherlands, Denmark, Finland, and Switzerland; more than 5,000 from Portugal and Mexico. There were more than a million Negroes, and more than 50,000 of other races, mostly Chinese and Japanese. From almost every country in the world there are enough people in the city to make up communities of thousands and tens of thousands with organizations, churches, a language, some distinctive culture . . .[3]

3. Nathan Glazer and Daniel Moynihan, *Beyond the Melting Pot*, Cambridge, MIT Press, 1964, pp. 1 and 7.

The result is that New York is an immensely complex city of over eight million people (one-twenty-fifth of the population of the entire United States), and it is exceedingly difficult for anyone to analyze. Moreover, this ethnic pluralism parallels other forms of our social pluralism, such as different forms of economic activity in the technological society:

To describe the economy of New York fully, one would have to point out that it is dominated at its peak (the banks, insurance companies, utilities, big corporation offices) by white Protestants, with Irish Catholics and Jews playing somewhat smaller roles. In wholesale and retail commerce, Jews predominate. White-collar workers are largely Irish and Italian if they work for big organizations, and Jewish if they work for smaller ones. The city's working class is on its upper levels, Irish, Italian, and Jewish; on its lower levels, Negro and Puerto Rican. Other ethnic groups are found scattered everywhere, but concentrated generally in a few economic specialties.[4]

Although ethnic heterogeneity is slowly decreasing in our society, as a result of certain cross-ethnic groupings and identities, every indication is that it will continue for a long time to come. As Milton Gordon has concluded in his important study of *Assimilation in American Life*:

Probably the vast majority of Americans, as revealed in their choices in primary group relations and organizational affiliations, desire ethnic communality, at least in essential outline. Their preferences are reinforced by the self-perpetuating pressures generated by the nature of subcommunity organizational life and by the demands and exhortations, grounded in ideological conviction, of their ethnic community leaders. As we have suggested, some individuals, as a result of their particular inclinations and perspectives, move out into an amorphously structured intellectual subcommunity which contains people of all ethnic backgrounds. All of these recurring processes are probably inevitable and basically irreversible.

4. *Ibid.*, pp. 4–5.

Thus the prognosis for America for a long time to come is that its informal social structure will consist of a series of ethnic subcommunities criss-crossed by social class, within which primary group relationships will tend to be confined, that secondary group relationships across ethnic group lines will take place in abundance as a result of the requirements of an urbanized industrial society, and that the intellectual subsociety will grow somewhat both in numbers and in institutional articulation as a result of the constant increase in the magnitude of higher education.[5]

The United States today remains one of the most ethnically heterogeneous societies in the world, not only in the composition of its citizenry but also in its openness to the rest of the world. The political position of the United States makes it a center of world activity, so that Americans are more involved in other societies than any other national group. Americans constitute the largest percentage of tourists in the world. Americans own large percentages of the corporations in many parts of the world. Americans work outside the United States more than any other people, and do more traveling on business. More American students are studying abroad than students from any other nation. American society is also more open to populations of other societies than almost any major nation. Although the great immigration ended before 1920, it has remained relatively open to foreign populations. Since the second World War there have been a number of major immigrations, including the immigration of displaced persons, such as Koreans, Puerto Ricans, and Cubans. America has more students from abroad in its schools than do other nations. There are probably fewer tourists and business visits to the United States than to nations such as France, but this is due mainly to the fact that most of the visitors to other nations are Americans. Most importantly of all, there are major constituencies within the United States

5. Milton M. Gordon, *Assimilation in American Life*, New York: Oxford University Press, 1964, pp. 263–264.

for many other nations of the world. An openness to world events has been accentuated by the rapid development of almost instantaneous international communications. Barring drastic change within the United States or in its world position, this increase in openness to the world will probably continue as the world is tied ever closer together by an international web of satellite communications and the international economy. All of these forms of openness and of pluralistic involvements in other nations of the world make the United States far more complex and changing than most other societies.

America today is also highly pluralistic in terms of its voluntary associations. The "nation of joiners" has created a web of overlapping and interlocking, yet independent, voluntary organizations for almost every conceivable social purpose, ranging from the preservation of redwood trees to the covert overthrow of foreign governments, both friendly and unfriendly. Americans have been known for their organizational entrepreneurship for almost two centuries, and the importance of this entrepreneurial activity must not be underestimated. As any political figure can easily attest, the private organizations remain very important in our society. Every day new groups of political vigilantes set out to transform the nature of our society; most never become foci of public attention. They include The Ladies' Home League for Decency and The Neighborhood Crew for Clean Streets, which are often only local groups and have no effect beyond their own neighborhoods. Sometimes, however, they are instrumental in producing basic changes in law, interpretations of laws by the courts, or new legislation. Some of these groups, even when very small, as in the case of Nader's Raiders, have great national effect. This group was able to humiliate the gigantic international automobile corporations and influence the direction of federal legislation. All men of practical affairs know how important these voluntary associations are in American society and, therefore, they court them by continual visiting, lecturing, and personal communication. Only abstractionists who insist on seeing this society in terms of some universal, over-arching structure or the relentless march of history fail to see the importance of such groups.

American society is pluralistic by design. It was that way to begin with and it was the intention of those who constructed the nation to keep it that way. The Federal structure of the government, of law, and of all governmental organizations has been purposely maintained to prevent too great a centralization of power. This decentralization of government and law has been directly paralleled by purposeful decentralization of economic activity and almost every other aspect of the society. In fact, this is so much the case that one danger one faces in analyzing American society is that the opposite tendencies to centralization, to the domination of many groups by a few giant ones, and the strains toward homogeneity in the society will be overlooked because of the ideology of pluralism.[6]

This emphasis on pluralism in American political philosophy, both in the abstract and in practice, has been so great that much of political science in America has been dominated by the pluralistic perspective on American society, at precisely the same time that much of sociology has been dominated by the systems perspective. The traditional emphasis on pluralism in political science has probably been due in part to the general ideological commitment to pluralism in our society. Whether for this reason or for another, Kariel and the other critics of the pluralist theorists have been quite right in arguing that the political scientists,

6. See the argument in Henry Kariel, *The Decline of American Pluralism*, Palo Alto, Calif.: Stanford University Press.

economists, and other social scientists concerned with pluralism (or decentralization and conflicting interests) have failed
to see the growing "threats" to pluralism (or the *possible
waning* of pluralism, if one wishes to leave out the value
judgment involved in most of this debate).

Trends Toward Homogenization and New Forms
of Pluralism in American Society

The primary forces tending to increase centralization and
homogenization in American society are the scientific-technological revolution, the related centralization of production
and marketing in the economic realm, and the growing
planning of business and government to deal with both of
these developments. There can be little doubt that the
scientific and technological way of thinking and acting has
increasingly become the ideal mode of thought and action
in the various realms of Western society.[7] Science and technology are the ideals for business, academic disciplines,
education, government, and to some degree even for such
previously sacrosanct areas as dating and marriage. Not only
has the scientific way of thought and behaving become an
ideal toward which other kinds of thought and activity are
directed and in terms of which they are judged, but science
and technology are ends in themselves, as is most apparent
in such massive social undertakings as the space program.[8]

At the same time, economic activity in our society has
been rapidly centralizing. Ours is the age of the Giant
Corporation, so much so that many people have begun to
argue that it is a corporate society, one dominated by the
one or two hundred massive corporations which span not

7. I have previously examined some of these questions in "Freedom
and Tyranny in a Technological Society," in Jack D. Douglas, *Freedom and
Tyranny: Social Problems in a Technological Society*, New York: Random
House, 1970.

8. *Ibid.*

only our continent, but much of the rest of the world.[9] In less than fifty years the independent producer and the small farmer have largely disappeared, to be replaced by the giant corporation. Although the government and much of the public have sought by various legal and governmental innovations to reverse the ever-accelerating pace of economic centralization, nothing has stopped the seemingly ineluctable growth of the giant organizations. Most working members of our society today work for some giant organization, and the majority of us are directly or indirectly dependent upon their policies. As W. Lloyd Warner, *et al.*, have shown in their massive review of this process in our society:

Well over four million small profit-making enterprises are a significant part of our economic life; there are thousands of small local governments and, by estimate, possibly several million small social, civic, and other voluntary associations. Although the number of religious denominations with more than 10,000 members is probably less than two hundred, there are thousands of small sects, storefront churches, and separate rural and village churches that have important functions in urban and rural change. At the foundations of our institutional structure, millions of small family units live their separate autonomous existence; yet all are part of the web of kinship that spreads from coast to coast. Extended clusters of friends and cliques and other groups of informal relations also form an important micro-social tissue of the national moral order. However, the "bony structure" of the emerging society, which gives form and mobility to its evolvement, is the large-scale organization. Of the 4,700,000 private business and industrial enterprises in the United States, only 21,000, less than one-half of one percent, have a net worth of over a million dollars. Yet this tiny fraction controls two-thirds of the national sales volume, employs four out of every ten workers, and pays half of all salaries and wages of private enterprise.

9. The actual number of giant corporations believed to dominate our society varies anywhere from one to many hundreds. It is all a question of how one wants to cut the pie.

Since its beginning the federal government has grown enormously. In 1790 there were approximately 1,000 civilian employees, according to estimations for that time; by 1800 perhaps some 3,000 were employed; by 1860 this number had grown to 37,000, an increase of some thirty-seven times; and by 1960 the number had increased to 2,400,000. Comparisons of the rates of growth of big government and the American society are revealing. From 1860 to 1960 the United States population and its work force increased approximately six times as against over sixty times for federal civilian employees. The Washington government work force increased one hundred times during that period. Meanwhile, the Gross National Product (GNP) increased some seventy times from 1870 (when figures are available) to 1960, whereas federal expenses increased over two hundred times.

In brief, although our society has greatly expanded in population, in economic ability, and in capacity to use its natural environment and its technological base, the institutions of the federal government have increased in size and probably in strer_th far more rapidly. Government in America is by far the biggest hierarchical organization.[10]

As John Kenneth Galbraith and others have tried to show, there appears to be a basic relationship between the growth of technology and the increasing centralization of economic activities in our society, with growing technology leading to ever more centralized production.[11]

The centralization of economic activity has been closely paralleled and reinforced by the centralization of population, communication, education, government, and many other realms of our social life. Because all of these have grown in size, because they have such basic effects on our society, and because their effects are so intertwined with each other,

10. See W. Lloyd Warner, et alia., The Emergent American Society: Large Scale Organizations, Vol. 1, New Haven: Yale University Press, 1967, pp. 5–6.
11. See John Kenneth Galbraith, The New Industrial State, Boston: Houghton-Mifflin Co., 1967, p. 20.

government officials have felt an increasing need to plan the various aspects of our society. Urban planning, economic planning, planning of scientific research and development work, and many other forms of planning have a growing influence on what happens in our society, even though the old laissez-faire dislike of planning has persisted and has resulted in a rhetorical defense of de-centralization, pluralism, non-planning, individual choice, private enterprise, and private initiative.

All of these developments have led Kariel and many others to conclude that our society is rapidly becoming a non-pluralistic society, a homogenized, centralized, systematized society. Analysts such as Jacques Ellul [12] have gone further by arguing that the modern technological society is a one in which individuals may *feel* free and may even have certain kinds of free choice, but in which they are inevitably constrained by the monolithic demands of the technological society. Herbert Marcuse has argued that our once free societies have unwittingly become monolithic *tyrannies:*

A comfortable, smooth, reasonable, democratic unfreedom prevails in advanced industrial civilization, a token of technical progress. Indeed, what could be more rational than the suppression of individuality in the mechanization of socially necessary but painful performances; the concentration of individual enterprises in more effective, more productive corporations; the regulation of free competition among unequally equipped economic subjects; the curtailment of prerogatives and national sovereignties which impede the international organization of resources. That this technological order also involves a political and intellectual coordination may be a regrettable and yet promising development.

The rights and liberties which were such vital factors in the origins and earlier stages of industrial society yield to a higher stage of

12. See Jacques Ellul, *The Technological Society,* New York: Random House. Also, see the collection of essays in the book I have edited on *Social Problems in a Technological Society, op. cit.*

this society: they are losing their traditional rationale and content. Freedom of thought, speech, and conscience were—just as free enterprise, which they served to promote and protect—essentially *critical* ideas, designed to replace an obsolescent material and intellectual culture by a more productive and rational one. Once institutionalized, these rights and liberties shared the fate of the society of which they had become an integral part. The achievement cancels the premises.[13]

The same kind of argument has been developed by C. Wright Mills,[14] who argues that the course of our society is increasingly being determined by a *power elite*, especially by a "military-industrial complex." This is really a modified theory of homogenization, since it begins by recognizing the existence, at least at some point in time, of independent segments of society and then argues that this independence has been undermined by coalitions between the two most important segments. This theory has gained considerable support at the common-sense level in recent years by the popularization of the Eisenhower Theory of the Military-Industrial Complex. The rapid growth in recent years of the giant conglomerates in business have accentuated these fears.

There can be no doubt that in some areas there has certainly been a rapid breakdown of previous boundaries and differences. Consider, for example, the relations between levels of government. Except for the doubtful exception of the South, regionalism and other ancient supports for federalism are rapidly decreasing in importance, especially as the mass of the population has come to live in a few giant metropolitan areas and has become nationally mobile and nationally oriented. There is rapidly emerging "one great

13. See Herbert Marcuse, *One Dimensional Man*, Boston: Beacon Press, 1967, p. 1.
14. See C. Wright Mills, *The Power Elite*, New York: Oxford University Press, 1956.

national community," as Warner and his associates have called it. The failure to change our governmental relations rapidly enough to deal with this change has been very important in producing some of our most trying social problems today.

But to jump from this to the conclusion that all of the old pluralism, or even most of it *has* disappeared or is disappearing is absurd. Much of this argument is, in fact, inspired by the assumption that American society is traditionally pluralistic and that this pluralism is only now being endangered by the "nightmarish" new forces of technology and large scale organization. There are many reasons for believing that we have not achieved that state and are a long way from it, even if it marks the general direction of much of our society.

The more extreme arguments are relatively easy to deal with because they are simplistic and extreme. The social analyses of Jacques Ellul, Herbert Marcuse and the other technicists who believe we have already seen the rise of a technological society and one-dimensional man are very largely moral arguments and seem impervious to contradictory facts. Even when they see differences and conflicts in our society, they see only a greater homogeneity: "Plus ça change, plus c'est la même chose."

Manfred Stanley has in fact analyzed the basic problems with this whole "technicist projection" and his arguments seem sound.[15] He concludes that it is difficult even to see how we would go about "testing" such arguments as the "technicist projection." This is partly because of the essentially political nature of some parts of their arguments, and certainly of the moral parts; it is also true because of the likely impossibility of ever getting sufficient comparative data to test some of the crucial aspects of such social theories. Very importantly, one feature of the argument over the

15. See M. Stanley, "The Technicist Projection," unpublished paper.

"death of pluralism" concerns the *effectiveness* of pluralistic structures in preventing the continual centralization of power by any one group or set of groups in society. The most commonly shared view of the pluralistic political theorists and practicing politicians in American society has been that the existence of many groups of nearly equal power is far more conducive to preventing such centralization of power than the existence of a few. This, for example, was the essence of Weber's theory of democracy in the Italian city states. When we consider the ease with which a few giant corporations—oligopolies—in any one industry are able to tacitly set prices through "price leadership" and to agree on many other things, we can see that there is a great deal to be said for this argument.

But there is a serious question, one which may be impossible to answer, concerning the optimal number for preventing this growing centralization of power—how many is "many"? At the present time there are somewhere between 200 and 500 giant corporations in American society. Is this the "many" that will insure optimal decentralization or must there be millions of small farmers? Might it not even be that 10 or 20 would be enough? Might it not well be that this kind of centralization of organizations is even conducive to further decentralization? Giant groups are more able to block each other than small groups. To this, of course, some of those accepting the technicist projection will simply object that the 200 or 500 are merely independent in "appearance," while "actually" (as known to these theorists, if not to those involved) having dominant, shared "class" and "corporate" interests. On certain things, such as "free enterprise," this is true of the majority of the corporations and they do act in concert on these few matters. But on the vast majority of issues they do not have such a commonality of interests and do not act in concert to centralize power in any one group. On the contrary, they jealously protect their own power by fighting such a centralization of power in any group, especially among their competing 200 to 500 firms.

On those issues where corporations do act in concert, they are at least potentially opposed by powerful labor, farm, political, professional, consumer, educational, and publishing groups. The one economic area in which there is clearly one centralized group in our society with one policy (though sometimes opposed by the ranks within the group) is that of labor, yet it is a serious question whether more labor groups would produce more effective pluralistic opposition to the centralization of power in our society. Although this is certainly an open and political question, it is at least plausible to argue that such a centralization of labor power can be conducive to a more effective block to centralization of economic power in our society because it then becomes more possible to check the (tacitly) concerted efforts of the 200 to 500 giant corporations. This is in fact the argument of the labor unions.

There are other obvious difficulties with the technicist projection which its proponents have simply refused to consider. For example, as we noted, the scientific-technological mode of thinking has become increasingly dominant in our society, yet we must not overlook the fact that in recent years there has been a growth in mysticism, astrology, Buddhism, Yoga, and other forms of the new "secret religion." Apparently, millions of people are involved in this underground movement and many of them are the educated young who have supposedly been "brainwashed" for years by the "scientistic" educators. So our society is still pluralistic and free enough to get rapid developments of oppositional points of view. This countermovement is now strong enough to inspire fears of a new wave of "irratio ism" among many, especially when seen in the light of the decreasing percentages of the best students enrolling in the sciences and engineering.

Some social scientists have even argued that this opposition to the bureaucratic forms of the technological society is producing a new form of existentially-oriented participatory-democracy. Bennis and Slater [16] have even argued that in the rapidly changing technological society only democracy, including democratic procedures *within* the technological corporations, will prove efficient enough to last.

The less extreme theories, the more middle range projections of homogeneity and centralization, are more difficult to evaluate, for, at the least, they are built on partial truths which we have already presented. What does seem clear is that most theories of the "death of pluralism" can be countered by a large body of evidence contrary to their assumption. An example of this is to be found in the literature on Power in American Society. The Marxian theory of the power elite has been systemically attacked, theoretically and factually, by such important works as Arnold Rose's *The Power Structure*.[17] In reviewing these works and analyzing the many arguments and facts contained in these opposite interpretations of power in our society today, that is, the non-monolithic theory of power and the pluralistic theory of power, social scientists have arrived at very different conclusions. Many agree with Mills' monolithic interpretation [18] and many others, probably more, agree with the pluralistic interpretation of Rose. What seems most apparent about the debate is that a strong case can be made for each position.

There is both growing homogeneity and difference, both growing centralization and decentralization in the United States today. Whether one trend will completely dominate the other in the long run it is impossible to say at this time,

16. See Warren G. Bennis and Phillip E. Slater, *The Temporary Society*, New York: Harper, 1967.

17. See Arnold Rose, *The Power Structure*, New York: Oxford University Press, 1967.

18. Mills' monolithic interpretation of power in American society has certainly been widely acclaimed by the members of the new left in recent years.

partly because the ultimate decision will be made by the individuals in our society who will choose between alternative paths of action. But it should also be noted that most social critics and social scientists have for some reason overlooked trends that appear to be gaining strength today and that are leading to *new forms of pluralism*. To some degree, critics and social scientists seem to have fallen victims to their own pessimistic theories, seeing the society as so massive, so stable, so centralized, so homogeneous, that they believe each individual must feel powerless in the society; they themselves have reacted as if they were powerless.

There are trends toward New Forms of Pluralism in our society partly because there are trends toward new forms of freedom, and there are new trends toward freedom partly because there are new forms of pluralism. In a society of massive, technologically-oriented, planned organizations, it is true that certain aspects of an individual's life, certain everyday situations, are not immediately under his control. The more centrally organized a society, the more small groups of individuals—especially experts—come to construct situations for the great mass of individuals in the society.[19] For example, as various political economists have long argued, the policies of the Board of Directors of General Motors and other giant corporations affect the lives of hundreds of thousands of individuals quite directly and of millions indirectly. Again, in any large city the planning boards and zoning boards have a very constraining effect on the everyday situations of home owners and business owners. No individual can build just any kind of building wherever

19. It is this ability of some small groups in society to construct situations for other far more numerous members of the society that produce much of the reality sociologists refer to as "social structure." To use a term like "social structure," however, obscures the realities of power. These realities are better dealt with in terms of differences in power. Rather than explaining the differences in power in terms of the "social structure," we must explain the apparent structuring of events far more in terms of differences in power.

he wishes without suffering some severe consequences, including the use of physical force to constrain him. In both cases, the individual has less freedom to construct his own situations than would an individual nineteenth century farmer who owned his own farm. The latter could build any kind of building he wanted; though he might have felt constrained by the views of his neighbors, he probably had more freedom in making his own decisions about production and about the amount of time he would spend at any given task during his day.

At the same time, the individual in modern American society has a far greater freedom in certain other respects. It is quite apparent, for example, that the nineteenth century individual had little choice other than to be a farmer, whereas any man today who acts "rationally" in view of the realistic alternatives can choose among literally tens of thousands of occupations. Again, he may be constrained by the planning board to some extent, but if he understands the nature of those plans and those zones, he can choose to live in dwellings such as apartments, trailers, cabins, boats, or types of houses, whereas the nineteenth century farmer was constrained to live in a cabin, a lean-to, or tent out of simple necessity. This conquering of natural necessities and this expansion of man's physical capacities have been the greatest contribution of technology and is, in fact, *the* purpose of technology in the modern world.

At this point the social critics of American society normally intervene to argue that the man who lives in a mass-consumption economy may be free to choose from the various alternatives, but that, in fact, these alternatives are extremely limited, even if he suffers from false consciousness to the extent of not being able to see those limitations. They would argue, for example, that individuals are, in fact, constrained to live in "ticky-tacky project houses," that they are forced to live next to the freeway, and so on. I would suggest that anyone who seriously believes this is either a victim of his own pessimism or has not known enough people in their home situations to see the absurdity of the idea. There are individuals working in every major city in the United States who live on nineteenth century farms and commute to the city to work. There are also many young Americans who have chosen to live in tents, or even in Mediterranean caves. The critics might then object that such choices can only be made at great cost, such as not being able to have a family, yet even this is not true when one examines the facts.

It seems impossible to think of trying to measure the degree of "freedom to" and "freedom from" today as compared to that in a previous day, especially since what counts most is whether individuals *feel* more free and even this is so difficult to determine. It is likely though that most Americans today are convinced that the freedom from natural necessity gained by technology and the greater promises of "freedom from" to be created by technology in the future are worthwhile. Those who have known older people from the nineteenth century, some of whom were pioneers, know how nostalgic such older people can be, and how resentful they often are of some of the changes in the modern world. Yet we know too that there are few of them who would choose to return to the simpler, more halcyon days of the frontier. They remember too well the backbreaking work of those days, the agonies of having one's children die soon after birth, the fear that the whole family might die in a plague—fears generally born of real experience of such things. However ambivalent they may be about much of the modern world—for, after all, it is a world in which to some degree they are aliens—the freedoms resulting from technology are very clear to these people.

Many of the other new forms of freedom and pluralism in our society today are also directly related to the freedoms from natural and social constraints born of technology and the affluence of the industrial society. Most importantly, there has been a great and steady increase in an individual's "free time" from the "drudgery of labor." There are, of course, the serious questions concerning the accompanying "alienation of modern men from work" which so many social critics have emphasized. Whether man in the industrial society is alienated from his labor or not is always subject to controversy. On the other hand, it is clear that modern man is plainly and simply escaping from many "labors" that he does not want to be involved in. The educated, the professionals and the executives in the society have chosen to continue working very long hours with intense concentration, presumably because they are seriously committed to their work, while the laborers have increasingly chosen to take more time off, even sacrificing some of the financial gain. There has been a steady decrease in the number of hours worked per day, per week, per year and per lifetime. Individuals start work later in life and stop earlier. Retirement age has gone down steadily while the average life expectancy has gone up. The number of hours worked during the day has gone down, the number of coffee breaks has gone up. The number of hours worked per week has decreased. All current trends point toward further decreases in hours worked by those who do not want to work. This development has had many profound consequences for the lives of large percentages of the individuals in our society.

An apparent consequence, but one which the social scientists have hardly begun to note, is that many individuals are no longer closely identified with their "occupational roles." A man need no longer identify himself or be identified by others primarily as a plumber, a carpenter, a factory worker. He is free to create for himself and dedicate himself to almost any new kind of activity. He can become a student, perhaps to develop a new occupational role. He can become a farmer, a gardener, or a moonlighter. He can choose to create a group in which he finds fulfillment. Today these possibilities are almost endless. Among the more frequently chosen today are the so-called leisure activities, such as golfing, bicycling, boating, fishing, auto-racing, motorcycle racing, sports-car racing, beach-combing, bird-watching, gardening. Each of these activities can, and freqeuntly does, become the basis for the development of a highly situated social activity of great personal importance to those who choose to become involved. Many individuals in our society choose to devote their status drivings primarily to these leisure worlds.

The critics argue that this is an "empty and false" form of pluralism. They will call it a "dropping out" or a rejecting of American society, and that it is in fact a sign of the monolithic nature of the technological society, for it so alienates individuals that they would rather not be involved. This is a possibility that must be investigated. There is also evidence that it is not true. The fact is that many of those who are involved in this kind of activity and who take their self-identities in the situated activities very seriously are also active in such things as politics. One would find that many bicyclists and even some surfers have been involved in political movements such as the Vietnam anti-war movement or more ordinary forms of political party action. Many of these people are professionals, or identify both with the profession and with their leisure world activities and with American society in general.

The growth of professional identities and groups is another new form of pluralism, possibly the most important form in the long run. As Durkheim long ago realized, in the Western technological societies groups of experts become a focal point of social identity, practical interest, and practical action. As most of the sociological studies of professions have emphasized, one of the essential aspects of professional groups in our society is independence or autonomy from most outside controls or influences. As the professional groups have grown in size and importance, they have come to have an ever greater effect on our national policies, so much so that powerful ones, such as the American Medical Association, have often been able to dictate national policies in their realm of interest and have, thereby, come to be seen by many as dictatorial and as requiring some degree of external constraint in the interests of all other groups. Since, as Machlup and other political economists have shown, the "knowledge industry" component of our society is an ever greater part of our society, involving a growing proportion of people and resources, there is every reason to believe this trend toward professionalism will continue and thus nurture a pluralism that affects the use of power at the highest levels in our society. Indeed, there is evidence that some of the professional groups, including sociology, are moving in the direction of becoming *ombudsman-professions* that seek to criticize and correct the "abuses" of professional groups and other powerful groups.

So great has the trend toward professional pluralism been that many, including scientists, have begun to fear that all unity may be lost in the society, for even the most influential and educated groups find themselves having few common interests and few means of effectively communicating with each other on important matters. The growth of specialized languages and world views reproduces some of the Babel-pluralism of the ethnically heterogeneous cities of the United States. As specialized professionalism or professional specialization has moved further downward in formal education, the dangers of disintegration have grown. In the long run this new form of pluralism could make American society more plural than it has ever been.

The freedoms from natural constraints made possible by a developing technology and industrial wealth have even begun to lead to a kind of pluralism in national identities within one nation, such as in the United States. A growing percentage of Americans are living abroad during important parts of their lives and in many cases for major parts of each year. Retired Americans are living all over the world and Americans with extended vacations are joining them. This is a reasonably recent development so it is not yet possible to say what its effects will be on the views or identities of the individuals involved; over the long run it may become one of the most important forms of pluralism in our society and in the world.

To summarize, the extreme positions on pluralism are both wrong. There are still many of the old forms of pluralism in American society. Some of these are clearly decreasing, though none seem to have disappeared. There are also new forms of pluralism that appear to be arising, though it is not yet possible to say what effects they will have on our political freedoms. At the same time there are trends toward centralization of economic and political power which could prove very dangerous for all pluralism and for freedom in our society.

On the whole, American society appears to be primarily a *social conglomerate* today, just as it has always been, rather than a social system, as many social scientists have thought. Insofar as we must make use of metaphors to inspire our thought about anything so complex as human society and human action, the *conglomerate* seems the only reasonable one. In one sense a conglomerate is a system, that is, a system with minimal assumptions concerning the interdependency of the parts: A conglomerate consists primarily of parts that are to varying degrees integrated within themselves, homogeneous in themselves, and yet not totally independent of other parts. In some way the parts are held together, are interdependent, and do move together. The question of concern to us is how the parts of the pluralistic American society are held together. What are the forms of interdependency? How do the parts move together? The basis of any adequate explanation of social order in American society will probably be found to be the relations between social power and social values.

Liberalism and the Functional Theory of Social Order

Functionalism in sociology is in part a direct outgrowth of classical English liberalism. At its base is a revised model of the liberal model of individual decision-making and its relation to social order.

The classical liberals firmly believed that social order was a direct outgrowth of individual decisions—or would be as long as government left individuals alone. In its barest and most ancient form, as found in Granville's *Analogy of the Bees*, the liberal economic assumption was that social order and the best interests of everyone would "naturally" grow out of each individual's devoting himself to his own best interest, just as beehives *supposedly* grow out of each bee's exclusive devotion to his own interests. Selfishness became the greatest virtue because it alone could insure the best interest of all, which must be social justice.

Implicit in this was that individuals would act "rationally" in making their bargains in the market, so that they would seek to maximize their own "profits," would have total information of the "real" situation, and would not seek to take advantage of the others by using power independently of rational considerations. The liberal economists, in other words, were taking all of the rest of the society for granted and assuming that they could in fact isolate economic exchanges from all considerations of the unmentioned factors. Indeed, they were even assuming that if one did focus on these factors, then all the rest could be explained and could be seen to flow from this fundamental bargain or exchange situation. This idea is compelling to men of the Western World even today, so much so that we still find even some sociologists who are transfixed by it and who spin out complex, formal theories to explain all of society on the basis of this "profit motive" and "exchange model" of human behavior, as found, for example, in the sophisticated works of George Homans.[20]

It was precisely this *radical liberalism* that the classical sociologists were unanimous in rejecting; it was precisely this rejection of the fundamental assumptions of liberalism that constituted a major stimulus to the formation of what in time was to be called functional theory. Marx, Durkheim, Weber, and most others who built classical sociology argued from many different viewpoints and with varying degrees of clarity that *the liberals had been assuming all important elements of society, the elements that in fact were essential for making any market economy and any individual exchange work—social values!* Without social values, they argued, not even exchanges could take place and certainly nothing so complex as economic contracts could be effectively used or even understood without sharing some social values. Most importantly, this economic exchange theory of society did not fit the facts and could not possibly explain social order. Indeed, if individuals were to live by contracts alone, society would almost immediately dissolve into Hobbes' nightmare of a war of all against all. In his first book, *The Division of Labor*, Durkheim was most explicit about this argument against the liberal theorists, even though his primary target, the much maligned (and unread) Herbert Spencer, was in no way a simple-minded radical liberal of the economic sort:

It is true that in the industrial societies that Spencer speaks of, just as in organized societies, social harmony comes essentially

20. See George Homans, *Social Behavior: Its Elementary Forms,* Boston: Harcourt, Brace and World, 1965.

from the division of labor. It is characterized by a co-operation which is automatically produced through the pursuit by each individual of his own interests. It suffices that each individual consecrate himself to a special function in order, by the force of events, to make himself solidary with others. Is this not the distinctive sign of organized societies?

But if Spencer has justly noted what the principal cause of social solidarity in higher societies is, he has misunderstood the manner in which this cause produces its effect, and, accordingly, misunderstood the nature of the latter . . .

. . . the conception of a social contract is today difficult to defend, for it has no relation to the facts. The observer does not meet it along this road, so to speak. Not only are there no societies which have such an origin, but there is none whose structure presents the least trace of a contractual organization. It is neither a fact acquired through history nor a tendency which grows out of historical development . . .

If this were so, we could with justice doubt their stability. For if interest relates men, it is never for more than some few moments. It can create only an external link between them. In the fact of exchange, the various agents remain outside of each other, and when the business has been completed, each one retires and is left entirely on his own. Consciences are only superficially in contact; they neither penetrate each other, nor do they adhere. If we look further into the matter, we shall see that this total harmony of interests conceals a latent or deferred conflict. For where interest is the only ruling force each individual finds himself in a state of war with every other since nothing comes to mollify the egos, and any truce in this eternal antagonism would not be of long duration. There is nothing less constant than interest. Today, it unites me to you; tomorrow, it will make me your enemy. Such a cause can only give rise to transient relations and passing associations. We now understand how necessary it is to see if this is really the nature of organic solidarity.[21]

21. E. Durkheim, *The Division of Labor,* New York: Free Press, 1964, pp. 200–204.

Durkheim went on to argue that this was not the basis of organic solidarity, but that, rather, the organic solidarity of modern societies is based on functional interdependency between the specialized tasks ("roles") of labor and on the *social constraint derived from shared values in society.*

By the time of his work on *Suicide* Durkheim had moved even further from the liberal economic ideas, with the consequence that he was no longer concerned with "social functions" (a point often overlooked by his functional admirers). He was now convinced that society is a "moral phenomenon," that the essence of the social effect on man is "constraint," and that constraint is derived from, and works because it is applied in terms of, the shared morality of the members of society.

This same path of development was much later to be followed by the greatest work of the entire structural-functional tradition, Talcott Parsons' *The Structure of Social Action.*[22] Beginning with his whimsical statement of his problem ("Spencer is dead. But who killed him and how? This is the problem."), and progressing through his massive scholarly comparisons of Marshall, Pareto, Durkheim and Weber, Parsons concludes that, indeed, society is a moral phenomena and that social order is the direct outgrowth of the common morality of the members of society.

But for all of their killing of Spencer, these functionalists still assumed that *individual values and decision making taken in the aggregate* are sufficient for the production of social order. (It is true that Durkheim's belief that social morals, or the laws, could not be directly inferred from individual consciousness was somewhat contrary to this idea, as are parts of the works of all of the others, but the general trend of their thought is still there.) This conclusion was the direct result of the assumptions of moral

22. See Talcott Parsons, *The Structure of Social Action*, Glencoe: The Free Press, 1949.

absolutism and moral determinism: if all individuals of society do have the same morality (or the same for all sociological purposes) and if that absolute morality is the basic determinant of what goes on in society, then it makes good sense to conclude that this absolute consensus will provide the basis for common decision making by rulers and ruled alike. *The result is that power can be ignored in one's analyses of society: power will necessarily be administered in accord with the absolute moral consensus, so it is not an independent determinant of what happens in society.*

The liberal theory had *de-politicized* economics, so that one would conclude that government should stay entirely out of economic activity and leave it all up to the "automatic and natural" workings of the market. Similarly, the functional theory *de-politicized power* in general, so that one naturally would conclude that the official power necessarily has authority, that social control by officials is necessary and "functional," and that deviance from official rules necessarily causes or even constitutes social disorganization or disintegration. It was this democratic de-politicization of social theory and methods that more than anything else prepared the way for the *official sociology of deviance* in the United States.

I have said that all of this was the outgrowth of the *structural-functional* theory. This is obviously not entirely true. As we all know, C. Wright Mills, at least in his later years, was a "structural-functionalist," yet he and many others like him, including Herbert Marcuse, who was greatly influenced by Mills' structural ideas, arrived at completely opposite conclusions. Mills and these others politicized almost everything and considered institutionalized power, now often called the "Establishment" by his very young friends, to be immoral and in conflict with the best interests of the great majority of the members of our society.

What we have here is a verbal confusion, caused primarily

by the recent preempting of the general terms of "structure" and "function" to cover the very special ideas of a small group of professional sociologists. The most basic meaning of *structure* is simply that of the *ordering of parts,* though there is closely associated with the term as well the connotation of a *stable* ordering of parts; and the most basic meaning of *function* is that of an *interdependency of parts.* In this sense, Mills and everyone in the Marxist tradition are very much structural-functionalists, because they believe that there is an absolute *ordering and interdependence of the parts* of society, yet they claim this ordering and interdependency is *caused by power,* not by any absolute shared morality. Indeed, to them, what is commonly called morality, such as the morals of Christianity, is merely part of the opiate of the masses, something engineered by the "oppressors" at the top of the "power structure." Generally "structural-functionalism" has come to be so exclusively associated with the positions of Durkheim, Merton, and Parsons, that most sociologists would probably define it as meaning that there is some structure based on shared values in which the parts are functionally related to each other in such a way that control agents enforce the shared values to maintain the boundaries of society. In this usage "structure" has come to be identical with the patterns of absolutely shared values and "functions" identical with the interdependency assumed to be reinforcing those shared values. The result is that both those who reject liberalism *in toto* and go to the extreme in politicizing everything, in making everything dependent on power independently of shared values, and those who merely revise liberalism to produce a system of thought that shares the democratic assumptions of liberalism and provides a "scientific" rationale for official power are called by the same name.

The differences, though, are very real. These are opposite points of view, each of which I believe had some element of truth but which totally distort the truth about our society by carrying a few points to the extreme and then insisting on interpreting everything in society in those terms.

Power, Moral Consensus and The Construction of Social Order in The Pluralistic Society

To the liberal social theorists power was in no way considered necessary for the maintenance of social order. Belief in an absolutely shared morality, absolute knowledge, and absolute rationality made power completely irrelevant. No central control of social activities was relevant because social order was believed to necessarily flow from rational market considerations.

To the traditional functionalists power was considered to be necessary, but only as *legitimate power* or *authority*. The absolute morality itself was believed to generate tendencies toward deviance (as we saw in our analysis of Merton's theory in Chapter 2), but, like all *simple systems*, society was assumed to be self-correcting and equilibrated. Power, then, would be used legitimately by appointed officials to control the socially caused deviants so as to "maintain the boundaries" of the social system. Whereas power was thus considered essential, it was not necessary to consider it explicitly in any analysis of society, for it was assumed to be completely dependent on the absolutely shared social values. Being solely a "dependent variable," it could be considered nonproblematic. Hence politics, as *conflictful* social action directed at controlling resources and people in society, was irrelevant.

Both liberal theory and functional theory fail in two interdependent ways. They fail in theory and, consequently, they fail in practice.

Liberal theory failed in practice first, because it was unable to predict or control the chaos of the market place (depression, panic, etc.) that had been created by a largely unbridled application of the theory. Second, it failed because *the very assumptions of liberal theory denied it the means to effectively resist its enemies.* Polanyi brilliantly recognized this in his analysis of the fate of the Weimar Republic and the subsequent siege of Western civilization:

Freedom's utter frustration in fascism is, indeed, the inevitable result of the liberal philosophy, which claims that power and compulsion are evil, that freedom demands their absence from a human community. No such thing is possible; in a complex society this becomes apparent. This leaves no alternative to either to remain faithful to an illusionary idea of freedom and deny the reality of society, or to accept that reality and reject the idea of freedom. The first is the liberal's conclusion; the latter the fascist's. No other seems possible. Inescapably we reach the conclusion that the very possibility of freedom is in question. If regulation is the only means of spreading and strengthening freedom in a complex society, and yet to make use of this means is contrary to freedom *per se,* then such a society cannot be free.

Clearly, at the root of the dilemma there is the meaning of freedom itself. Liberal economy gave a false direction to our ideals. It seemed to approximate the fulfillment of intrinsically utopian expectations. No society is possible in which power and compulsion are absent, nor a world in which force has no function. It was an illusion to assume a society shaped by man's will and wish alone. Yet this was the result of a marketview of society which equated economics with contractual relationships, and contractual relations with freedom. The radical illusion was fostered that there is nothing in human society that is not derived from the volition of individuals and that could not, therefore, be removed again by their volition. Vision was limited by the market which "fragmented" life into the producers' sector that ended when his product reached the market, and the sector of the consumer for whom all goods sprang from the market. The one derived his income "freely" from the market, the other spent it "freely" there. Society as a whole remained invisible. The power of the State was of no account, since the less its power, the smoother the market mechanism would function. Neither voters, nor owners, neither producers, nor consumers could be held responsible for such brutal restrictions of freedom as were involved in the occurrence of unemployment and destitution. Any decent individual could imagine himself free from all responsibility for acts of compulsion on the part of a State which he, personally, rejected; or for economic suffering in society from which he, personally, had not benefited. He was "paying his way," was "in nobody's debt," and was unentangled in the evil of power and economic value. His lack of responsibility for them seemed so evident that he denied their reality in the name of his freedom.[23]

This same failure of liberalism has been repeated many times in Western societies, especially in the more complex ones, for it is the pluralism of values and political groups that ultimately frustrates liberalism. Indeed, so contrary is it to the liberal's world perspective that he is utterly dumbfounded when his beliefs are overturned by the facts of reality; often he is unable to make any sense out of what has happened. He is trapped by his liberal perspective and cannot respond adaptively to the new situation. (Those of us who have at some time lived inside the liberal perspective know how totally foreign the idea of using force is, even to uphold *the* fundamental value and assumption of the whole perspective—freedom. Power becomes unthinkable.) This is all the more true when the liberals have in fact lived in a relatively homogeneous society or part of society in which the liberal can find his only home. (It is certainly no accident that England, one of the few homogeneous Western societies, was the only nation in which classical liberalism was highly developed and briefly held sway in practice. But, then, the English did not practice this liberalism in their relations

23. See Karl Polanyi, *The Great Transformation*, New York: Holt, Rinehart, 1949.

with the Scotch or Irish, especially the revolutionaries, or the colonies.)

In recent years this ancient fate of liberalism has had to be acted out again in American universities. Since their foundings the American universities have been among the only relatively homogeneous public groups. Their students, faculties, and administrators have been middle-class, white, and Northern European in origins and in goals; they have been planted in the Medieval traditions of academic, cloistered life. Sometime in the 1930's a change began that accelerated after the Second World War. The universities became the mobility path for ethnic groups, meaning the lower class; the faculties fractionated as specialization rapidly increased; the administrators moved away from the ancient life of learning to find money for the great building programs and for more specialists; and increasingly the faculties left the cloister to become official researchers and businessmen. Through all of this the academics remained totally liberal in their views on politics and force, while eschewing all liberal views in economics.

When the growing differences within the universities were then inspired by the passions of war and race the inevitable use of power by some groups against others began. The liberal perspective was confronted with its one impossibility, the one thing that cannot be considered—force. Liberals then began their ancient search for "their mistakes," assuming that they must have somehow failed to be totally rational in their bargaining with the students in the great market place of ideas. The use of force grew, presumably because its users recognized how effective it was against what they saw as the "Great Jelly-Fish." The liberal academies' understanding was dumbfounded by this "irrational" use of force, they were further fractionated, and action was paralyzed.

The ancient fate of true liberals was acted out once again:

they were forced to give in to all demands backed by force, with the result that they supported measures opposed to freedom and totally contradictory to all of their fundamental principles.[24]

Classical liberalism failed in practice because its theory of social order proved false for such a highly pluralistic society as America. It fails to see the fundamental problems of morality, beliefs, and practical decisions that inevitably occur. It fails to see that any given idea, policy, or decision for action in a pluralistic society will inevitably be seen as morally and ideationally wrong by some important parts of the society; that is, it fails to see that the pluralistic society at any given time is necessarily absurd, both morally and ideationally, for part of its population. This absurdity cannot be bridged by any simple appeal to morality, though the appeals to overlapping morality and beliefs and the appeals to future benefits—compromises—to be gained by going along with the present absurdities are the most important tactical devices used to maintain social order in situations of this sort. Given this social absurdity, and the obvious human proclivity for appealing to force as a continuation of serious political arguments by other means, *the use of power independently of moral considerations becomes a necessity in constructing social order in a complex and pluralistic society.*

This theoretical failure of classical liberalism to see the necessity of independent power is also the fundamental failure of the functional theory of social order, but the practical failure of functionalism has never been so complete, both because it does not share the fundamental weakness of liberalism on and because it has never been given much of a test. The practical application of functional analysis would consist in treating society as a simple system, primarily by seeking to apply to society a set of values assumed to be absolute.

24. This is quoted in Carl Friedrich, "Democracy and Dissent," *Political Quarterly* 10(October, 1939), pp. 571–582.

The whole tendency would be toward repression of any "deviance": that is, the practical functionalist would seek to "maintain the social patterns" at all cost. Presumably, such a society or group would be some kind of functional theocracy in which those dedicated most to the absolute values would institute "social control" measures to "control" the deviance inevitably caused by society. These officials would indeed use power to maintain "social control," but it would be authority, since they would be presumed to be acting in terms of the unchanging values to truly maintain the eternal patterns of society. So the exercise of power would not itself generate the deviance that tends to make for less "pattern maintenance."

There have been many theocracies in the Western world in which the theocrats sought to create and maintain "The City of God" on earth. And they have in fact made precisely the same kinds of "simplifying assumptions" about man and society made by the functional analysts, which have then led them to totally repressive measures. Calvin's Geneva is an obvious example, but the best examples would be the hundreds of utopian communities started in the United States. All of these simple societies have failed, in spite of their highly repressive measures intended to "maintain social boundaries" (quite literally in most cases, since they felt they could succeed only if they cut off their "Cities of God" from the surrounding "Cities of Mammon"). There is something inimical in our complex world to the existence of simple societies, something that even those who strive mightily to maintain their "social boundaries" cannot overcome. That something is complexity itself, which makes it impossible to live by morals alone.

In our own "Cities of Mammon," probably the only major attempt to apply the functional theory to society is that of the official agents of control, who, as we have seen, have been a major source of support for this kind of sociology as well as originally a source of such a theory. Although there are undoubtedly many instances in which officials look at themselves as the upholders of righteousness and seek to carry out the mandates of the absolute morality, we have every reason to believe that these fits of righteousness are infrequent. The reason is simple. Any official who seriously tried to uphold the absolute morality would soon be overwhelmed in every way—and dismissed. For example, if any police department suddenly decided to arrest all those individuals they discovered committing felonies, the department and all legal and judicial organizations in the area would be overwhelmed in a day or two. The officials would also be faced by angry outcries from every major group in their area, and be dismissed. The officials may believe in the absolute morality, at least for the "public" who are assumed to need protection from themselves, even if the officials have to violate some of that morality to provide that protection. But their public support for it is primarily rhetorical and their public statements about acting in terms of it are primarily self-presentations. As we have seen, they in fact invoke and enforce rules very selectively.

Having argued the need for the exercise of power independently of social values and beliefs in order to construct social order, we must hasten to insist that this independence will only be partial if the attempts to construct social order are to be successful. The social power will not be successful in achieving this goal if enough people resist, and in America the willingness to actively resist official power is great. In fact, though the power of the official agents of control has increased in the last hundred years, the legally sanctioned power of these agents is still relatively small compared to that exercised by officials in many societies. Because of their relatively small legal power, officials have to rely primarily on something other than power to construct social order.

One thing they utilize is shared meanings. As the functionalists have argued, there are important shared meanings in American society. But the important questions here concern the degree of sharedness, which shared meanings are really important in constructing social order, and how they are important.

Certainly it is clear that there are disagreements about everything within a society so complex as ours. There are undoubtedly many thousands of individuals who are privately in favor of anything, even the most heinous of crimes. While there are few *public* supporters for these crimes, there are large groups of public supporters for almost any other position. Motherhood and apple pie are frequently used in platitudes as examples of the universal agreement in our society, yet today there are thousands of people who are vociferously against motherhood for anyone, and certainly there are thousands who are against apple pie, at least for themselves. It would make little sense, then, to search for universal agreement. When we say that there are certain shared meanings, values, and beliefs in America we are not speaking of universality. We are speaking of those shared meanings about which the most important groups are publicly agreed, so much so that the opponents of such views would find it difficult to get much of a hearing. And if they did get a hearing, they would generally be attacked by the others.

Citizenship is one of these meanings. Like members of other national groups, Americans are so firmly agreed on the nature and importance of membership in American society that these are taken for granted. The majority have a clear idea of what constitutes an American and how it fits themselves. In addition, this self-identification is taken to be extremely important and not something that more than a small minority would consider giving up. Even the so-called "radicals" who attack American policies and styles of life rarely consider the possibility of giving up their identity as Americans. When the radical right attacks them and argues that they should "love it or leave it" they hardly know how to respond. Contrary to what many on the radical right appear to believe, most radical leftists show no inclination to leave America.

This common conception of membership and of the importance of this membership is of relevance in determining what happens in the society. The sense of all being in the same boat and, therefore, of all having to live together in some way, becomes a very important support for compromise strategies which we shall soon discuss. In general, it helps greatly to prevent the polarizations that can lead to secession movements and civil wars. In this way, it is a vital element in constructing social order.

Other meanings which appear to be almost universally shared and which contribute to the construction of social order are the *procedural rules*. The procedural rules are those concerning the ways in which individuals will go about agreeing and disagreeing about anything. They are the rules by which individuals seek to govern their relations with each other, for reaching common decisions that will be accepted by all parties to the decision. There are no doubt disagreements about the procedural rules that anyone might propose to use in any one situation. But there is an almost universal agreement about the rules called "democratic government." Most Americans are fundamentally in favor of democratic procedures, though they may at times disagree about some of the situational interpretations of this abstract agreement.

Most Americans take it for granted that the right way to reach a decision when there is disagreement or conflict of interest is to take a count of how many people are in favor of what position, and then to proceed in accord with that position. This *rule of the majority* is learned at a very young age and applied in almost every realm of everyday life, from presidential elections to sandlot baseball games. It is omnipresent, so that the individual who explicitly opposes it, rather than covertly going around it, will find that most Americans react with a sense of horror at his "total unfairness" or his "dictatorial view." This is almost certainly the basic reason for the explosive sense of outrage expressed against the New Left, which explicitly opposes the rule of the majority. This rule is so taken for granted that it often overrides those other procedural rules that have been built into many of our political institutions. For example, the rules protecting the rights of minorities are often violated because the rule of the rights of the majority is overriding. There are problems involved in the concrete interpretation of this procedural rule, and there are many conscious violations of it in the United States, yet it is probably the most universally shared rule that is of direct relevance to the construction of social order.

In addition to sharing this kind of procedural rule, Americans generally agree concerning the specific structures established in our society for reaching decisions through the use of such procedural rules. There is a general acceptance of the local, state, and federal governments as the appropriate bodies for making public decisions in the society. Few people seek to overthrow the government at any level.

Few other social meanings are so generally shared by members of our society; yet even the importance of these in maintaining social order have been disputed by some of the theorists of political pluralism. The classical theory of political pluralism in the Anglo-Saxon societies, as proposed by Balfour, assumed that some underlying agreements were necessary to prevent the differences in our pluralistic societies from producing social conflicts that would lead to the disintegration of such societies: "Our whole political machinery presupposes a people so fundamentally at one that they can safely afford to bicker."

But this assumption has been attacked many times by

political theorists in the twentieth century. Probably the most important attack was that made by Carl Friedrich in 1939. Arguing that this insistence on some kind of fundamental unity is the basic assumption of totalitarianism, which goes back to Hobbes and to Rousseau's theory of the general will, Friedrich argued:

It seems highly questionable whether fundamental agreement, or the absence of dissent in matters of basic significance, is really a necessary or even a desirable condition for a constitutional democracy. When one considers the frantic efforts which the totalitarian regimes are making to secure uniformity of opinion and belief, one is bound to ask whether this insistence upon agreement on fundamentals, far from being an essential concomitant of democracy, is not really alien to its very conception.[25]

Friedrich then proceeds to argue that the constitutional democracies are found to exist and to be most secure in those societies in which there is the least basic agreement on such matters as cultural customs, values, and beliefs. Switzerland and the United States are the obvious examples and he made the most of them, arguing that in the American case there is fundamental disagreement among the many ethnic groups on just these matters.

Then he turns to "fundamental agreements." Must there not at least be some agreement on fundamental procedural questions? Must there not at least be fundamental agreement to disagree and to seek some compromise solution without fighting about it? This is the most widely shared and accepted interpretation given to the classical theory of order in a pluralistic society, so it is crucial to his argument. Friedrich concludes that no such procedural agreement is necessary because there are in fact common behavioral patterns lying behind such procedural agreements:

25. *Ibid.*

In a recent discussion, Professor Hula, in insisting upon agreement on fundamentals, has said: "Democracy is doomed when there is not, or is no longer, common agreement at least on the point that political decisions have to be based rather on consent than on force. There can be no doubt that such an agreement presupposes in itself common fundamental objectives." W. Y. Elliott added that "one of the most fundamental points of agreement is the ability to put up with disagreement." In speaking thus, Elliott and Hula undoubtedly expressed opinions which are widely held today. And there can be no argument that up to a certain point the disposition and readiness to agree to disagree is a concomitant of democratic life. But is not this true of all social life? It seems to me that what we are dealing with here is not a fundamental view on which people agree, but a behavior pattern according to which people conduct themselves.[26]

It would appear here that Friedrich has simply given a different meaning to "agreement on fundamentals" than most of us would expect. He is apparently arguing that no agreement on the fundamentals of idealogy—of abstract values and beliefs—is necessary as long as there is agreement in the patterns of behavior, some customary working-out of differences in everyday, practical activities. And this impression is strongly reinforced later:

There must, of course, be common objectives. Democratic behavior is pragmatic in that it tends to concentrate upon practical tasks in the realization of which men of very different general outlook can collaborate. Such common objectives as security and order permit of a large measure of effective collaboration, when the concrete aspects of their content are emphasized.[27]

Basically, then, Friedrich was arguing that the capacity to rule ourselves by democratic procedures comes not from some abstract agreement about the value or morality of doing

26. *Ibid.*
27. *Ibid.*

such a thing, but, rather, from the practical realities of everyday life, which involve the use of customary ways of handling people with potentially conflicting points of view and interests. We have more than an interesting linguistic shift here. This view is relevant because it is a reasonably clear statement of the views of some of the most important practicing politicians in American history and because it hits a fundamental truth.

The classical common-sense theory of pluralism and democratic procedures, as practised and partially expounded by American politicians has been well summarized by Robert Dahl:

The theory and practise of American pluralism tend to assume, as I see it, that the existence of multiple centers of power, none of which is wholly sovereign, will help (may indeed be necessary) to tame power, to secure the consent of all, and to settle conflicts peacefully:

Because one center of power is set against another, power itself will be tamed, civilized, controlled, and limited to decent human purposes, while coercion, the most evil form of power, will be reduced to a minimum.

Because even minorities are provided with opportunities to veto solutions they strongly object to, the consent of all will be won in the long run.

Because constant negotiations among different centers of power are necessary in order to make decisions, citizens and leaders will perfect the precious art of dealing peacefully with their conflicts, and not merely to the benefit of one partisan but to the mutual benefit of all the parties to a conflict.

These are, I think, the basic postulates and even the unconscious ways of thought that are central to the American attempt to cope with the inescapable problems of power, conflict, and consent.[28]

28. See Robert Dahl, *Pluralist Democracy in the United States: Conflict and Consent,* Chicago: Rand McNally and Co., 1967, p. 24.

Dahl was able to present evidence from the writings of the Founding Fathers to show how much they thought in such terms: pluralism and democratic procedures require each other for very practical reasons. The same point of view is found repeatedly in the most diverse sources. A good example is the recent argument by Bennis and Slater that some kind of "participatory democracy" will necessarily grow in modern industries and that democratic governments will become more common around the world because only the democratic procedures are efficient in a rapidly changing technological society.[29]

Although most of these scholarly and common-sensical theories miss some crucial points about pluralism, democratic procedural rules, and social order in our society, they generally include several fundamental truths that have come out of their observations of the ways things are done in this society. The major insight is the recognition that *the democratic procedural rules grow out of practical, everyday attempts by those involved to achieve practical purposes (at-hand) as a result of the recognition that compromise is necessary in situations involving pluralistic differences over basic values, beliefs and interests.* The democratic procedural rules are those ways of achieving compromise solutions to conflicts in a pluralistic society or situation that involve the minimum potential loss to the maximum number involved. In other words, the democratic rules are a kind of minimax strategy for the most people, the majority, involved in any situation in which no coalition can hope to achieve enough power in the situation to dictate the terms to all others.

However, a basic mistake, often made by theorists such as Friedrich and Dahl, is to believe that this kind of procedural rule grows *naturally* out of the pluralistic situation. This is another variant of the error of total situationalism,

29. See Warren G. Bennis, and Slater, *The Temporary Society, op. cit.*

of seeing the meanings of things as coming entirely from the situation at hand. If that were the case, then all pluralistic situations and societies would arrive at democratic-compromise procedural rules. Clearly, this is false. Russia is one of the most pluralistic societies in the world, but it is also one of the most tyrannical.

The democratic-procedural rules in certain Western societies came about only as the result of centuries of experiences involving crucial situational constructions of meanings for the purposes-at-hand that were then transmitted to other situations (as abstract meanings). We have mentioned the long tradition of feudal compormises, such as the Magna Carta, which grew out of special situations and were transmitted. It took almost a century of religious wars to produce such simple compromises as the acceptance of the principle that "cuius regio, euius religio" (who rules shall have the right to determine religion) or the theory of tolerance, which made religious pluralism not only a fact of life but an abstract idea that could be transmitted and used in different situations. Centuries of struggle lay behind the principle of free speech as a way of preventing violent conflicts between differing groups.[30] All of these were partially embodied in the everyday lives of the American colonists and were known to the founders of the American Constitution and to many later politicians. Their constructions of the Constitution, of various American institutions, and of much later legislation made use of both their practical experience involving these ideas in taken-for-granted form and their scholarly understanding of these ideas and of centuries of experience with them. Historical studies were important to almost all of these "practical" men. When Jefferson, Adams, Madison and most of the others wanted to understand something or to convince their fellows of a point, they often made extensive

30. Historians have generally dealt with this problem in terms of the development of "tolerance."

use of historical evidence. But it is equally true that they used history in the light of their practical experience and of what they were trying to get done at the time: they were theoretical and practical in the same way most men are. They were social planners on a grand scale and all effective social planning involves a marriage of convenience between abstract theory and concrete practice.

The democratic procedural rules are only the most important and widely shared forms of compromise used by Americans to construct social order. In addition, there is a generalized recognition and acceptance of pluralism and the resulting need for compromise, though this by no means prevents the simultaneous existence and use of absolutism. The recognition and acceptance of compromise are fundamental reasons for the basic separation of public and private in our everyday lives and for the insistence on such compromise values as tolerance in the public realms of life. In politics, which is the one realm in which the pluralistic parts of our society come together systematically to clash over conflicting values, beliefs, and interests, there are many ways in which the need for compromise is explicitly recognized. Compromise itself has become a major value of political activity in our society and any group that refuses to compromise its position may be stigmatized as fundamentalist and largely excluded from participation.

This is not to say that these matters are not extremely problematic. The very question of what is public is problematic. The question of what aspects of a group's life has such bearing on the general welfare of all groups that they must compromise on that aspect is highly problematic. This has arisen many times over the ethnic or religious control of the education of the children of any group. The bitter conflicts over community control of education and Black studies are only the latest in this unending battle. The uses of rules concerning compromise are almost as problematic as the uses of other rules. It is common for individuals to make demands in anticipation of using the rule of compromise to better their position; that is, they initially demand much more than they expect they can get so that when the other side does compromise they will, they hope, be better off than if they had made lesser demands at the start. This "anticipatory compromise" strategy is even institutionalized in certain realms of our society, such as in our present system of "bargain justice." The same insistence on "give-and-take," runs throughout our society.

The insistence on compromise solutions and the exclusion of everything but what is seen as necessary from the public realm, hence from the realm of public control, leads to a pervasive *negative rule of decision-making* in American public life. As almost all experienced politicians, salesmen, government workers, bureaucrats, and teachers know, working with the public involves conflict. There are so many different ways of looking at things, so many conflicting interests, and often so many problems in communicating, that most of those dealing with the public develop a *trouble-avoidance strategy.* They have the "interactional radar" that Riesman thought so characteristic of all Americans today: [31] They watch for the differences and try to avoid them by simply leaving them alone. They seek to leave everything alone that is not essential to getting the job at hand done. Perhaps this is the key to the vaunted American "genius of organization"—a high degree of *situational specialization* that goes beyond role specialization.

For public officials this rule is carried further to become the all-purpose rule of bureaucracy: don't do anything until it is necessary, until someone complains or threatens to cause you trouble if you don't do it. This may look like a rule of laziness, but it is really a rule for minimizing trouble and,

31. See David Riesman, *The Lonely Crowd,*

since the public realm is the realm of troubles, it makes good sense from the standpoint of the public worker.

In the realm of political decision-making this rule leads to the *crisis-intervention strategy* that so many social scientists have criticized. That is, the government, whether liberal or conservative, tends to avoid doing anything until a sense of "crisis" has grown so that the public is demanding immediate action, complaining that the government is not doing what is necessary to solve troubles. Then the government acts to avoid the troubles, or the public sense of troubles. This strategy is intimately tied up with the strategy of doing for the people only what they cannot do for themselves. The two combined help to avoid, or appear to those involved to minimize, the troubles they face from a set of groups with conflicting ideas about what should and can be done. By avoiding trouble in this way one also avoids potential conflicts in the society. If a given group must do what it wants for itself, then the other groups are far less apt to attack the government for helping "them" and not "us." From the standpoint of most Americans in many situations most other Americans are "thems," that is, people with whom one does not have sufficient common interest to benefit by their good fortune.

At the same time, and for the same reasons, all levels of government must seek goals that are general enough (or vague enough) to be or appear to be common to a large number of the conflicting groups. As the government has increasingly initiated and maintained investment and financial policies (especially taxation policies), it has become necessary to emphasize *least-common denominator goals*, that is, goals calculated to appeal to the greatest possible number of people. Apparently, the most successful least-common denominator goals have proved to be those of national security (we're all in this together), gross national product (everyone benefits to some extent through the trickle-down system), and health (everyone has a body that will someday cause him pain and death, both of which almost everyone wants to avoid). Increasingly the government officials present their policies to the public in terms of their potential contributions to the attainment of these goals.

While Galbraith and many other social critics have attacked this policy as failing to meet many of the "real needs" of the society and inspired by the needs of the giant corporations,[32] they too have failed to see that these may be the only goals for which sufficient consensus can be created to allow the government to act. In many cases the politicians use these goals as umbrellas to gain support for projects with only very limited, if any, relevance to the immediate goals of health, wealth, and security. (Certainly this is true of much of the social science research that has been "bootlegged" by the defense department, and all experienced social scientists are well aware of how to go about relating their research to "mental health," whatever the research might be.) These are abstract goals which can be used to construct situational legitimizations for other concrete goals.

If these measures fail, the politicians can fall back on a call to "patriotism," to being in favor of something because it is good for the country. This does have some appeal because, as we have argued, almost all Americans do have some commitment to being Americans and to the best interests of the whole nation; but the appeal seems to be weak in any instance other than that of a foreign threat because everything else involves our internal conflicts.

All attempts to construct social order in this society would probably be quite ineffective, without the use of far greater force, if there were not certain other characteristics of this conglomerate society. (In fact, the use of totalitarian methods to integrate such pluralistic societies as Russian society may

32. See John Kenneth Galbraith, *The New Industrial State, op. cit.*

be due primarily to their lack of these other factors.) Probably the most important is the overlapping of memberships and identities. If individuals lived and identified entirely within their own segments of the society, so that we had a Byzantine type of society, then they would have little reason other than the fear of force to work together or not to use force against each other. When memberships and identities do overlap, it becomes hard to attack the other groups in which individuals also have some involvement. These overlappings create blocks to the spreading of conflicts in the same way in which overlapping clan loyalties block the spread of clan warfare in some simple societies (such as the Tiv of Nigeria). Given a multiplicity of interests and identities resulting from different, overlapping involvements, and given the great multiplication of compromises resulting from having to consider possible future relations with other groups, we get a vast number of checks against spreading conflicts.[33]

We find the greatest potential for conflict in our society when overlapping of memberships and identities decreases. The dangers of such segmenting in the society are so great and the members of our society so conscious of the problems involved in constructing social order and in avoiding social conflicts, that it has been given a special name in our society, *polarization*. If carried to the extreme, polarization can produce groups with completely opposite points of view, attacking each other as enemies. The classic example in our society is the Civil War, which was preceded by several decades of increasing segmentation and isolation of the South from the North and the West. In the beginning of the conflict there were many Southerners who openly supported the Northern policies of doing away with slavery and weak-

33. See Clifford Geertz, *The Religion of Java*, New York: Free Press, 1960, pp. 355–381. Also, see Henry Magid, *English Political Pluralism*, New York: AMS Press, 1966, pp. 77–79.

ening State's rights. But as the conflict grew, as Southerners withdrew from the North, as they came more and more to see the North as their enemy, these overlapping memberships and identities decreased considerably. In our present period of great conflict among ethnic groups, class groups, and other groups, there is much talk about polarization and most members of the society, certainly those writing in the mass media, see it as a grave danger portending social conflicts of ever greater proportion. If such polarization continues, then they probably will prove to be quite right—conflict will increase.

Because of this consciousness of the dangers of polarization, Americans have created many ways to increase the amount of overlapping membership and identity. The attempt to move people into the "mainstream of American life," as it is called these days in the mass media, has taken several forms. Probably the most important form is the *melting-pot institutions* that we find throughout our society.

The public schools are probably the foremost example of the melting-pot institutions. Their purpose is to "bring all peoples into the Mainstream of American life," to teach them the fundamentals of the public morality so that they can act "correctly" in the public realm, regardless of what they do privately. Schools do this by teaching English, the basic methods of making a living, courtesy, patriotism, tolerance, and so on. For almost all ethnic groups the public schools have been the primary method of entering the public realm ("mainstream") of American life, and it has been the schools, as a result, which have contributed most to breaking the earlier exclusive identification with the parent's ethnic group. The schools have been the place where the children learn to be ambivalent about their ethnic identity and to assume the public ways of life, at least for public purposes.

In recent years there has been great conflict over the melting-pot effects of the schools, from the elementary to the college levels. Many public officials have complained that the schools have for some reason been failing to effectively "melt" the Negro population in the large cities. One sector of the Negro population has made growing attacks on the schools for the very idea of trying to "melt" the Negro children into the mainstream. While there may have been some exceptions, most ethnic group members have probably had the same feelings. They have no doubt resented the ways in which the schools have made their children ambivalent about their original ethnic cultures. The fact is that the American schools, like most all important public institutions, have been dominated by the Anglo-Saxon groups. American public life is distinct from that of any other major national society in the world, including English society; American public life is also more like English life, and, perhaps, like life in other Northern European societies, than it is like public life in the other societies from which the major ethnic groups have come. As many critics of the melting-pot institutions have argued in recent years, this dominance in the public realm of a very few of the many ethnic groups in our society is a partial "failure" of pluralism. It is one of the ways in which the essential pluralism in our society is modified such that social order becomes possible without the use of a high degree of independent force.

Contrary to what many have argued in recent years, this domination by the Anglo-Saxon American groups in the public realm has not been due to any conspiracy to keep down the other ethnic groups. Certainly there have been important movements against the various Southern Europeans (especially Catholics) and other new ethnic groups over the last one hundred or more years in the United States. We have had an undercurrent of no-nothingness throughout this time, but opposition to these new ethnic groups has not differed in kind or degree from the opposition of the new ethnic groups to the old ones or from the opposition of the new ones to each other. Moreover, while some of the no-nothing movements *have* temporarily triumphed at the local and state levels and have elected many national political figures, they have never had a dominant influence at the national level.

The public morality at the national level has always emphasized tolerance and the irrelevance of "nonessential" characteristics; rather than conspiracy or dominance by numbers, there would appear to be a primacy effect at work. The Anglo-Saxon groups were very numerous and, therefore, dominant in almost all realms of public life until about 1850. As each new wave of immigrants entered the United States, they found themselves faced with a public morality that stressed the use of English, as well as Anglo-Saxon rules of public decency, virtue, and puritanism. Although each new group struggled against these older public values, beliefs, and customs, each with varying degrees of success, none were able to overthrow them, even after the new immigrant groups had come to outnumber and politically dominate the old groups. The reason seems to be that each successive wave had accommodated in the public realm to the public morality established by the earlier group. While the public morality was probably changed by each successive struggle over its content, the Anglo-Saxon public morality had a continuing and cumulative effect. Hence, each assimilated group came to support the public morality for their public purposes, while maintaining their separate private ethnic lives. However fortunate or unfortunate it may be, there was never a large enough wave of new immigrants able to combine formally or informally in a coalition against the earlier public morality. Thus the "primacy effect" has continued up to the present day, and has apparently been the dominant influence in setting the tone of public life in America.

This same kind of primacy effect has acted in the realm of work to produce a dominant public morality. In the beginning the Anglo-Saxon groups owned almost everything. They owned the country and enlarged it through purchases from France and other countries. The desire for geographic expansion and economic growth, combined with the competitive economic arrangements in American society, led to the "Open Door Policy" on immigration and the succeeding competitive gains of the new immigrant groups. But even in one of the most competitive societies in the world, those who had the most to begin with were apt to have the most at the end of the game, because some of the informal criteria for selecting the winners in the game are that they come from or resemble the original group of owners.

This economic primacy effect and this policy of selecting in terms of social attributes has probably been decreasing in recent decades as the criterion of technical knowledge and the degree of the competitive struggle have increased, but its effects are still felt in the dominance of the Anglo-Saxon and Northern European groups in the most important forms of finance and the control of corporations. In selecting those who are to have important economic influence in our society partially in terms of their social characteristics, the Anglo-Saxon groups have been more able to set the tone of public life in American society. This dominance in the economic realm has combined with the dominance in the realm of public institutions, especially that of education, to produce a strong emphasis on conformity to the dominant public morality in American society. This dominance has led many people to mistakenly conclude that American society as a whole is dominated by a Puritan Ethic today almost as much as in an earlier age. Even in the public realm this is not exactly true, as we can see from the general public expressions of attitudes toward divorce, nudity, and almost anything else. It is, however, true that the public realm today remains more like the public realm in an earlier day than the private realms do.

This mistake of taking American public behavior as the whole life, rather than seeing it as a very special realm of life carefully and systematically situated from much of private life, has been a primary prop for the *myth of middle class morality*. And the myth of the all-dominant middle class morality has supported and been supported by the *myth of the Founding Fathers,* that is, the belief that it has always been this way, that the Founding Fathers decreed a set of sacrosanct values and beliefs that have been transmitted in all of their pristine purity. Both myths have been very successfully maintained in our society, and both certainly have some relevance to describing what can be observed in public by a stranger, or by the many millions who know better in private practice but prefer not to talk or think about it in public. These two factors combined probably account for the incorporation of the myths into the functional theories of American society, which were maintained by social scientists who, like so many millions of salesmen, were privately engaged in activities that they themselves could see as systematically violating the assumptions of the theory. Like the rest of the American "public," their belief in and espousal of these two supporting myths were also probably encouraged by other things as well.

In the first place, these social scientists are strangers to most of American life. From the standpoint of most others, they are always distrusted outsiders who must be treated as outsiders, that is, in terms of the public morality. For this reason, it is hard to see that the idea of a dominant middle class morality transmitted from the Founding Fathers over the centuries is a myth.

Another reason for most individuals' support of the myths is that their belief is itself normatively defined. As with all important social myths, it is morally wrong to attack them: it is morally wrong to say that this "social reality" is a myth. One who denies that there is this dominant, absolute middle-class morality may well be attacked as "Un-American," "a corruptor of youth," or "undermining the moral foundations of the society." He may even be "harassed" by the official control agents, the upholders of the absolutist public morality.

The proscription of any denials that there is such a set of absolute moral standards in our society, even when there are many ways in which all individuals violate this assumption, is an indication of the importance of this "social reality" in our society. It is of vital importance in our society precisely because there is so little agreement on fundamentals. In a pluralistic society there is an ever present danger of social disorder, even of social chaos. And the belief in the dangers of chaos is probably greater than the realities. These beliefs take the form of diffuse anxieties, of impending chaos and of conflicts. These fears can be seen in the fears of "crime in the streets," which bear little relation to the actual nature and patterns of crime in our society, and in the intense fear and hatred of the "anarchists" and others who "threaten the very foundations of our society." These fears and hatreds go beyond anything like the fear of losing one's property or freedom by a "Communist take-over." They are independent of most realities, but they are based on an insight into the very real problems of constructing social order in such a highly pluralistic society.

Our everyday lives are rarely torn by "senseless," "mindless" violence, and our society is rarely torn by the violent confrontations between enemy groups, yet the fact remains that most of our lives are touched *at times* by individual acts of violence and by violent conflicts between some of the massive groups in our society. We are only a few generations away from one of history's worst civil wars, a war which still has great personal importance to millions of Americans. Who is to decide that it is unrealistic to believe that it will happen again or that it is beginning to happen again? Even the most seemingly stable societies have eventually experienced great turmoil and violence. If we cannot unravel the nature of human society far better than previous societies have done, then we may expect that our society, like all previous ones, will experience chaos that can be ended only by the use of severe force. The only remaining question is when this will happen. Surely the tremendous uncertainties and conflicts being unleashed by the fundamental changes wrought by our increasing commitment to technology could be the source of such violent internal chaos.

In such an uncertain and conflictful society, the belief in an absolutist set of moral rules is important not only because it is reassuring, because it helps one to control his nightmares of social chaos and violence, but also because it helps the individuals involved in political action to solve the fundamental problems of constructing order. It does this, first of all, because the belief that a rational and ordered society is both possible and already existing gives individuals the belief that their attempts to construct social order will be successful. It gives them assurance that their nightmares are not realistic evaluations of the state of the society. It does this also by discouraging any actions that would disrupt the order in the public realm of our society which is so important in maintaining or constructing social order. The belief that there is an absolute morality governing our lives, a dominant middle-class morality, makes it appear absurd to expect or hope that one could publicly act contrary to the public morality. In seeing public morality as unassailable, they tend far more to act in accord with that morality, even if privately they do not agree with the rules, than would be the case if they believed other individuals also disagreed with the rules.

But there is, in fact, more reason than this to act in public *as if* one agrees with and supports the public morality. We have already seen some of these reasons, such as the importance of such public morality in economic success. Most importantly, enforcement of the public morality is entrusted to, or left up to, the official agents of control who make use of severe physical force to enforce public compliance with public morality.

The Official Agents of Control, Social Rules, and Social Order

Official agencies of control have grown rapidly in our society in the past century. Little thought has been given to this singular growth of official agencies of control or research done on such questions as their rate of growth, but there is reason to believe that they have been among the most rapidly growing segments of our society. Indeed, it is possible that these agencies of control have grown more rapidly in the proportion of our working population and the resources devoted to them than most other segments of our society in the past century. A century ago there were very few control agents in American society. Today there are millions, working in hundreds of massive bureaucracies and expending billions of dollars every year to survey and control the behavior of the other members of our society. These agencies are already a central fact of life in our society. Certainly few would doubt the direct or indirect importance in their lives of such agencies as the police, the FBI, the FDA, the FTC, the FCC, the ICC, the CIA, the SEC, the NLRB, the draft boards, the social security administration, treasury agents, border patrol agents, customs officials, boards of the agriculture department, federal mediators, federal marshals, federal water pollution control agents, the forestry service, the civil service commission, school psychologists, state agencies paralleling many of these, local zoning boards, planning commissions, and so on.

The official agencies of control have been created for

different purposes, in different situations, with different mandates, with different powers, and with different built-in constraints on their activities. But the central idea is that of controlling what goes on in our society: they act in some way, either by planning beforehand or intervening afterward, to constrain individuals and groups to move in identified directions, to act in identified ways. Lying behind much of this conception of control is the feeling of the need to bring "order" into otherwise too "disorderly" a situation. The official agencies of control, then, are used by the members of our society, or, at least, by the government officials who construct them, to try to produce both order and orderings.

Probably the agencies with the broadest mandate of social control, the official purpose of maintaining order in its broadest sense, are the urban police bureaucracies. The prime slogan by which the police are known and make themselves known is "law and order." But there were laws and legal proceedings to control members of society long before there were police departments. The police were not created, maintained, and vastly expanded in size and power, because they were a more efficient means of using law to govern society.[34] On the contrary, as many researchers have shown in great detail, throughout much of their history the police agencies have systematically and purposefully violated many important laws—for the ostensible purpose of maintaining social order.[35] The mandate of the police is to "maintain social order" and they have always understood that this is to be done even at the expense of violating some of the most important and cherished laws in our society, especially concerning "civil rights." In addition, the police have always

34. See Allan Silver, "The Demand for Order in Civil Society: A Review of Some Themes in the History of Urban Crime, Police and Riots," in David J. Bordua, *The Police, op. cit.*, pp. 1–24.

35. See the essays in Jack D. Douglas, ed., *Crime and Justice in American Society*, Indianapolis: Bobbs-Merrill, 1971.

lobbied to eliminate laws that constrain them in pursuing the "maintenance of social order."

The persistent linking of police activity with both law and order and the upholding of police as the "guardians of the law" has been primarily a rhetorical attempt to legitimate their activities, to provide them with the social support needed to carry out their mandate. The myth of police dedication to upholding the law has been strongly supported in public by the headline linkage between mass murders, rapes, and other violent or heinous crimes and police work. It is certainly true that the police do such work and are concerned with doing it effectively, since this is the only time most people take much note of them; however, this "glamorous" side of police work is very different from the less prominent facts of their daily lives. In the relatively rare instances of these heinous crimes, which threaten and outrage almost all groups the police work primarily to "solve" the headliner cases and give little attention to the murders of skidrow bums and other outsiders. But in the mass of their daily work they choose not to invoke or attempt to enforce most legal rules, both because it is impossible to do so and because doing so would not advance their taken-for-granted purpose in life—maintaining social order—and might even make it impossible to achieve this purpose. The typical policeman on the local beat senses that he must overlook most illegal activities by local groups who do not see such laws as legitimate, if he is to have sufficient legitimacy to maintain the minimal social order demanded of him by others, including his superiors.

But as we have noted, "social order" is an essentially problematic, abstract symbol in our society. One man's social order is another man's social disorder. What one group sharing a given set of social meanings would see as "ordered," because they would "see" the unseeable, taken-for-granted meanings that lie behind the visible activities, may well be seen as chaotic by someone who does not share those meanings. This is most true in a pluralistic society such as ours and for individuals involved in the management of complex public social relations in the way the police are The questions, then, are what the police situationally define as "social order," as bearing on social order, how they believe this social order is to be constructed, and how the police have come to construct these situational meanings for social order.

There are, as Roy Turner has shown,[36] many practical concerns that enter into any given situational construction of these meanings by policemen (even such facts as how much longer the policeman has to work that night); and there are many factors that have gone into the compromise constructions of meanings they have committed themselves to over the years. Perhaps the one overriding fact about police constructions of the meanings of "social order" is that they have been determined primarily by the conceptions of the absolute public morality shared by the dominant groups in our society, namely, the Anglo-Saxon morality. This is clear when we look at the history of the police. The urban police bureaucracies were created in this society a little more than a century ago just as the cities were being populated by the waves of lower-class, Catholic immigrants, especially the Irish; and, as Allan Silver and others have shown,[37] they were created for the specific purpose of "maintaining social order" among these "unruly mobs," which meant in large part that they were to make the new groups conform to the older American morality (or moralities). In a society with a basic separation of public and private realms, this demand for conformity could be maintained only in public, so it would have to be public lives that would be "controlled" or "ordered." In addition, since the police were

36. See Roy Turner, "Police Work," unpublished paper.
37. See Allan Silver, "The Demand for Order in a Civil Society," op. cit.

also given limited resources and powers to produce this public order, it meant that they would have to concentrate on the aspects of the public morality that were seen as most important by the older groups, or else their continual "harassment" of the poor in their everyday lives would so alienate them that the police would be completely ineffective. (Where the police have not sufficiently pursued this compromise strategy for minimizing their troubles with their different publics, as they appear not to have done in recent years, they have found themselves almost unable to enter many of the everyday public settings of these groups.)

The pressures put on the police by the most influential groups in our society, and the resources provided them for specific forms of work by those who control state legislative bodies, have led them to concentrate on several fundamental aspects of the public morality. First of all, the police have been concerned with invoking and enforcing those laws concerned with the property rights and physical safety of the dominant groups. As we saw in Chapter 4, the police have been increasingly used by the more powerful groups in our society to survey and control the kinds of criminal activities that lower class groups are most apt to become involved in, while many violations of the dominant groups, such as anti-trust violations, have been defined primarily as civil violations, so that they are not directly subject to police activity.[38] All of this means that police work will be directed primarily at surveying and controlling the newer immigrant groups in American society.

Second, the police have always focused upon prevention of acts of violence in everyday life. To some extent this refers to individual fights, but mostly it means controlling the spread of any violence. That is, they have been primarily concerned with preventing private disputes from becoming

38. See my essay in *Crime and Justice, op. cit.*

public disputes. In this sense, "maintaining social order" has a reasonably specific meaning that could be agreed upon by most groups of the society and most groups appear to support police work of this sort. Even today the urban, lower class Negroes, who are for the most part profoundly alienated from the police, give a majority vote in favor of police action intended to prevent the use of violence in their neighborhoods by their fellow Negroes. In fact, studies have shown that most urban Negroes are upset because the police do not give them enough of this "protection." [39]

Third, the police have also defined their purpose to be the general maintenance of "social order" in the broadest sense. They have probably done so both because of the tendency of bureaucrats to try to extend their own power and span of control and also because the dominant ethnic groups have always applied pressure to them to do so, both directly through budgets and appointments and indirectly through vigilante citizen movements or mass media pressures. In taking this broadest definition of their purpose, the police have attempted to control those activities that they believed would tend to "undermine or destroy social order," even if this means committing illegal activities on their part. Presumably because of the pressures put on them by the dominant groups in our society, the police have come to define these "threats to public order" to be any violations of the public morality. The police, then, have come to see themselves, and to be seen by many others in our society, as a respository of the public morality. Moreover, they take an absolutist view of that public morality even though they do, in fact, invoke and enforce the great majority of laws very selectively. They also maintain a public stance of absolutism toward the laws and the public morality in general.

This insistence on the absolutism of the rules they enforce

39. This was reported in *Crime in a Free Society, op. cit.*

and the absolutism of their own relation to those rules is probably due partly to their desire for more power. There is another reason for this absolutist stance. All public officials in our society are subject to very critical evaluation and to intense criticism from major groups. The police have many powerful enemies, who themselves commonly invoke the absolute public morality in judging the police. Perhaps the police know from their own experience that it is impossible to act in accord with any absolute morality, especially one so complex as our own, and perhaps they feel that this method of judging them is intensely unfair. Nevertheless, it becomes strategically difficult to fight such absolutist arguments by anything other than a counter-absolute argument. As noted previously, absolutism in the use of rules tends to drive out relativism. The police, then, present themselves *as if* they were invoking and enforcing the rules absolutely and present themselves as the repository of an absolute morality. However purposefully done this tendency may be in the beginning, in the case of the police it has become more than a strategy. They have developed a very "moralistic" attitude toward those kinds of activities, which they see as being "destructive of social order."

Every indication is that the police actually decide by very complicated processes toward which laws, which group of people, and which kinds of activities to take an absolutist stance. They apparently make use of their commonsense ideas about the nature of persons, the relations of such personality types to types of actions, and the relations of types of actions to "social order" to decide which kinds of people and which activity in which situations are dangerous to social order.[40] Even practical considerations, such as the budgets of the department become important in these considerations. Once the police do decide to invoke and enforce

40. See especially Aaron Cicourel, *The Social Organization of Juvenile Justice, op. cit.*

any given laws through the use of arrest, their work tends to take on an absolutist stance and, through the stigmatization process, to have an absolutist effect on people.

Legal stigmatization tends to transform the *substantial self* of the individual from a normal, morally right and trustworthy person into the opposite, an abnormal, morally wrong, untrustworthy person. Legal stigmatization, then, is an absolute phenomenon. While there is much opportunity to keep knowledge of one's troubles from becoming public, or to change one's social identity, arrest by the police is the crucial stage in legal stigmatization in our society.[41] It is arrest, not conviction, which makes an individual into a *distrusted outsider*. It is arrest that has such an important influence on an individual's friendships, job, and whole social situation. This is not because most individuals in our society believe that anybody arrested is actually guilty; most people who think about it know cases of arrest that were mistakes or injustices. Rather, arrest by the police has this stigmatizing influence primarily because it so easily produces a sense of distrust. In our society most of an individual's relations are with other individuals who do not know much about his background, his person, or his activities at any time. That is most social relations are highly situational. Because this is so, most individuals must rely upon situational factors to build trust, but this makes trust itself relatively situational. When an individual is arrested by the police for anything, it creates a suspicion in the minds of most members of the society. How are they to *check out* the charge? Surely the police, who are seen as the experts on such matters, know something about his activities that warrant such suspicion. Since individuals in public life, such as employers dealing with the public, are basically

41. There is actually very little good evidence concerning stigmatizing by police and legal action in our society. See, however, the essay by Richard D. Schwartz and Jerome H. Skolnick, "Two Studies of Legal Stigma," in Howard Becker, *The Other Side, op. cit.*, pp. 103–118.

concerned with "avoiding trouble," just as the police themselves generally are, the creation of such a suspicion that cannot be checked out leads individuals "rationally" to distrust the individual in general. Hence avoid those kinds of relations that necessitate continued trust. In a complex society, then, the official agents of control potentially have very great power over individuals. This power is constrained only by the capacity of the individuals and groups to "make trouble" for them.[42]

It should be apparent, then, that the official agents of control, especially the police, are of tremendous importance in maintaining the myth of the absolutist middle class public morality. Any individual who chooses to violate that morality in public, or who chooses simply to question the absolutist nature of that morality, might find himself subject to police "harassment," even arrest. The very uncertainty of police action adds to this *conformity effect;* the individual has a tremendous incentive to *play it safe* by not publicly violating or challenging the morality. Because the police are apt to see anyone who challenges the public morality as an even greater "enemy of social order" than one who happens to violate it, there is incentive for individuals to *act as if* they believe in the public morality. In this way they build up "deviance credits" with the police. If they get caught violating the public morality, they may even find it to their greatest advantage to admit that they have violated it (by giving a "mea culpa" speech) while maintaining they did not intend to do this and then insisting that they should be in some way (minor, of course) punished for such a violation because the public morality must be upheld at all costs. In other words, the nature of police activity is an incentive for "hypocrisy," for presenting oneself as being the opposite of

42. For a discussion of the importance of "trouble" in police work, see Peter K. Manning, "Police Trouble," in Jack D. Douglas, ed., *Crime and Justice in America, op. cit.*

what he knows himself to be. While this is not to say that all members of our society are Elmer Gantrys, it is to say that there is a genuine incentive for becoming Elmer Gantrys.

Besides the danger of police action against any challenge to the public morality, there is a continued danger of informal invocations and enforcements of the rule, either directly or, more often, indirectly without explicit invocation of the rule. This is so because there are important groups that continue to support most of the public rules. The "little old lady" vigilante groups can be instrumental in forcing official action where the officials themselves would prefer to do nothing. This is the case today with charges of "pornography." The vigilante groups often work behind the scenes, threatening to make trouble for the police, D.A. or politician, if they do not control the sale of magazines and books in local stores. The officials then threaten to make trouble for the local store owner if he doesn't comply with these wishes; he normally finds it to his advantage to comply.

Fundamentalist or conservative groups are further important to politicians and help to prevent their taking any public action to change the laws that would make it harder to maintain such rules in society. Even when they constitute only ten percent of the vote, pressure groups can be the difference between victory and defeat; so officials will not cause trouble for themselves by raising an issue which does not have an *organized* constituency behind it. And, even if most members of the society wanted such changes, they would probably find it very "unwise" to try to organize, because, as long as there are such laws and such pressure groups, reformers are subject to the severe penalty of legal stigmatization.

For these reasons, even if an individual suspects from his own experience that most individuals agree with him in his opposition to some aspect of the public morality, he will find it risky to commit himself publicly against that rule.

The result of this is that the official enforces of the public morality serve to slow change in the public morality. Where they do seek to change laws and enforcement procedures they almost always seek to add new rules to the public morality, to make enforcement more effective, or to make the penalties for violations more severe. That is, the only change they seek is to make the public morality broader and more absolutist.

But the official agents of control cannot wholly prevent change in the public morality and behavior, for there are always *moral provocateurs* who challenge that morality and there are always those who will choose open conflict over quiet subversion and circumvention. Their general effect is to make change much slower and to produce a growing difference between public morality and behavior and private morality and behavior. This is especially important in a society that is changing at an accelerating rate.

Official Agencies of Control and the Individual Construction of Social Order

Insofar as the official agents of control have served to maintain the public morality, and insofar as a generally shared and enforced public morality has served to prevent conflicts in our pluralistic society, the official agents of control have served to decrease conflict in our society, in particular, the violent social conflict that leads to an increasing polarization of groups. They have been the independent force that is necessary in constructing social order in a pluralistic society. However unjust some may find it, however unfortunate it might be that the world cannot be run by morality alone, and however "cynical" it might appear to even say these things, we have needed official agents of control and we shall continue to need them as our source of power to be used in constructing social order in our society. In some respects,

paradoxical as it may seem on the surface, the more pluralistic we are and the more free we are, the more we shall
need them.

But this must not be interpreted to mean that the agents of
control necessarily *help* in constructing "social order," or
that their actions are necessarily compatible with the greatest
freedom for the greatest number. Whether their actions are
in fact conducive to "social order" and to social freedom is
dependent on the concrete things that individuals in our
society choose to do. *Social order in our complex and plural-*
istic society is only possible if individuals purposefully go
about constructing that social order and if they choose wisely
in doing that constructive work. If people in our society
should for any reason choose not to continue their efforts to
construct American society, or if they should make some
fundamental mistakes in their constructive work (which is far
more likely), then we shall experience the violent conflicts
between groups that can lead to the fundamental reconstruction or the destruction of societies. At the least, misunderstandings of the nature of our society and the unwise decisions that can come from such misunderstandings can lead
to greatly increased conflicts that would produce an "im
miserization" of our daily lives.

As the pace of change in our increasingly technological
society has accelerated, and it has become ever more complex,
the difficulties of understanding it and of making wise choices
in our attempts to construct social order have grown rapidly.
Indeed, millions of Americans have apparently decided that
it is not even worthwhile to try, that we must have a return
to a simpler society and, if we cannot do that, then we can
at least have a return to simpler understandings and decisions.
They have decided to use force to eliminate some of the new
complexities and to stop many of the social changes; and
they have decided that the public morality must be enforced
absolutely, at all cost. They have been joined in this effort

by a large percentage of the official agents of control, whose position in our society and whose self-image give them a singularly absolutist approach to social rules and social order. Nothing is certain in human existence, so it is possible they will succeed. But all indications in recent years have been that they are only helping to produce that one great source of the most violent forms of conflict in a pluralistic society —social polarization.[43]

There have been other attempts by minorities or small majorities in the history of our society to enforce their private moralities upon the other groups in private as well as in public. But these absolutist attempts to legislate private morality for large groups in our society, as opposed to attempts to legislate public moralities for public purposes only, have generally led to greater social disorder rather than greater social order. The Prohibition movement was such an attempt and those involved in it must have felt elated at finally winning their struggle when it was made part of the Constitution. Yet this great act of "idealism" and "purity" soon had the opposite consequences from what its firebrand proponents had expected. Prohibition not only failed, it also produced widespread alienation from law and was important in creating the economic incentives to the establishment of organized criminal syndicates that still plague us. Prohibition was presented as a cure for all kinds of social evils, especially as a cure for urban violence and crime. It only increased these.

In American society, only when there is a general coalition of social groups supporting what is in fact an accommodative public morality will the enforcement of the public morality as absolute (but only for public purposes) serve to produce social order. In any other situation such absolutist treatment of the public morality will lead to greater social conflict or social disorder. This is true simply because the basic legal

43. For a discussion of the nature and importance of "social polarization" see my book on *Youth in Turmoil, op. cit.*

distinctions between public and private situations so reinforce the pluralistic structure of social groups in our society that it is not possible for the official agents of control to use enough force to enforce such rules. They could only do this if our society were fundamentally reconstructed, if the ancient sources of our individual and social freedoms were eliminated.

Those individuals and officials who have chosen in recent years to treat certain legal rules as absolute seem to have created the same massive circumvention and alienation from the law and from officials, and in some cases from America in general, as the enforcers of prohibition did a generation ago. For example this seems clearly to have been the case in the attempts to enforce the laws against marihuana use.

Unless we choose to move in the direction of using ever greater force and eliminating the ancient protections of our individual freedoms, we shall find it increasingly necessary to circumscribe the realm of the absolutist public morality in order to avoid polarization. Only by coming to understand better which particular kinds of activities have bearings on the general welfare, and which do not, and by seeking to control only those that do have such public effects, are we likely to avoid polarizing important segments of our society and turning them into the "enemies of society." Only by *deabsolutizing* all social rules except those necessary for the construction of an "optimal" social order are we likely to avoid violent disorders as our society becomes more international, changeable, open, complex, and pluralistic.

8. The Challenge to Sociology

Intellectual disciplines are commonly guided by certain taken-for-granted ideas that lie behind and determine much of the everyday work of its practitioners. The absolutist ideas of social rules and social order were such ideas for those sociologists who shared the structural-functional and statistical-hypothetical perspectives on society. By the twentieth century these absolutist ideas had become so taken for granted by these theorists that they hardly realized their existence and did not subject them to any critical analysis. These theorists uncritically used only those methods and examined only those social phenomena that they could plausibly use and analyze in terms of these absolutist and derivative ideas. Among other things, this led to their passive use of official information to construct and test social theories that unwittingly allied them with the official agents of control in our society.

Much of our difficulty up to now in developing more creative and effective understandings of our society has been the result of our inability to see and understand these underlying absolutist ideas. They were so fundamental to many of our common-sense understandings of everyday life that to question them aroused many of our ancient fears of chaos: the groundwork of our everyday lives was threatened. This is why so much of my discussion consisted of scholarly analyses and critiques of the absolutist ideas underlying the structural-functional and statistical-hypothetical perspectives on society.

Undoubtedly, the overriding idea of the theoretical perspective I have developed here is *the necessity of remaining true to the phenomena*. It is this that sets this perspective in fundamental opposition to all absolutist sociologies. And it is this that allies our efforts, at least initially, with those of some of the phenomenologists, existentialists and analysts of language.

Once we recognize that the phenomena of our common-sense experience are the fundamental data for any sociological ideas and theory, we look upon a world that was previously irrelevant to our work as sociologists. *We discover everyday life*. We no longer simply live everyday life independently of our sociological enterprise.

But this discovery is not simply the result of our looking at the everyday world in the way a member of society would normally do, that is, by taking the natural stance toward it. Rather, we seek to analyze the phenomena of everyday life to identify their basic properties or dimensions. This commitment to analysis and to scientific understanding distinguishes the discipline of sociology from everyday life.[1]

Analyzing social rules on their own grounds consists largely of analyzing the ways in which members construct the meanings of rules and use them in their everyday lives. When do they invoke what rules? How do they invoke them? Why? What are the responses? The consequences?

Probably the most crucial property we have discovered

1. For a discussion of these issues see my essay in *Understanding Everyday Life, op. cit.*

of these everyday constructions and uses of the meanings of rules is that they are very problematic for the members, in particular, for the members of such a pluralistic society as ours is. The problems of deciding what rules are relevant (if any), what should be made of them in a given situation, what to do about others' decisions of the same sort, and so on, have fundamental effects on all human social life. These problems assure us that we shall of necessity live in a world of conflict, a world in which men will arrive at different sets of conclusions about what is right and what is wrong for situations, even when they begin with highly shared social meanings. These problems mean that our social world will be morally absurd in some ways.

Yet this absurdity and these conflicts must be managed in some way that will enable human beings to live together. They must be managed to allow people to feel that their world is adequately ordered for the achievement of their purposes in their everyday lives. They must be managed in some way that produces adequate social order. At the same time, and especially in our own society where we prize freedom so highly, they must be managed so as to preserve our individual freedoms of thought and action.

The problems of meanings and social order can probably be solved adequately only by some wise use of social power. At the least, this is one of the elements men of practical affairs always seem to have found necessary in constructing any solutions to these problems. But the wise construction of effective solutions to such problems is itself problematic, especially when the demands for order must be constrained by and balanced against strong demands for personal freedom, which in some ways is antithetical to social order. Since any solutions to the problems are themselves problematic, we can be certain that they will inevitably prove inadequate at some time. Human experience shows that the best solutions to the problems eventually fail. Injustice and social disorder inevitably return, in spite of the best intentions and wisest efforts of men. This social flux continues today and we have no assurance that chaos will not be our fate tomorrow.

The primary justification of sociology and any other social science is its promise of helping to find better solutions to these problems, though we know that any solutions will only be partial. (Indeed, the problems could be finally eradicated by eliminating human freedom, which is hardly the intention of any social scientist.) This practical justification of sociology remains an unfulfilled promise, one which sociologists today must accept as their challenge if they are to justify their work to our society. I believe it remains an unfulfilled promise largely because the absolutist ideas to which sociologists became so deeply, if inadvertently, committed distort the picture of our society. No social theory or research committed to seeing American society as an unproblematic, unconflictful, and well-equilibrated system could ever be useful in solving the very problems denied by those assumptions. Such absolutist ideas could only be useful to those officials who seek to use absolutist rhetoric to control society.

To meet this challenge of practical relevance, we shall also have to meet the many fundamental challenges that remain to develop better theoretical understandings of social rules and social order in American society. I believe we have made a beginning in the important work of reconstructing our sociological understanding of American society, but this beginning has hardly taken us beyond the statement of the basic questions and the proposal of what now seem the basic principles and their relations. I believe there is already more than enough empirical evidence to show the great fertility of the new perspective and the value of the proposed principles. But the accumulation of evidence in the years ahead will surely produce new questions whose answers will clarify and change many of the principles of the theory.

Certain problems that remain to be solved should be clear

from this work. In keeping with the *progressive strategy* of not prematurely closing analysis by proposing formal theories ungrounded in empirical evidence, but, rather, of seeking to develop formal analyses progressively as the necessary evidence does become available, I have felt it best not to try to solve certain problems which the careful reader of this work will have recognized. Although I have tried to clarify the issues at certain points, I have left the meanings of "meaning" and "social order" largely at the common-sense level. I have done so for the simple reason that both are complex common-sense ideas that will necessitate far more investigation and analysis before we can hope to understand them in any more formal way. I have chosen to ground that part of the work in our common-sense understanding in the hope and belief that this has allowed me to get on with other parts of the theoretical analysis where I already have enough evidence to make considerable progress. I leave these basic problems as challenges to future work which I hope will be undertaken by many sociologists.

I believe the many basic challenges to sociological theory are clearer today than they have ever been. I also believe it is clearer than ever before that we must successfully meet these challenges if we are to meet the even greater challenge of wisely reconstructing our everyday lives.

Index